Also available at all good book stores

9781785316302

9781785315329

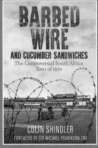

9781785316340

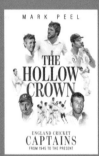

9781785316630

9781785316395

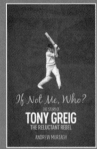

9781785316418

9781785316876

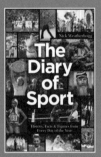

9781785316289

9781785316197

CRICKETING CAESAR

A BIOGRAPHY OF

MIKE BREARLEY

CRICKETING CAESAR

A BIOGRAPHY OF
MIKE BREARLEY

MARK PEEL

First published by Pitch Publishing, 2020

Pitch Publishing
A2 Yeoman Gate
Yeoman Way
Worthing
Sussex
BN13 3QZ
www.pitchpublishing.co.uk
info@pitchpublishing.co.uk

A CIP catalogue record is available for this book
from the British Library.

ISBN 978 1 78531 662 3

Typesetting and origination by Pitch Publishing
Printed and bound in India by Replika Press Pvt. Ltd.

Contents

Introduction

F RIDAY, 10 July 1981 was no ordinary evening in the life of a professional cricketer, even one as distinguished as Mike Brearley, since he was a guest at Westminster School's Election Dinner, held annually at the end of the summer term. While guests, dressed in all their finery, were being greeted with Latin and Greek epigrams, Brearley couldn't help but contrast this ancient ritual with major disturbances in neighbouring Brixton, a multiracial community with a long history of social deprivation and fractious relations with the police.

The previous week the disaffected youth of Toxteth in Liverpool and Moss Side in Manchester had taken to the streets to vent their fury at the economic and social policies of the Thatcher government in the worst riots in living memory. Such a surge of popular discontent threatened to overshadow the forthcoming marriage of Prince Charles to Lady Diana Spencer, unless the nation could look outward and unite around something more inspirational.

Although sport seemed an obvious force for social cohesion, the fortunes of the England cricket team hardly suggested they would provide the Midas touch. One down after two Tests to Australia and without a win in 12 matches, the England selectors had taken the drastic step of dismissing the embattled captain

Ian Botham and recalling his predecessor Brearley in a caretaker capacity. While Brearley reaffirmed his intention not to tour again, he was happy enough to oblige and was welcomed back with open arms by his former team-mates. As they assembled at Headingley, venue for the third Test, he went out of his way to restore morale and convince Botham in particular that he remained a class player. His show of confidence was soon vindicated as Botham's 6-95 and half-century was the one redeeming feature of a lacklustre England performance over the first three days. Bowled out for 174 in reply to Australia's first innings of 401/9 declared, and forced to follow on, their position appeared near hopeless when they joined their bullish opponents for a barbeque at Botham's home on the Saturday evening.

Monday brought no improvement in England's fortunes as they slumped to 135/7, still 92 runs short of avoiding an innings defeat. With the ship slowly sinking and nothing to lose, Botham and his new partner, Graham Dilley, opted to go down fighting. Striking the ball to all parts, they put on 117 in 80 minutes and, after Dilley's departure for 56, Botham kept playing his shots. Taking advantage of a tiring attack and enjoying his fair share of fortune, he raced to 144 not out at the close when England were 124 to the good with one wicket left. After Bob Willis, England's number eleven, was out early the next morning, Australia needed 130 to win. It looked a mere formality but the pummelling they had taken the previous evening had exacted a dreadful toll. England, on the other hand, had rediscovered their sense of purpose and with Brearley back in charge they fancied their chances, even when Australia proceeded cautiously to 56/1. Switching his strike bowler Willis to the Kirkstall Lane End to give him the advantage of the slope, Brearley encouraged him to run in as fast as he could and not to worry about bowling no-balls, a fault that had dogged him in the first innings. Boosted by this show of confidence, Willis responded in style. Rediscovering a level of pace and hostility of yesteryear, he bowled like a man possessed. Well supported by his team-mates, he ripped through the Australian batting to return match-winning figures of 8-43 to complete the most remarkable comeback in the history of Test cricket.

The match captivated the nation and helped fuel a mood of euphoria that expressed itself the following week at the royal wedding and at the Edgbaston Test immediately afterwards. In a taut, low-scoring contest, England's batting failed throughout and only a ninth-wicket stand of 50 in their second innings between Bob Taylor and John Emburey kept them in the game. This time the Australian target was 151 but on a frenetic fourth day the England bowlers, cheered on by a highly partisan crowd, made their opponents fight for every run. Thanks to a dogged 40 from Allan Border, Australia were in sight of the home straight, but at 105/4 he was caught at short leg by Mike Gatting off a brute of a ball from Emburey. Thereafter the floodgates opened as Brearley persuaded a reluctant Botham to re-enter the fray. It proved the defining moment. Sweeping all before him, the now-imperious Botham captured the remaining five wickets for one run as England ran out victors by 29 runs.

At Old Trafford in the fifth Test, Botham's genius was once again to the fore when his brilliant 118 in England's second innings gave his side an unassailable lead. Set 506 to win, Australia lost by 103 runs, enabling England to win the series and retain the Ashes. With the final Test ending in a draw, Brearley once again vacated the national stage to enter the pantheon of great England captains, his reputation forever forged by the events of 1981. When he published his classical treatise on leadership, *The Art of Captaincy*, in 1985, his reputation grew ever greater so that his captaincy became the yardstick by which subsequent England captains were assessed.

Given Brearley's youthful pedigree as a batsman and captain it would be all too easy to see his rise to national eminence as inevitable, but in truth the road he travelled contained many a bump along the way. Had the game of cricket entirely consumed him as it consumed his contemporaries such as Ray Illingworth or Geoff Boycott, he might well have emerged as a greater player, but cricket had to compete with his academic vocation.

The son of a Yorkshire schoolmaster with a fine sporting pedigree, Brearley, born in 1942, excelled at City of London School (CLS) and St John's College, Cambridge, where his first in Classics and an upper second in Moral Sciences was matched by his success at cricket. Having established a record aggregate of 4,068 runs during his four years in the Blues team and captained them in his last two, he was voted Young Cricketer for 1964, the year he was chosen for MCC's (Marylebone Cricket Club) tour to South Africa that winter. His failure to live up to expectation helped persuade him that his future lay primarily in academia, and for the next five years his research at Cambridge and his teaching at Newcastle University greatly restricted his appearances for Middlesex, his indifferent form offering few hints of future higher honours. Even when he assumed the captaincy of Middlesex in 1971, his batting continued to pale, until a chance encounter with Tiger Smith, the former England wicketkeeper-batsman and Warwickshire coach, in 1974, brought about a change in his technique. Rediscovering some of the fluency of his youth, his progress over the next two years was such that he made his Test debut against the West Indies in June 1976 at the advanced age of 34. He made little impression and was dropped after two matches, only to be recalled as vice-captain to Tony Greig for MCC's 1976/77 tour of India. He began with an effortless double century against West Zone but was never able to reproduce that form in the Tests. This failure to impose himself at the highest level continued throughout his 31 Tests as captain, a defect that heaped additional pressure on his leadership. Robin Marlar, the *Sunday Times*'s cricket correspondent, wrote:

> Time after time, one recalls sitting in a stand either here or in Australia, thinking and even writing ... that this simply could not continue, that England ... must never again in the future take the field behind a man whom unkind critics could describe as a non-playing captain. [1]

At first the critics held their fire because of Brearley's success in bringing home the Ashes in the summer of 1977, but a slew of low scores against the unfancied Pakistan and New Zealand attacks the following year gave them fresh ammunition. He owed his survival to his immense popularity with his team and the lack of a viable alternative, but his poor form continued in Australia that winter when his first six Test innings yielded a mere 37 runs. After scores of 1 and 0 in the third Test at Melbourne, England's first defeat under his captaincy, he momentarily thought of dropping himself only to be talked out of it by his fellow selectors. A painstaking fifty in the next Test at Sydney helped save his blushes, but he ended the series – won 5–1 by England – with an average of 16.73. Thereafter he continued to struggle among the game's elite aside from the return series in Australia in 1979/80 when he averaged 34.20, his best return for England. 'Had he played under a captain as sympathetic as himself, the problem might have been solved,' wrote the renowned cricket writer and broadcaster John Arlott. 'In the event, although he often batted freely and fluently in county cricket, when he played for England anxiety drove him constantly into over-care. This frequently cost him his wicket. In short, he was, like all good batsmen, basically an instinctive player: not even he could quite impose thought on the high-speed reactions of batting against pace.'[2] 'He tinkered with his style, his stance, his back-lift, but nothing really worked,' noted Boycott, his regular England opening partner. 'That did not surprise me, because it was all too manufactured. Batting has to feel right and there is no way you can be thinking about technique when you face the next ball. It must not be intrusive.'[3]

If Brearley's underwhelming batting kept him awake at night, the same couldn't be said for his captaincy. Leading Middlesex to the county championship in 1976, their first title for nearly three decades, helped win him the vice-captaincy of MCC's tour to India. There he proved himself a loyal and capable deputy to Greig and when Greig lost the captaincy on return because of his leading role in the formation of Kerry Packer's World Series Cricket, (WSC), Brearley stepped up to take charge. 'Replacing Tony Greig with Mike Brearley, as England cricket captain, is a bit like replacing one of the Bash Street Kids with Little Lord Fauntleroy,' wrote *The Sun*'s chief sports writer John Sadler. 'Rarely can so little be known by the majority of cricket fans about the man set to assume the most coveted role the game can offer.'[4]

Unlike the flamboyant Greig, Brearley's aversion to publicity was entirely genuine. 'Perhaps I shall be known as the Greta Garbo of cricket,' he commented on his appointment. While invariably polite to strangers, he disliked being pointed out in the street, interrupted in restaurants or appearing on television game shows. A man of few close friends, he shunned the camaraderie of the bar or the pool table on tour for a solitary meal in his room or an evening at a concert. Similarly, he would opt for an energetic day's sightseeing, or for voluntary work at a local hospital, in preference for a leisurely stint on the beach. Even when lack of entertainment in some remote Indian outpost called for some home-grown amusement, Brearley's erudition was manifest. 'We played charades a lot which we enjoyed until Mike Brearley and Mike Selvey started doing Keats's poems,' recalled the former England opening batsman Dennis Amiss. 'We were all right on things like Bambi, but when those two started doing the highbrow stuff we walked out.'[5]

Yet despite his privileged education, his urbane tones and the classical allusions which littered his conversation, Brearley was no old-style amateur in the tradition of Plum Warner or Gubby Allen. 'His clarity of mind enabled him to pierce the woolly romanticism and anachronistic feudalism which for so long obscured the truth of cricket,'[6] remarked Arlott, who fully shared Brearley's support for the underdog and his rigorous opposition to the apartheid regime in South Africa. Invited to play for the Gentlemen against the Players at Scarborough in 1961, the young Brearley, always a casual dresser, found the idea of wearing a dinner jacket for dinner unduly pretentious. 'Michael, there is such a thing as inverted snobbery,' the crusty cricket correspondent of the *Daily Telegraph*, E.W. Swanton, admonished him when Brearley spurned his offer to become a member of the Free Foresters Cricket Club because he didn't want to play 'that kind of cricket with ex-colonels and so forth'. A leading member of the Cricketers' Association, Brearley fought as hard as anyone to increase their pay and it was his sympathy for their financial plight that accounted for his more moderate stance towards WSC than most of his England team-mates. 'I have always felt that Mike would have made an outstanding trade union leader,' wrote Trevor Bailey, the former England all-rounder turned cricket journalist, 'with the considerable advantage of being more intelligent than the bosses, and just as determined.'[7]

That same determination governed his approach to captaincy and opponents who underestimated him did so at their peril. 'He was the antithesis of an Australian; he was establishment,' recalled Kim Hughes, his opposite number in the 1981 series. 'He had nothing going for him apart from being intelligent; and we didn't trust blokes who were too intelligent.'[8] After Hughes had been outsmarted by Brearley, he later revised his opinion, calling his captaincy outstanding. 'Brearley's the hardest man I've ever played with,' recalled Roger Tolchard, the former Leicestershire and England wicketkeeper-batsman. 'He was clever enough to know how to be nasty and cruel – Brears saw everything, knew everything, hated losing, loved winning. Never missed a trick. You felt that pressure with him all the time as an opponent.'[9] 'He was certainly not averse to gamesmanship,' wrote his England team-mate David Gower. 'He would talk about a batsman, from slip, loudly enough for the victim to hear – and discuss field placings with the bowler as though the batsman was no more a difficulty to remove than a fly brushed off the nose. A number of people who suffered this kind of treatment were put off Mike and termed him arrogant.'[10] When challenged by the cricket writer Peter Hayter that he could be 'quite nasty on the field when necessary', Brearley replied, 'I'd like to say tough, but, yes, I suppose I was sometimes. I'm not very proud of it.'[11] Declaring him a less diplomatic captain than the mercurial Nasser Hussain, the *Sunday Telegraph*'s Scyld Berry wrote that had he played in a later era his confrontational style 'might have copped a few fines from match referees'.[12]

His ruthlessness was evident in the Edgbaston Test of 1978 when he was unstinting in his support of fast bowler Bob Willis for felling the Pakistan nightwatchman Iqbal Qasim with a bouncer. As far as he was concerned, he saw no reason why a lower-order batsman should be protected from short-pitched bowling, a view that brought him into conflict with Australian umpires that winter when Botham bowled bouncers at their tail.

Brearley's uncompromising ethos alienated opponents and spectators alike when England returned to Australia in 1979/80 following the settlement between the Australian Cricket Board and WSC. In the first one-day international (ODI) between England and the West Indies, he thought nothing of placing every man, including the wicketkeeper, back on the boundary to guarantee victory in the closest of finishes. Unrepentant over the storm he'd unleashed, he risked further opprobrium by remarking that he would have liked to have done it in front of 50,000 Australians. Although the target thereafter of persistent abuse from Australian crowds, he literally stood his ground by repeatedly fielding in front of the rowdiest sections of the ground.

A keen student of the game, Brearley would rarely allow a match to drift. He was always willing to experiment and despite his sharp intellect he conveyed his thoughts to his players with admirable clarity. Invariably calm under pressure, he handled his bowlers and fielders with aplomb, ruthlessly preying on the weaknesses of opposition batsmen. When Middlesex played Nottinghamshire at Trent Bridge in 1982, he noticed that Clive Rice, Nottinghamshire's leading batsman, was looking to force the ball away through cover off the back foot. Two years before, he recalled Rice slicing the ball over the slips from a thick edge so he moved Clive Radley from orthodox gully to fly slip some 25 yards from the bat. Next time Rice tried the shot, the ball went straight to Radley. When Nottinghamshire followed on, Brearley, knowing Rice was inclined to flick the ball off his legs in the air, switched Radley to deep square leg, and in the same over Rice holed out to him.

As impressive as Brearley's tactical expertise was, so was his capacity to empathise with his players. Shunning favourites, he reached out to one and all and won their allegiance by taking them into his confidence. 'When I played for Brearley he was an expert at blending a diverse group of characters into one successful unit, wrote Boycott. 'Brearley understood that each man needed something different if he was going to give his best in the middle.'[13] According to Boycott's Yorkshire and England team-mate Chris Old, Brearley was indisputably the best captain he played under. 'He used his training in psychology on the people he played with and against. He knew when to put an arm around players and when to kick them up the backside. He knew the right buttons to press.'[14]

This rapport was never better illustrated than in his relationship with Botham. It was to Brearley's advantage that he was 13 years his senior and intellectually his superior, but while brooking no nonsense from him he liked him as a person, respected him as a tactician and was in awe of him as a player. Responding to this mixture of firmness and friendship, Botham gave his all to his captain. 'No one could match Brearley's knack of getting the best out of Ian,' wrote England opener Graham Gooch.[15] 'He was without doubt my greatest captain,' concurred Botham. 'He encouraged me when I needed it, and restrained me if he thought I was in danger of overstepping the mark. More important though, he listened to me.'[16]

Not everyone fell for the Brearley mystique. One such person was his Middlesex and England team-mate Phil Edmonds who, as a Cambridge graduate, was one of the few people who could master Brearley in argument. Although they began as firm allies against the fusty old regime at Middlesex, their relationship gradually deteriorated as they quarrelled over tactics and Edmonds's worth in the team. Their simmering feud boiled over in the Perth Test on England's 1978/79 tour of Australia after a flustered Brearley openly disparaged Edmonds for his deficiencies as 12th man. It was at this point that Edmonds, frustrated by his demotion from the Test side, saw red and only the quick intervention of their team-mate John Lever kept the two from trading blows. Later Edmonds alluded to the retirement of Brearley as his biggest break in cricket, while Brearley admitted that his inability to handle the talented but volatile Edmonds ranked as the greatest failure of his captaincy.

Others have questioned Brearley's enviable reputation by pointing to his good fortune in having Botham at his peak when playing against some mediocre opposition in the Packer era, but if the great Australian captain Richie Benaud was correct when he pronounced that captaincy was 90 per cent luck and 10 per cent skill, then Brearley exploited his luck better than most.

Chapter 1

His Father's Son

JOHN Michael Brearley was born in the north London suburb of Harrow on 28 April 1942. Few things used to irritate his father Horace more than Geoff Boycott's contention that Mike was part of a gilded elite compared to his own humble provenance. Not true, he professed, since their ancestry was of lower stock compared to the Boycotts', who, as miners, were the aristocracy of the working class. Horace's grandfather, Joseph Brearley, was a mechanic from Triangle, a village four miles south-west of Halifax in west Yorkshire, who married Emma Normanton in 1868. After the birth of their son James in September 1872 they moved to Heckmondwike, a former mill town, nine miles south-west of Leeds, on the edge of the Pennines, where Joseph continued his work as a mechanic. James, too, began in the same trade, graduating to become an engine fitter who travelled all over the north of England mending and fitting crucial pieces of mill machinery. He was also a fearsome fast bowler for Heckmondwike. Once when Horace came off the field after scoring a century there, an old man in the pavilion congratulated him but told him that he wouldn't have scored it if his father had been bowling.

In 1896 James married Lydia Ann Gregg, the feisty daughter of Michael Gregg, a former carrier turned publican, and his wife Elizabeth Ann. Originally from Commonside, Dewsbury, a mill town with a radical tradition, they later moved to the village of Gomersal, north of Heckmondwike. They had eight children, the youngest of whom was Horace, born in 1913. The two eldest brothers, Joseph and Percy, both fought in the First World War, along with five other Brearleys from Heckmondwike. Joseph, a clerk in the rate office and choirboy at the local church, enlisted in the Yorkshire Hussars, the county's senior yeomanry regiment, aged 16, in September 1915. In 1917 the regiment was converted to infantry as the 9th West Yorkshire and later that year they were engaged in the bloody battle of Passchendaele, the Flanders offensive which claimed 250,000 British casualties. It was while volunteering for an advance attack that Joseph was shot through the lung and died instantaneously. He has no known grave, but his name is on the Tyne Cot Memorial near Ypres and on several war memorials in Heckmondwike. His commanding officer commended him for his bravery and unselfishness, qualities which won him the Victory Medal and the British War Medal. The fourth brother, Arthur, was a fine cricketer and led Heckmondwike to a hat-trick of wins in the Heavy Woollen Cup, the oldest club cricket competition in England, between 1936 and 1938. In 1938 he married Mary Crowther, a member of Spen Valley lacrosse team, and Horace was best man.

Horace, born in 1913, always said it was only because he was the youngest child, and the older ones were earning, that he was able to stay on at school and go into higher education. At Heckmondwike Grammar School, he won a maths scholarship to Leeds University, where he gained a first. A superb all-round sportsman, he played squash for the university and captained it at both hockey and cricket. In addition, he captained the

Combined British Universities cricket team, as well as playing hockey and cricket for Yorkshire, albeit a solitary appearance in the case of the latter.

Making his debut for the Yorkshire 2nd XI in 1935, he topped the averages the following year, scoring 449 runs from ten completed innings, and according to *Wisden*, 'stood out above any of his colleagues'. He was markedly less successful in 1937 but he did make his championship debut against Middlesex as an amateur, a late replacement for the England batsman, Maurice Leyland. Batting at number five in a side that contained legendary names such as Herbert Sutcliffe, Len Hutton, Hedley Verity and Bill Bowes, he made 8 and 9, sharing a brief partnership with Hutton in the second innings during which he complained that Hutton kept monopolising the strike.

That same year Horace began teaching at King Edward VII School, Sheffield, and it was there that he met Marjory Goldsmith, a fellow mathematician who taught at the sister school. Brought up in Surrey and educated at London University, Midge, as she was known, was a warm, sprightly person whose love of sport, especially netball and tennis, made her the ideal wife for Horace. They married, and on the outbreak of war they moved south when he enlisted in the Royal Navy. On being ordered to report to HMS *Hood* in March 1941, he was delayed on the railway and arrived in time to see the battleship putting out to sea. Two months later, she was sunk by the *Bismarck* with the loss of all but three of her crew of 1,418.

With Horace away for much of the war either on the high seas or in South Africa, where he taught navigation and meteorology to ratings, life was hard for Midge. After a spell living with her mother in Ealing, west London, she was evacuated to Yorkshire before moving to Portsmouth once Horace, now a Lieutenant Commander, was stationed there. On his discharge in 1946, he returned to teaching, first as head of maths at Sloane School, before joining CLS in January 1950 and remaining there till his retirement in 1978.

A warm, friendly man with a droll sense of humour, Horace was a natural schoolmaster liked and admired by his colleagues for his reliability and integrity. Never one to get embroiled in petty disputes, his down-to-earth bluntness and Yorkshire common sense ensured that the common room maintained its sense of perspective.

A gifted teacher of maths and mechanics, he made his lessons both interesting and fun. Having explained a topic for 10 or 15 minutes he would then give the class examples to work on, making himself available to those who were in difficulty. On occasions he would invite individuals to explain solutions and Terry Heard, later head of Maths at CLS, recalls that it was the satisfaction gleaned from such an experience that persuaded him to become a teacher.

Horace's ability to empathise with the less able was his particular forte. In later years, ex-pupils would come up to Mike and share their delight at his father getting them through their O-level Maths, and how both he and they did a jig of celebration when they heard the result. 'I had a great affection for Horace,' recalled former pupil John McGeorge. 'He was a very warm character; both as teacher and friend. He did not tell us how to solve a mathematical problem: he would solve it with us, as our friend.

'Horace displayed a pastoral interest in us, very important during our turbulent teenage years, and to me personally he showed great kindness.'[1]

In addition to his work in the classroom, Horace played a leading role in the life of the school: organising the timetable, singing in the choir, coaching rugby and hockey and running the school cricket. Although the least sentimental of men, he would always help those in trouble, on one occasion standing up for a boy whose strong right-wing views had alienated the School Society, even though his own politics were very different. It was a measure of the man that when Mike was in his class, he didn't favour him over other pupils and that Mike, in turn, was never embarrassed by having his father teach or coach him. He thought his father a 'terrific teacher' and once commended his style of 'invisible leadership' to a panel of international cricket umpires.

From 1945 the Brearleys lived at 62 Brentham Way in Brentham Garden Suburb, Ealing. It was the coming of the Great Western Railway in 1838 which opened up Ealing to the rest of London and led to a surge in development. Brentham Garden Suburb, built between 1901 and 1915, was the original garden suburb built on co-partnership principles, primarily by Henry Vivian, a trade unionist, the chairman of the Ealing Tenants Ltd and later a Liberal MP. Committed to the ideal of communal living in beautiful surroundings, the directors of Ealing Tenants designed cottage homes for working people in the Arts and Crafts style, each with their own garden. It was in this 'paradise' that Fred Perry, the greatest of all British lawn tennis players, grew up in the years after the First World War, and its green open spaces held a special appeal to Horace. Hailing from the industrial north, he used to marvel at the sight of trees in the street.

Growing up in their modest, terraced home, one of 600 or so on the Brentham estate, Mike and his two younger sisters, Jill and Margy, enjoyed a happy, secure childhood. Both Horace and Midge were warm, loving personalities who provided the most stable and caring of environments. Friends of Mike such as Brian Waters, John McGeorge and Martin Smith, who were guests at their home, recall the gracious hospitality. Shunning her teaching career for the responsibilities of motherhood, Midge was very happy with her close family, cooking, walking and playing the piano, as well as supporting them in all their endeavours.

Inheriting their parents' sharp intelligence, all three children succeeded at school and developed a wide range of cultural interests, but it was sport that most preoccupied them, with Mike persuading his sisters to bowl at him. His requests couldn't have been too taxing, since they remained very close to him and, in later years, they accompanied their parents to Lord's to watch him play.

At the heart of the Brentham estate was the Brentham Club and Institute, a focus for social and sporting life, adjoining 12 acres of cricket, hockey and football fields, as well as numerous tennis courts. Situated two minutes from the Brearley home, it became the centre of their universe, Horace playing cricket and football for Brentham, Midge and Jill active on the tennis courts and the young Mike an avid spectator. In the football season, when play was safely down the other end, he would chat to the Brentham goalkeeper Paul Swann, who, along with his brother, John, was one of his great heroes. Not only were both of them excellent footballers and cricketers, especially John, a classic left-hand bat, an accurate leg-spinner and a fine fielder good enough to have played for Middlesex, they were both men of sterling character who, like Horace, exemplified the very best of sporting values.

The coming of peace saw the re-emergence of Horace's cricket career. Aside from playing twice for Middlesex in 1949 – his second match against Somerset marked Fred Titmus's debut, aged 16 – and gaining his 2nd XI cap, he became a pillar of the Brentham club, scoring 15,000 runs for them as a solid opening batsman. David Bloomfield, a leading player for many years and now the club president, recalls how he had a great influence on everyone at the club, a source of encouragement to the younger members. Always kitted out in plimsolls, fast bowlers would try to hit his toes with a yorker but he was more than capable of looking after himself.

By the age of two, Mike was batting in the garden. Immediately captivated by the game, he laid out his own little pitch, mowed it and rolled it, before playing out his fantasy matches, his hero being Jack Robertson, Middlesex's prolific opener in the post-war era and a professional version of his father. 'From a very early age, my father was instilling in me not only a straight bat and a pointed left elbow[which had a suspiciously Yorkshire quality],' he later wrote, 'but also a sense of who was bowling and why someone else should have been; of where certain fielders stood and why they ought to have been elsewhere.'[2] Encouraging and supportive, Horace would spend hours making him dive for catches, but if they were playing catch uphill he'd be at the higher point so if Mike missed it, he would have to go all the way down the hill to retrieve the ball. It was the same when his father bowled to him at the recreation ground near the house they rented in Bognor each year, since Mike would have to run to fetch the ball whether he missed it or hit it.

At the age of seven his mother escorted him to Lord's for the first time to watch Middlesex and, shortly after joining CLS, his father took him to Jack Hobbs's sports shop in Fleet Street to buy him his first cricket bat, signed by 'The Master'. That same year he played in his first official match at Middleton-on-Sea in Sussex, near Bognor, where his family holidayed throughout the 1950s. As a small boy Mike would wander along the beach asking to join cricket games in progress, inducing a certain exasperation from those who couldn't get him out, before he gravitated to something more challenging.

Every August from 1945 to the 1960s, a local parish councillor, Betty Richards, organised a month of sporting activity for children at the Middleton Sports Club, including a colts' cricket week. When Middleton found themselves one short against Worthing Colts, a team comprising boys as old as 18, Brearley stepped in as a late replacement. Clad in his long whites which his aunt had managed to send him in time, he batted at number ten and scored 5*, a hook and an off-drive. Two years later, he was photographed in the local paper playing for the colts alongside Mike Griffith, later a team-mate at Cambridge; then aged 14, he scored two fours off the Bognor Colts' opening bowler John Snow, the spearhead of the England attack in the late 1960s and early 70s. As he hit his second four, Brearley's mother heard Snow's father say that her son would one day play for England. Such praise wouldn't have gone to his head because Horace's down-to-earth Yorkshire mentality wouldn't stand for it. Days later he had cause to quietly rebuke him for boasting as they walked round the Middleton boundary. 'I felt and can still feel the shame,' Brearley later wrote. 'I had been both arrogant and falsely modest, commenting to Mike Griffith and my father that my wicketkeeping was not "quite as good as Mike's on the leg side".'[3]

That same year, playing for the Middleton Sunday XI, Brearley came up against another future great cricketer, the Nawab of Pataudi, later captain of India, at Wisborough Green. Between them they barely troubled the scorers but this was the exception rather than the rule as Brearley began to make his mark, impressing Mike Griffith with his talent and application, 'one of those people who meant business'. A Middleton XI, comprising two Brearleys and two Griffiths – Billy, a former England wicketkeeper who made 140 on his debut against the West Indies in 1948, and his son Mike, a future captain of Sussex

– took some beating. Playing against the Musketeers, the 16-year-old Brearley hit Freddie Brown, the former England captain, for four off the back foot before Brown gained his revenge, bowling him for 33.

Back in 1955, Brearley had made his debut for Brentham, aged 13, against South Hampstead, making 0*, and he followed this, weeks later, with 3* against Malden Wanderers, a raucous side who felt miffed that they couldn't bowl short at him. 'After his father had scored 64 valuable runs …,' reported the local paper, 'young Michael Brearley batted like a veteran to ensure a draw for his club.'[4]

Aside from the odd appearance over the next couple of years, he played in the Sunday team in 1958, the club's golden jubilee, and although not that productive his promise was clear to all. The secretary reported: 'Michael Brearley, not yet 18, is a batsman of the future who also bowls and keeps wicket. It has been said he will be a better player than his father.'[5]

The comment would have amused Horace since he gave no quarter in any contest with his son. Always physically strong and immensely competitive, he would let Mike lead 20-16 at table tennis before he'd come back to win 22-20, and it was only when aged 59 that he lost to him at squash. Still top of the Brentham averages at the age of 57, Horace continued to turn out for the CLS staff well into his sixties, when his evident despair at a missed opportunity by the captain was all too apparent. His competitiveness rubbed off on his son. 'My father is a Yorkshireman … and I think I've got something of his attitude. I like to try to win,' Brearley later informed the *Sunday Times*.[6] 'His father approached his cricket intellectually, the sort of man who wanted to discuss all the intricacies of the game,' noted David Bloomfield. 'Michael was very much in that vogue. He was a very correct, strict player.'[7]

After attending North Ealing Primary School, one of the best schools in the borough, with his sisters, Brearley graduated to CLS, aged ten, a 40-minute trip down the District line from Ealing Broadway.

CLS, an independent day school for nearly 900 boys between the ages of 10 and 18, was founded in 1834 by a private act of parliament following a bequest from John Carpenter, a former town clerk to the City of London, who died in 1442. His bequest was administered by the Corporation of London for the benefit of local children. When a report by the Charity Commission in 1823 revealed that the accumulated funds had greatly exceeded the educational expenses, the decision was taken to found a permanent school. Originally established at premises in Milk Street off Cheapside by the Corporation of London, the new school appealed to progressive sentiment because of its non-denominational status and its emphasis on subjects such as science and commerce, as well as more traditional ones such as classics. As its popularity soared, its pupil body including the future Liberal prime minister Herbert Asquith, it soon outgrew its site and it moved to a new one, just west of Blackfriars Bridge on the Victoria Embankment, in 1883. The imposing new building, high Victorian in style, housed the Great Hall with its stained-glass windows and impressive organ, where the school gathered every day in assembly.

Compared to its older, prestigious neighbours, Westminster, Dulwich and St Paul's, CLS was more socially diverse, with many of the suburban middle class taking advantage of its low fees and generous number of scholarships. The school contained a sizeable Jewish minority who benefited from its ethos of tolerance and diversity. The poet and novelist Sir Kingsley Amis, who was a pupil there between 1934 and 1942, wrote:

I have never in my life known a community where factions of any kind were less in evidence, where differences of class, upbringing, income group and religion counted for so little.

The academic teaching was of a standard not easily to be surpassed, but more important still was that lesson about how to regard one's fellows, a lesson not delivered but enacted.[8]

His words still applied in the 1950s following the school's evacuation to Marlborough during the war years. The common room contained many schoolmasters of dedication and brilliance who left a lasting impression on their charges, none more so than the classicists, the Rev. C.J. Ellingham, who also taught English, and H.C. Oakley. Ellingham was a gruff muscular Christian, who inspired both Kingsley Amis and, later, the renowned literary critic John Gross with his love of poetry, while Oakley, a committed Baptist of sheer goodness, nurtured generations of Oxbridge classicists. According to Barrie Fairall, a contemporary of Brearley's, who recalls his schooldays with much pleasure, they had some marvellously kind and long-suffering teachers.

What disturbed the tranquil waters of the common room was the arrival in 1950 of the new headmaster, Dr A.W. Barton, from King Edward VII, Sheffield, the school where Horace Brearley had previously taught. Unlike his revered predecessor, Dr F.R. Dale, a distinguished classicist and war hero, Barton was a physicist from Nottingham and his provincial roots bred in him an insecurity that he was never able to shed. His autocratic style and rigid insensitivity won him few friends among his colleagues, especially after sending home the director of music because the jacket and trousers of his suit didn't fit. Yet behind his austere exterior, he wanted the best for the boys and he set out to achieve this by appointing younger masters, raising academic standards and advancing the cause of music.

Helped by a free education available to all staff children, Brearley entered CLS in September 1952 and immediately flourished, singing in the choir, playing the clarinet in the orchestra and excelling both at work and sport. In his book, *The Art of Captaincy*, he relays his earliest memories of leadership when captaining the CLS under-12 football XI against Forest School. Awarded a penalty by the Forest referee with the score still tied at 0-0, he admitted to shirking his responsibilities of taking the penalty but having failed to persuade anyone else to take his place, he stepped up to the mark. Without any thought as to placement, he ran in and kicked the ball as hard as he could in the general direction of the goal. The ball hit the bar and bounced back but, despite knowing the rule that stipulated that after the penalty kick some other player must be the next to touch the ball, Brearley still kicked it into the net. The referee rightly disallowed the goal and CLS went on to lose 5-0. 'Even as I write this,' he wrote in *The Art of Captaincy*, 'I tremble and sweat from reliving the anxiety of the awful moment as well as from embarrassment at my absolute lack of coolness, followed by misguided coolness. Captaincy material, was I? It is hard to believe.'[9]

On a happier note he scored his first century aged 11 when scoring 120* against Forest, an achievement that won him a copy of the MCC coaching book from Rev. Ellingham. A stalwart of the under-13 XI for two years – in 1954 he excelled as a leg-break bowler taking 5-22 against Forest and 8-21 against Dulwich – he was promoted to the under-14s a year early in 1955 to give him stiffer competition.

CLS, in line with its location at the heart of the capital, boasted a rich extra-curricular life which appealed to someone of Brearley's all-round interests. While prominent in the major sports, and participating in boxing, tennis, athletics, cross-country and swimming at house level, he also acted and debated alongside a talented group of contemporaries: the film director Michael Apted, the philosopher Jonathan Barnes, the poet Anthony Rudolf, the actor John Shrapnel, the businessman Peter Levene (later Lord Mayor of London) and the political scientist Michael Pinto-Duschinsky.

Terry Heard, a classmate of Brearley's in the middle school, where he frequently won classics and English prizes, remembers him as one of those outstanding characters who excelled at everything but was very nice and unassuming. His view was endorsed by Barrie Fairall, later a sports journalist, who noted his photographic memory and ability to assimilate information very quickly. He recalls that one of Brearley's essays about squashing an annoying fly flat on his masterpiece was shown to his class as an example of imaginative writing.

Compared to many independent schools, field sports at CLS lacked kudos and, consequently, the captains of rugby and cricket weren't revered figures. In keeping with the character of the school, 1950s sport wasn't compulsory. On Wednesday afternoons, when games for the all-age groups were held at their playing fields at Grove Park ten miles away, boys who did not wish to participate could wander off into central London.

A natural ball player with excellent hand-eye coordination and the quickest of reactions, Brearley proved adept at Eton Fives – a form of handball in an oddly shaped court – so much so that in the opinion of his team-mate Anthony Rudolf he could have been something special had he really concentrated on the game. On one occasion he was due to play against Eton the day after the house cross-country run. The fives master, Tom Manning, didn't want him to participate, so that he would be fresh for this prestigious match, but Brearley refused to withdraw and the headmaster ruled in his favour. He duly ran and came tenth, but paid for it the next day. Two sets up, Brearley ran out of steam and he and his partner lost 3-2.

Playing first pair with Robert Thatcher in 1958-59, they reached the semi-final of the Public Schools Eton Fives Championship, CLS's best-ever result, before losing 3-1 to the eventual winners Aldenham. 'One of the best players we have had. If he lacked anything it was real crispness,' declared *The City of London School Magazine* as it assessed his contribution to CLS fives. [10]

At cricket, Brearley's promise was such that, aged barely 14, he made his debut for the Ist XI, beginning a five-year stint in the team, which, even allowing for the relatively low profile of cricket at CLS, was some achievement.

Batting at number seven, he made 18* in his first match against Emanuel and followed up with 18 against St Dunstan's College in his next innings. Runs became harder after that, his last eight innings yielding a mere 37 runs, and against the Staff he was stumped for 5 off his father. 'A promising bat with a sound defence and correct technique,' recorded *The City of London School Magazine*. 'He must learn to hit the loose ball harder.'[11]

Promoted to opener the following year, he became the ballast of the CLS team, his 73* against MCC being the highlight. 'Most encouraging was the batting of Brearley, who scored over 400 runs at the age of 15,' noted *Wisden*. [12]

He maintained his progress in 1958, with half-centuries against the Frogs, a prominent wandering club, and the Haberdashers' Aske's Boys' School, although his liking for the pull led to his downfall on several occasions. A useful leg-break bowler, he took 17 wickets, including 5-35 against Chigwell, and had the satisfaction of dismissing his father for 80 in the Staff match, but as he grew, he could no longer spin or control the ball, so he took up wicketkeeping instead.

On inheriting the captaincy in 1959, Brearley really came into his own in a year in which CLS only lost one school match. His progress was helped by the hiring of Reg Routledge, the former Middlesex all-rounder, as coach. He got him to move his top hand behind the bat and drag the bat down with it, as well as constantly telling him, 'Let the ball come to you.' After beginning with 26 and 5 he then showed his class with 83 against Forest, 77 against Merchants Taylors', 103* against the Forty Club, 126 against Eltham, 107 against the Old Citizens, 111* against Chigwell, 79* against Bancroft's and 111 against the Staff.

In those days it was a school tradition that anyone who scored a century for the school, a fairly rare occurrence, was given a cricket bat by the headmaster. John McGeorge recalls an assembly presided over by the second master Cyril Nobbs, who, after making reference to another Brearley century, commented wryly, 'That will cost the headmaster another bat.' In actual fact, according to the novelist Julian Barnes, several years his junior, Brearley gallantly declined to claim more than one bat a season, no doubt on the advice of his father.

Even though the CLS circuit wasn't that strong, Brearley's average of 84.58 for 1959 was remarkable. Only once before had a City batsman scored two centuries in one season, let alone four, and no one had ever scored 1,000 runs. While *The City of London School Magazine* suggested he should lean into his off-drive, instead of getting most of the power from his arms, it commended him for his excellent defence, his reliable wicketkeeping and his intelligent captaincy. Used to discussing tactics with his father since the age of eight, Brearley, according to Lionel Knight, then a member of the 2nd XI, had a transformative effect at both encouraging teams and individuals. He recalls playing under an unenterprising captain in the 2nd XI whose overriding aim was not to lose and Brearley, playing on the adjoining pitch, suggested to this captain that he could win the match. His words changed everything since Brearley was the one person whom the 2nd XI captain would listen to.

He was also an impressive ambassador for his team. Barrie Lloyd, who twice played for the Frogs against CLS when Brearley was captain, recalls him as a charming young man, testimony to a father whom Lloyd found both warm and encouraging as he strove to establish himself in club cricket.

During the winter of 1958-59, Brearley had attended nets at Lord's and had come under the supervision of the former Middlesex leg-spinner Jim Sims, a genial, humorous man inclined to utter platitudes out of the side of his mouth. 'Michael,' he would say, 'a straight ball has a certain quality about it. If you miss it you've 'ad it.'

That summer Brearley opened the batting for the Middlesex Young Amateurs, striking gold in their final match against Surrey at The Oval. Batting first, Middlesex struggled early on against their giant opening bowler Richard Jefferson, fresh from a highly successful season at Winchester where he'd taken 56 wickets. With the ball moving all over the place, Brearley was fortunate to avoid facing Jefferson before the latter broke the heel of his boot, forcing him to leave the field for the rest of the morning while he went shopping for another pair of size 12s. By the time he returned after lunch, Brearley had reached his century. He was finally out for 115, lbw to Jefferson.

With his captaincy of cricket, his high profile in the school and the esteem in which he was held, Brearley appeared a strong candidate to be head of school. Rumours to that effect circulated after he was made a prefect halfway through his penultimate year, but he had to be content with being senior prefect and head of Carpenter House. It has been suggested that the headmaster didn't appoint him to avoid accusations of favouritism, given Horace's position in the common room, but this is to speculate.

Contrary to its progressive ethos in matters of religious toleration, voluntary games and the absence of fagging, CLS had a more repressive side. Not only was the Combined Cadet Force compulsory – Brearley was in the Naval Section and passed Advanced Naval Proficiency – the powers of the prefect body were considerable, not least the power to beat. Compared to some prefects who flaunted their authority to excess, Brearley was very self-effacing, staunchly resisting any form of bullying. He was also a model diplomat. When his good friend John McGeorge flouted school rules by eating a sandwich in the classroom, Brearley said to him, 'John, you are putting me in a very difficult situation,' a conundrum which McGeorge readily accepted. He thought Brearley a natural leader since success in no way turned his head. It was a view endorsed by Anthony Rudolf. Brearley commanded respect, he recalled, because he was friendly, intelligent and unassuming, while *The City of London School Magazine* noted that he led Carpenter House 'with an enthusiasm that prompted even the youngest boys to follow his example'.[13]

Given his outstanding intellect, his choice of subjects for the sixth form wasn't entirely straightforward. Shunning maths which both his parents had specialised in, he opted for classics 'largely because I was good at it, it was well taught, and it seemed the respectable thing to do'.[14] It proved an apt choice because under the tutelage of the head of classics, Dennis Moore, and Stanley Ward, he won both the Latin and Greek Verse Prizes in 1959, in addition to the Sir James Shaw Classical Prize, and elected to sit the Cambridge entrance exam.

Once he'd set his sights on Cambridge, Horace asked Colin Ranger, a young biology master, if he would give some time to take Mike through the evidence and principles of evolution, since the evolution of species was one of the topics covered in the Oxbridge General Paper. So Brearley went to Ranger on a one-to-one basis in the biology library for an hour or so on a couple of Wednesday afternoons. 'It goes without saying that he was assiduous in his work, made use of the literature in the library and came prepared,' recalled Ranger. 'MB was much reported in the staff room with interest and pleasure, partly because his father was on the staff but mostly because he was a pleasing character who generated a presence, something to do with leadership qualities I would venture.'[15]

His efforts reaped their reward with a minor scholarship at St John's College, Cambridge, part of his roll of honour in his final year: winner of Dr Conquest's Gold Medal for the best overall academic achievement, winner of A Special Prize for all-round service to the School Games, winner of the Classical Association (London) Greek Reading Prize, first pair in the fives team and 1st XV rugby colours. 'His first-class handling and deceptive side step made him a formidable three-quarters in attack,' commented *The City of London School Magazine*. 'However, here he was handicapped by a certain lack of speed. He was strong in defence and his touch kicking was very good.'[16]

He also became a leading thespian. Each year the school play was exquisitely produced by the debonair Geoffrey Clark, who managed to make all kinds of boys exceed their capacity. Martin Neary, later Organist and Master of the Choristers at Westminster Abbey, remembers a reluctant Brearley being given a small walking-on part and being coaxed into something more positive than might have been expected. After previous minor parts in *Androcles and the Lion* and *Henry V,* he performed as one of the citizens in scenes from *Julius Caesar* before the renowned actress Dame Edith Evans on Beaufoy and Mortimer Prize

Day, and played Horatio alongside John Shrapnel's Hamlet and Michael Apted's Claudius in *Hamlet*. 'Brearley was very steady and dignified in speech and bearing contrasting nicely with the volatile Prince,' remarked *The City of London School Magazine*; 'he gave the noble concluding lines very firmly.' [17] He then participated in a sixth-form modern dress performance of *The Frogs* by the Ancient Greek playwright Aristophanes in the theatre of the Guildhall School of Music. 'J.M. Brearley as Dionysius sustained his difficult and exacting part well, in the double character of the unheroic god of wine and the patron of drama.' [18]

Overshadowing all his accomplishments was his success on the cricket field. 'City of London will be captained again by J.M. Brearley, a batsman with quite a phenomenal record behind him,' commented *The Times* in their preview of his final season. 'It is a tall order to have to build a side round one man, but Brearley is the only full colour left.' [19] After a quiet start with one fifty in his first seven innings, he returned to form with 99 against the Frogs, 109* against Chigwell, 60 against Haberdashers' 95* against the Staff and 89* against Bancroft's, the next top score being 9. Robin Sengupta, later a good friend, recalls bowling chinamen for Haberdashers' when Brearley was dispatching his team to all parts, and appealing loudly for lbw out of sheer desperation. 'It was a rank bad appeal because he was quite a distance down the wicket. I felt bad about it and apologised to Mike at the end of the over. His response left me stunned. He said, "Don't worry about it." But then went on to say, "You would have had to worry if I had been given out."

'That for me embodied everything Mike was ... competitive, yet witty and with a double dose of intelligence.' [20]

'Although he was not quite so prolific as in the previous season, his batting developed in maturity and power,' wrote

The City of London School Magazine. 'Shots off the back foot went through the covers for fours instead of ones, while his on-driving became, at times, very aggressive. A neat and effective wicketkeeper. A first-class captain with a thorough knowledge of the game and a keen appraisal of the tactical situation.'[21]

'Brearley in his final year averaged 68 for 615 runs,' wrote the *Evening News's* cricket correspondent E.M. Wellings in *Wisden.* 'He spent five years in the school team, and his complete aggregate was 2,651 runs with an average of 53. Brearley headed the averages in the last four years. The importance of his batting in 1960 was shown by the fact that the second average was merely 17, 51 below Brearley's mark.'[22]

He continued his summer in prolific form for the Old Citizens, the alumni cricket club for CLS. 'Michael Brearley has, of course, been a great asset when he has been able to play,' commented their journal *The Gazette.* 'In his first eight innings he has scored 556 runs, including three centuries, and averaged over ninety.'[23] He also captained the Middlesex Young Amateurs, scored several half-centuries for Middlesex 2nd XI, and played for both the Southern Schools against the Rest and the Public Schools against the Combined Services at Lord's. In both matches he kept wicket and opened with Edward Craig, a prodigious run scorer at Charterhouse who exceeded Peter May's aggregate and average there, making 0 and 34 in the first match and 2 and 46 in the second.

For all Brearley's accomplishments at CLS, he remained a grounded, self-effacing individual. The headmaster, Dr Barton, at his final speech day in November 1964, looking back at his 14 years in charge there, cited Brearley's career at school and university as one of the highlights. 'With all his remarkable achievements he remains a modest young man, one of the most remarkable ever produced by Oxford and Cambridge.'[24]

Others drew a similar picture, but while mentioning the high esteem in which he was held, they stress there was no adulation, since it wasn't that kind of school.

For several years after leaving, Brearley remained in contact with the school, playing fives and cricket for the Old Citizens. Thereafter, despite attending the annual dinner of the 1960 Society, comprising all the prefects of that year, he has had little to do with the school till more recent times, perhaps a reflection of his mildly anti-elitist outlook manifest throughout his career.

Chapter 2
'Shades of C.B. Fry'

FEW personalities have adorned the history of cricket more than C.B. Fry. Not only was he one of England's best-ever batsmen, he was the greatest all-rounder of sport of all time, representing England at football, equalling the world record at the long jump and excelling at almost every other sport. At Oxford between 1891 and 1895, he won three successive blues in cricket, football and athletics in his first three years, which, combined with his prowess as a scholar, writer and debater, made him something of a phenomenon. No England cricketer has come close to emulating him but Brearley evoked some comparison with his intellectual and sporting accomplishments at Cambridge.

With its honey-stone quads, immaculate green lawns and leisurely punting on the river, Cambridge appeared locked in a timeless world of gilded charm, none more so than St John's College, one of the university's largest and most prestigious colleges. Founded in 1511 by Lady Margaret Beaufort, mother of King Henry VII, it could boast seven prime ministers, ten Nobel Prize winners, the romantic poet William Wordsworth and two former England captains, Norman Yardley and Freddie Brown, among its alumni. Yet amid such grandeur and tradition,

Cambridge wasn't immune to the winds of change blowing across the Fens. No longer merely a haven for the wealthy elite, the university was becoming more middle class, meritocratic and socially conscious as the first stirrings of a vigorous youth culture appeared. It was a development which appealed to aspirational types like Brearley, as it did to a whole cluster of budding Conservative politicians on the make such as Kenneth Clarke, Michael Howard and Leon Brittan. Clarke, an undergraduate at Gonville and Caius College between 1959 and 1963, wrote:

> Those of us at Cambridge all assumed that we were on the way to securing lifelong careers with whomever we afforded the eventual privilege of employing us. There were full-time rugby players, some of whom played internationally, full-time actors and entertainers and full-time cricketers … The staggering undergraduate success was Mike Brearley, who combined captaining the first-class cricket team in the summer with getting a starred first in his degree. [1]

As someone troubled by the ongoing debate between art and sport, not least at university, Brearley tried to ride both horses, a delicate balancing act he pulled off most of the time despite occasionally coming unseated. During his second term, the Cambridge Greek play, Aristophanes's *The Clouds,* clashed with the University lacrosse match, which was to be played at Oxford that year, and Brearley, who'd been given the significant part of the leader of the chorus by the eminent theatrical director Dadie Rylands, chose the latter. He later recalled that when he informed him at the first rehearsal that he was having to withdraw, Rylands announced to the rest of the cast, 'This dear young man is going off to play netball for the university'. But he kindly permitted him to play the god Hermes, appearing with winged sandals on a pedestal to pronounce the last two lines, on those nights he was in Cambridge.

With St John's renowned for its reputation in the classics, it wasn't surprising that Brearley's fellow classicists in college were a talented group. Aside from his good friend, Michael Scholar, later a top civil servant, he was friendly with Michael Silk, later professor of Classical and Comparative Literature at King's College, London, and Malcolm Schofield, later professor of Ancient Philosophy at Cambridge. Silk recalls Brearley as pretty self-confident, secure in his studies and sport but holding something back, and Schofield recollects a bubbly individual with a great twinkle in his eye who liked teasing people, yet difficult to get close to. 'He was never a person who wanted to tell you things. He was better at listening and he would have been a good civil servant.'[2]

For all the prestige of the Cambridge classics department, the course lacked breadth and relevance. With the emphasis overwhelmingly on linguistic purity, the opportunity for exploring the meaning of ancient texts and independent thought was limited. According to Silk, who recalls discussing English and German poetry, the reading of Homer today and T.S. Eliot's *Murder in the Cathedral* with Brearley as they leaned out of their respective windows in college, he was very able. Although he appeared to lack the time to spend on scholarship, he came across as a natural, a view endorsed by his results. In Part 1 of the Classics Tripos, he secured a first with distinctions in Latin and Greek verse composition. It made a fitting end to his study of the classics as he, along with Scholar and Schofield, switched to Moral Sciences, the formal name for philosophy. Silk recalls being unsurprised by Brearley's decision, since he didn't appear attached to the classics. 'My objection to classics was that at the end of it I couldn't, or at least didn't, read Virgil fluently,' Brearley later wrote. 'Also, I began to doubt the shibboleths about discipline and classics. I think there is discipline involved in learning anything.'[3]

In his second year he went to lectures on Greek philosophy by Renford Bambrough, a former miner who won a fellowship at St John's in 1950 and became a notable Cambridge figure thereafter as a lecturer, broadcaster and administrator. A philosopher in the tradition of G.E. Moore, Ludwig Wittgenstein and John Wisdom, the professor of philosophy at Cambridge, Bambrough's calm rationality made a deep impression on his students. Although his northern dissenting background bred in him a seriousness of purpose for life's great issues and a lofty disdain for those who affected facile opinions, his warmth and compassion endeared him to generations of Cambridge undergraduates. Having helped persuade Brearley to switch to philosophy with the clarity of his teaching – 'he made things that seemed completely crazy sort of thinkable' – he later became his supervisor and good friend.

In a department where most of the lecturers took their eccentricity to extremes, philosophy, with its lack of answers, posed a more challenging discipline than classics, but Brearley found the exchange of ideas liberating. He specialised in metaphysical and ethical philosophy and the history of modern philosophy, being drawn, like Bambrough, to the human kind of philosophy – what matters in the world.

In addition to Bambrough, he was greatly influenced by John Wisdom. A lively, quirky personality with a great love of horses, he would appear at 9am lectures in his riding kit and place his crop down on the desk. According to Schofield, a lot of his teaching consisted of sitting around and looking deeply puzzled, not knowing what to say. A follower of Wittgenstein, the great Austrian-born British philosopher and esteemed Cambridge professor, Wisdom lived out the truth of his famous dictum that philosophy is not a doctrine but an activity.

When Brearley first attended Wisdom's lectures on 'Other Minds and Metaphysics' in 1963, he was disconcerted by his silences, his apparent puzzlement and his direct questioning. He fled. A year later he tried again and stayed. Gradually he came to see that his teaching method, too discursive for some, reflected his ideas about philosophy as he drew out of his students thoughts which many felt might be unconscious and inaccessible. It was his argument that the uncovering of unconscious ideas and assumptions was an important element in dealing with philosophical perplexity, as it was in psychoanalysis, that opened Brearley's eyes and enlarged his sense of human emotions. The two formed a close attachment. 'Brearley was a fair-minded and sympathetic man,' Wisdom later recalled. 'He never set out to demolish another man's argument, before making any objections, he would look for something valuable in what the man was saying.'[4]

Despite Brearley's many commitments, especially his captaincy of the cricket XI for two successive years, his studies in no way suffered. Schofield recalls that he worked hard and was extremely well organised, rising early to get through his busy schedule. 'The exams only lasted three weeks so I didn't find them a problem,' Brearley later remarked. 'I worked hard in the mornings and had a great time playing cricket for the rest of the day.'[5]

Although lacking the knowledge and range of arguments and a sharp enough focus on the question to replicate his first in Classics, his reward was an upper second in Moral Sciences. A further boost came shortly afterwards when he came joint top in the civil service examination, a career he briefly considered.

When it came to sport, Brearley was spoiled for choice. He continued to play some fives but this took second place to lacrosse, the oldest half-blue sport at Cambridge. Introduced to it by his friend Jon Prichard, who'd played it at Manchester Grammar School, he made remarkable progress with his tireless probing and harrying. After helping St John's to win Cuppers, the inter-collegiate sports competition, in his first year, a feat they repeated in the following two years, and gaining his half-blue, he went on the Oxford and Cambridge tour to the USA that March. In his second year, he and K.F. Winterbottom were prolific in front of goal, none more so than against Oxford at Grange Road, when he shot the best two goals of the afternoon in their 9-1 victory. His efforts, described as 'outstanding' by *Varsity*, the Cambridge undergraduate newspaper, as well as Cambridge's subsequent victory in the South of England Flag, their seventh in nine years, won him selection for the South against the North. 'Brearley's selection is particularly noteworthy at the end of only his second season in lacrosse,' reported *The Times*. 'As a natural ball player, with a remarkable instinct for the tactics of the game, he could eventually achieve considerable distinction on the lacrosse field.'[6] It wasn't to be. After helping the South to a rare 9-5 win against the North, he gave up lacrosse the following year, considering it an unsatisfying game unless played at a high level of skill. Taking up hockey instead, he developed into a gifted inside-right who excelled as a thinker and distributor, for the Wanderers – the Cambridge 2nd XI – and even managed some games for the Blues.

Following in the footsteps of such sporting giants as Hubert Doggart, Peter May and David Sheppard, Cambridge University cricket had flourished throughout the 1950s, its wickets at Fenner's among the best in the country. It was here that Ted Dexter had risen to eminence but now, in the twilight years of the amateur, the cricket club was beginning to suffer from ailing finances and declining attendances, especially at the Varsity match, as the game lost some of its sparkle.

Since 1938 Cambridge University cricket had revolved around the stalwart figure of its groundsman, Cyril Coote. Renowned for the quality of his pitches, Coote, an accomplished batsman for Cambridgeshire in his day, acted as coach and mentor to generations of undergraduates, and soon Brearley was benefiting from his throw-downs in the nets as he tried to get him to hit through the ball with a straight bat. He later wrote that one of the big regrets of leaving Fenner's for good was losing the help of Coote. 'No one knows more about the game than he does.'[7]

In an inexperienced Cambridge side, captained by David Kirby, later the long-standing master in charge of cricket at St Peter's School, York, and containing the future England captain Tony Lewis, Brearley was preferred as wicketkeeper to his friend Martin Smith. He made his debut against Surrey, which marked the return of Peter May to first-class cricket after an absence of over a year through illness. May made 68 out of his side's 290 before the attack, led by England's Peter Loader and Tony Lock, went to town on the university batting. Entering at 60/6, Brearley didn't let the situation faze him. He opened his account with an on-drive off Eric Bedser and proceeded to prosper in partnership with Mike Edwards, the future Surrey opener. Together they put on 106 and, after the former was dismissed for 51, Brearley went on to make 76 before he was run out. It was largely due to his effort that Cambridge were able to escape with a draw.

He continued to look the part in the next match against the county champions Yorkshire after the opening attack of Fred Trueman and Bob Platt had reduced Cambridge to 29/6 in their first innings. Undeterred by Trueman's pace or reputation, he played him with confidence and finished with 33*, more than double the next score. Although easily beaten, the university had clearly unearthed a cricketer of genuine pedigree. 'If the past fortnight has yielded a "find", it is Brearley,' commented Jack Davies, an ex-Cambridge blue and honorary treasurer of the university cricket club, in *The Cricketer*. 'He has kept wicket with uniform competence and he has batted with a soundness and judgement few freshmen, except Lewis, have shown us in recent years.'[8]

After two unremarkable matches, Brearley gave further notice of his potential with scores of 73 and 57* against Sussex, during which he helped save the game with Richard Jefferson. It was useful preparation for the visit to Cambridge of Richie Benaud's Australians. On the truest of Fenner's surfaces, the first four Australian batsmen all scored centuries in their 449/3 declared before their bowlers made serious inroads into the Cambridge batting. Entering at 107/6, Brearley batted with great composure and judgement to make 73 before he was last man out – lbw to medium-pacer 'Slasher' Mackay. Because of an injury to Cambridge opener Nicholas Alwyn, Brearley deputised and returned to the middle as the university followed on. Despite losing Edward Craig early, he again exuded confidence as he and Lewis added 70 for the second wicket with strokes all around the wicket. From 69* overnight, he continued to display defiance the next morning before he tried to cut a full toss from left-arm spinner Ian Quick and was caught at the wicket. His innings of 89, containing 15 fours, wasn't enough to save his side from a nine-wicket defeat, but his performance won him some glowing reviews. Michael Melford in the *Daily Telegraph* wrote:

> For a 19-year-old freshman to bat for five hours against the Australians and make 162 is remarkable enough. Yet it was the way the runs were made that stirred the thoughts and hopes for the future.

There are no strokes which he does not seem to be able to produce if needed and his footwork throughout was something to bring joy to a coach's soul.

His running between the wickets and his ability to monopolise the strike when No 11 was in with him yesterday was testimony to his cricket sense, inherited no doubt from his father, an eminent London club cricketer.[9]

The Australians, too, were impressed. 'His 73 and 89 and a neat exhibition of wicketkeeping were surely the work of a potential England Test player,' wrote Benaud, while Jack Fingleton, the former Australian opener turned critic, thought he'd seen a great batsman in the making.[10]

Brearley continued his bountiful run at Fenner's with a maiden century and 42* in the next match against the Free Foresters followed by 145* against Kent, 100 of which were in boundaries, and 52 against Lancashire. Another centurion against the Free Foresters and Kent was opener Edward Craig, who Brearley described as his superior both as a scholar and a batsman. It wasn't false modesty since Craig secured a first in both parts of Moral Sciences, a pointer to his later career as Knightbridge Professor of Philosophy at Cambridge, and topped the Cambridge averages that year with five centuries. According to Jefferson, 'Whereas Craig was verging on genius – he had incredible talent – Mike was much more of a fighter and a grafter.'[11] Standing next to each other through many long sessions in the field, they traded philosophical niceties such as 'Did a biscuit have a soul?' and Brearley found these conversations so stimulating that they helped bring about his switch to philosophy.

Away from Fenner's when on tour, Brearley proved less prolific aside from a polished 74 against an MCC attack which included Frank Worrell and Gary Sobers, on the eve of the

University match. Over the course of the season, Oxford had looked the more accomplished side but a serious car accident had deprived them of their charismatic captain, the Nawab of Pataudi. On an abbreviated first day, Cambridge, after winning the toss, had their work cut out to reach 90/5. *The Times* cricket correspondent wrote:

> Brearley has batted so far for 85 minutes and has been more at ease than anyone. There are those who see him as a budding Test match batsman, in the May and Sheppard class as an undergraduate, and he has matured perceptibly since I saw him make two fifties against Sussex in May. The impression then was of self-effacing promise.
>
> On Saturday, with the same boyish approach, he played with bat and pad closer together and offered some well-made strokes when the chance arose. For one straight from school he shows a surprising understanding of batting on an awkward pitch and a welcome determination to play an attack on its merits. So long as he pursues his uncomplicated way, without becoming grave and theoretical, his success should continue. [12]

He only added a single on the second day before he was lbw for 27 and Cambridge were indebted to an aggressive 54 by Jefferson to reach 173. Oxford declared at 232/8 with a lead of 59 but any hope they harboured of victory was foiled by a painstaking century from Craig. In its review of the Cambridge season, *Wisden* commended Craig and Brearley for easily exceeding 1,000 runs and singled out the latter for his technically polished style and wide range of shots, alongside his competent wicketkeeping.

Brearley and Craig returned to Lord's the day after the University match to play for the Gentlemen against the Players, an all-but-unique experience of two freshmen playing in this fixture within less than a year of leaving school. Neither distinguished themselves as the Gentlemen were comfortably beaten. Brearley then made his debut for Middlesex, keeping wicket in the absence of John Murray who was on Test duty, but he achieved little in his two matches and was subsequently demoted to the 2nd XI. He returned to the spotlight for the traditional Gentlemen-Players end-of-season fixture at the Scarborough Festival but, once again, he failed to shine.

Not for the first time, he encountered, at Scarborough, the genteel traditions of the first-class game which offended his free-thinking spirit. Raised in progressive environments at both Brentham Garden Suburb and CLS, he developed quite a disdain for social elitism and institutional protocol. Not only did he upset E.W. Swanton by refusing to play for the Free Foresters, deeming them to be a group of crusty old colonels, a view he later admitted to be somewhat harsh, he adopted a similar attitude towards the Frogs, a club he'd briefly represented. (In one match for them at Harrow, he and fellow opener Barrie Lloyd began with a century partnership, whereupon, on dismissal, he read Chester Wilmot's *The Struggle for Europe,* an acclaimed history of the Second World War.) His social sensitivities may well have been heightened by the assumption of others that he was grander than he actually was. In *The Art of Captaincy,* he recalls playing for the Middlesex 2nd XI at Hove as an amateur because he wasn't paid. 'I was still at school; this was only my second game with a mainly professional side. I was told to change in a large room, plush with carpets and sofas, along with our captain R.V.C. Robins (Esq). The other ten – all professionals – were changing in a tiny makeshift room virtually under the showers. Perhaps it was not entirely a coincidence that I was run out twice in the match.'[13]

The next year Brearley arrived at Scarborough for the festival unaware of the need for a dinner jacket when dining in the Cricketers' Room at the Grand Hotel. 'All this seemed pretty anachronistic to me and I felt the sooner we saw the end of the distinction between amateurs and professionals the better.'[14]

That distinction ended the following year but old habits lived on for some time. When Brearley took over the Middlesex captaincy in 1971, he was surprised to be asked by one of the committee whether he had a private income and, for some years afterwards, he battled against the blimpish attitudes of MCC, most notably over standards of dress.

Following his auspicious first season, Brearley was appointed Cambridge secretary, effectively deputy to captain Tony Lewis, an urbane Welshman with a deep hinterland. Lewis later recalled the pleasure of watching Brearley and Craig bat in their many fine partnerships, 'both thoughtful, chanceless but overflowing with humour. Indeed, when we fielded together in close positions we spent a lot of our time giggling.'

He thought he detected Brearley's later success as captain. 'He was always the man who enquired, thought the matter through to the root and took positive action even if it went against convention, or, I suspect, especially if it did. He was direct with people, often argumentative, suspicious of formality. I was keen to have my Cambridge team photographed at Lord's wearing scarves knotted and tucked inside the light blue blazer. I liked that. It reminded me of misty old pictures. Mike argued that it was unsuitable because it was hot and unnecessary. It had no sense. He was right, but a dreamy-eyed nostalgia won.

'What Mike had in his Fenner's day, sure to stand by him, was humour and the common touch. He never adopted a stylized Oxbridge posture, it would have been abhorrent to him. He was a clever, determined and a stimulating companion. You could see the determination in his batting.'[15]

While Cambridge lacked decent spinners, they had three class batsmen in Lewis, Brearley and Craig, plus a hard-hitting South African, Ray White; an effective opening bowler in Tony Pearson, who'd taken ten wickets in an innings against Leicestershire the previous year; and two promising all-rounders in Tony Windows and Richard Hutton. Lewis and Brearley's reluctance to select Hutton at first earned them an invitation to dinner with his father at the Garden House Hotel in Cambridge. 'He can play, you know,' Sir Leonard assured them. Over the succeeding years, Sir Leonard came to Fenner's to watch Richard play and Brearley became fond of them both.

Brearley began the season in poor shape, his first 12 innings yielding a mere 174 runs. After missing three matches because of exams, he celebrated his return with a century against Combined Services, followed by 99 against Sussex and 68 against Leicestershire, but, overall, his form remained patchy. With Oxford experiencing a wretched season, Cambridge, despite winning only one match, approached Lord's as favourites. They batted first and Brearley once again displayed his big-match temperament by becoming the third wicketkeeper, all from Cambridge, to hit a century in the University match since the First World War. As he battled through the early stages with Craig, the *Daily Telegraph*'s E.W. Swanton was moved to write:

> We now had a First in Classics joining a First in Moral Sciences, but this massive intellectual combination was obviously occupied with higher things than the mundane matter of running between the wickets. [16]

Brearley's 113*, consisting of many admirable cover-drives among his 18 boundaries, enabled Cambridge to declare at 259/6. Oxford, after early alarms, recovered to 237 all out and then pressed for victory by reducing Cambridge to 68/5 before a painstaking century by Lewis saved their blushes. His declaration wasn't a generous one and, although Oxford began in enterprising fashion, the loss of three quick wickets forced them to put up the shutters.

Consigned to the Middlesex 2nd XI thereafter, Brearley did little of note before winning promotion to the county side for the final two matches of the season. He responded with 45 and 15* to help beat Lancashire and 83* in the rain-interrupted match against Kent, sharing in an unbroken seventh-wicket stand of 118 with Fred Titmus, the England all-rounder.

On assuming the Cambridge captaincy in 1963, Brearley had the makings of a talented side with Craig, Hutton, Windows, White and Pearson still in harness, along with Roy Kerslake, a capable off-spinner who later captained Somerset, and a promising wicketkeeper-batsman in Mike Griffith. The latter recalled Brearley not only as a very workmanlike batsman who never gave it away, but also as an exceptional captain who displayed a much more professional approach than anyone he'd previously encountered.

On one occasion the team went to a May ball and arrived at the ground the next morning in an inebriated state, except for Brearley who scored a hundred. Besides telling his batsmen what he expected, he could get quite aggressive in the field if his players didn't concentrate. Once, Griffith was fielding on the boundary and let the ball come to him, a lapse which earned him a wigging from Brearley, who berated him for not attacking the ball. Yet for all his competitiveness, Griffith admired him for his terrific sense of fun, the interest he took in people and the help he gave them, not least by providing an alternative view of themselves.

Brearley in turn received sound advice from Cyril Coote and Jack Davies, an alumnus of St John's, who besides taking a first in Classics, bowled Bradman for nought at Fenner's in 1934, Bradman's first duck in England. After playing cricket for Kent and rugby for Blackheath, Davies became chief psychologist at the War Office during the Second World War, before returning to Cambridge in 1952 as secretary of the university appointments board. With their many interests in common and Davies's sense of humour, Brearley looked up to him, placing him very high on his list of those with whom he'd like to share his last dinner.

Griffith's presence helped persuade Brearley to give up the gloves and concentrate on his batting. After two matches at number three, he moved up to open and, after laying down firm roots, he burst into full bloom in mid-May with 100 against Leicestershire, 75 against Nottinghamshire, helping Cambridge to their first victory over a county for two years, and 79 against Sussex. As with the previous two years, scoring away from Fenner's proved more taxing, but the team, nine of whom were to play county cricket, had gelled under his leadership and they approached Lord's with optimism.

Oxford had benefited by the return of the Nawab of Pataudi and would take some beating. In the event, despite the good intentions of both teams, another draw resulted. With bad weather interrupting the second day, Pataudi declared 45 runs behind Cambridge's first innings and Brearley responded in kind by inviting Oxford to make 194 in two hours and 20 minutes. They began with intent but their enterprise appeared their undoing, and at 101/6 with 35 minutes still to go, defeat seemed a real possibility before all-rounder John Cuthbertson, top scorer with 62 in the first innings, again, came to the rescue.

When a draw appeared all but inevitable, Brearley came on to bowl underarm, tactics he'd previously employed against Sussex, much to the consternation of Test umpire Frank Lee. 'To me, this was terrible,' recalled Cuthbertson with some amusement as he negotiated several grubbers which reminded him of prep school. 'The thought of being bowled by Brearley was too much to bear. He was always thinking some strategy up his sleeve.'[17]

Although experiencing a double failure with the bat, Brearley had captained the side imaginatively and helped restore the flagging reputation of one of cricket's oldest fixtures.

The year 1964 was when Brearley really came of age. The first person to hold the office of captain in successive years since F.S. Jackson in 1892/93, he impressed not only as captain and opening bat but also capped a memorable year by his selection for MCC to tour South Africa that winter.

Although he was unable to coax Craig away from his studies for another season, he had all his other leading players, Pearson aside, and the team provided opposition for many a county visiting Fenner's with only Northamptonshire and Leicestershire winning there. On tour their record was less spectacular, but two of their five defeats were close affairs and a third, against MCC, was on the back of two declarations. In one of those defeats – against Kent at Folkestone – Alan Knott, batting on his first-class debut, recalls Hutton wasting time in the closing overs by running in to bowl from the sightscreen. 'Brearley became very cross and told him to complete the over more quickly. He then bowled off a couple of paces and conceded more runs than he might have done.'[18]

After a quiet opening match against Glamorgan, Brearley scored 53 and 31* against Middlesex and 157 and 50 against Gloucestershire, 29 and 45* against Essex and 7 and 13* against the Australians. Arriving late for the game against

Northamptonshire after a three-hour exam, Brearley went in at number seven with Cambridge reeling at 48/5. For the next three and a half hours his dominance was such that he scored 92 out of the remaining 129 runs. He excelled again in the second innings with 75 and it was largely due to his efforts that Northamptonshire won by only two wickets.

After signing off at Fenner's with 21 and 2 against Lancashire, his run spree continued with 169 against Combined Services. He performed consistently on tour and in the course of his 106 against MCC he became the second person in the country to reach 1,000 runs for the season. Despite his achievements, however, his team hadn't played to their potential. When taxed about this by *Varsity*, he admitted that they ought to have produced 'a win or two by now', but there was an inability to capitalise at the crucial moments. It was this slightly amateurish lack of finality which prevented them from being a top-class side.

With Oxford beset by injuries and dismal form, Cambridge certainly started as overwhelming favourites for the Varsity match. Having dismissed their opponents for 142, Brearley, in company with Griffith, then gave a masterclass in batting as they added 167 for the third wicket. Scoring his second century in the series, the former was at his stylish best, his 17 fours comprising many a classical drive, especially off the front foot. 'For those who say that academics and games at Oxford and Cambridge can scarcely now be mixed this is a redoubtable answer,' declared Swanton.[19] 'If he can give the time to it, Brearley should have much to offer the game of cricket,' commented John Woodcock in *The Times*. 'Even a tour this winter to South Africa is not beyond the bounds of possibility. He has marked ability, a sound method, a level temperament, and a fine University record.'[20]

With 119 from Brearley, 82 from Griffith and 89 from White, Cambridge declared at 363/8, 221 ahead, after half an hour on the final morning, but despite an encouraging start they were foiled by a resolute fourth-wicket stand of 130 between Maurice Manasseh and Richard Gilliat, later captain of Hampshire. The former finished 100* to earn Oxford an honourable draw. Although the result disappointed Brearley, he could derive much satisfaction from his final season at Cambridge in which he'd scored 1,313 runs at an average of 57.08. Only three other Cambridge cricketers had scored more runs in one term and he took his career aggregate there past 4,000 runs, surpassing the record of David Sheppard, although he had nearly twice the number of innings as the latter. 'It was uncommon for an undergraduate to stay at the head of the first-class averages or thereabouts for a period of six weeks,' wrote Jack Davies in *The Cricketer*. 'Brearley's performances this year undoubtedly justify his exalted position. He has fulfilled amply the promise he showed during his successful first year in 1961. In defence his head is right over the line of the ball. He plays mainly off a firm right foot, but the operative leg is always very near the oncoming delivery. He concentrates admirably, is continually on the look-out for the scoring stroke and has no particular weakness for the bowler to attack.'[21]

Brearley's success guaranteed him a regular opening slot at Middlesex and together with Eric Russell he formed one of the most successful opening partnerships in the country. In his third game he scored a second-innings century against the Australians, the latter part against exhibition bowling, putting on 135 with Russell, a prelude to further opening partnerships of 110 and 107 by them in the next two games against Gloucestershire and Surrey. Two weeks later, they went one better with an opening stand of 174 in the first innings against Northamptonshire at Northampton. Russell made 138 and Brearley made 75 but Middlesex still lost by ten wickets.

A further honour came his way with his appointment to captain the President of MCC's XI against the Australians at Lord's. He was perhaps fortunate that that year's president was Gubby Allen, formerly of Cambridge and Middlesex, captain of England and one of the most influential people in the game. Disillusioned by the recent drift in English cricket, he looked to youthful brio to revitalise it and in Brearley he saw a kindred spirit. His enterprise was rewarded as Brearley and his team lost nothing in comparison with the tourists and won their spurs for their spirited effort. In dank conditions, he inserted the Australians and his bowlers exploited a helpful wicket to good effect, dismissing them for 162. The President's XI responded with 193/9 whereupon Brearley declared and saw fast bowler David Brown once again bowl Bobby Simpson for nought, the first pair in the Australian captain's career. A second-wicket stand of 186 on the third day between opener Bill Lawry and wicketkeeper Barry Jarman avoided any further embarrassment, before Simpson declared, leaving the President's XI to score 228 in two and a half hours. A scintillating opening stand of 112 in 84 minutes between Brearley and Geoff Boycott, a centurion in the Oval Test against Australia days earlier, gave them the perfect start and it was only after the former was brilliantly run out for 67 that their victory charge faltered. 'They failed,' wrote the *Daily Mail*'s Ian Wooldridge, 'but not before Brearley had demonstrated his full range of powerful strokes and a dynamic approach to a challenge.'[22]

He'd demonstrated his prowess at the most opportune of moments, because the final six places for the MCC tour to South Africa were due to be chosen the following day. The selectors' deliberations were complicated by Colin Cowdrey's last-minute decision to make himself available for the tour having previously ruled himself out for family reasons. After a four-hour discussion, they decided that the reserve opening batting slot should go to a specialist opener and hence Brearley was preferred to Cowdrey, a decision that baffled Richie Benaud. 'Brearley is a fine lad and a promising cricketer – Cowdrey is so far ahead in class and skill that one wonders in fact just why he was left out.'[23] According to Mike Smith, the captain to South Africa, the general thinking at that time was to pick a promising youngster and Brearley had strong backing from Gubby Allen. His selection elicited a mixed response. Swanton called it 'a sound and imaginative choice', and Woodcock, while regretting the omission of the Surrey opener John Edrich, a recent centurion against Australia in the Lord's Test, accepted the logic of taking him. 'Brearley could well be an England captain of the future if he stays in the game. He has great promise and is improving fast.'[24]

Edrich's omission dismayed Denys Rowbotham, the cricket correspondent of *The Guardian*. 'As plucky, determined, and concentrated a player as England possesses, he is at once more experienced and defensively more comprehensively equipped than is Brearley, who, even in success at Lord's, looked frighteningly vulnerable on a trusting front foot. Brearley is an attractive stroke maker, but Edrich is no less forceful and lucrative. In cricketing insight, there can, as yet, hardly be comparison between them. Has the mere idea of youth run to MCC's head? Or is an outmoded concept of amateurism buried but still not yet dead?'[25]

Others adopted a similar view. 'Much as I support Brearley,' wrote Alex Bannister, the *Daily Mail*'s cricket correspondent, 'I cannot believe at this moment that he is a more qualified opener than Edrich, Eric Russell, who is technically supreme, or Stewart. All are consistent run scorers, and have been for several seasons.'[26]

Brearley's inclusion coincided with Middlesex's match against Kent when, needing three to become the first man to complete

2,000 runs in the season, he was out for a pair dismissed in both innings by opening bowler John Dye. (Ironically that distinction now went to his fellow opener Russell.) He reached the milestone in the next match against Lancashire and finished his season in style with 78 and 55 against Derbyshire. His exploits won him the Cricket Writers' Club Young Cricketer of the Year award for 1964, and with a tour to South Africa pending his future looked a gilded one.

Chapter 3

Growing Up in South Africa

WHILE England's home record in the mid-1960s was indifferent, their only defeat overseas during the whole decade was in India in 1961/62, and that was with a depleted side. Mike Smith's side to South Africa lacked quality among its pace bowlers with no Trueman, controversially discarded, or Statham, but the batting led by Boycott, Barber, Dexter and Barrington looked formidable and Brearley would need to play above himself to gain a Test cap.

Although the players were warned to stay aloof from politics following growing opposition to the apartheid policies of the white Nationalist government, their departure happened to coincide with election day in Britain. Ted Dexter had abandoned the England captaincy in order to represent the Conservatives in the Cardiff South East constituency against the future prime minister Jim Callaghan, a contest he lost comfortably, and as the team assembled outside Lord's to make their way to Heathrow, the Conservative candidate for St Marylebone, Quintin Hogg, later Lord Hailsham, drove past canvassing support through a loudhailer. His chutzpah prompted Cartwright, a lifelong socialist, to wave a fist and shout something derogatory at him, and Brearley did something similar. 'I remember that moment,' Brearley later told Stephen Chalke, Cartwright's biographer. 'I could never vote Conservative, and Tom could certainly never vote Conservative. Somehow we knew that about each other straightaway. So there was an immediate pleasure in each other's company.'[1]

While Australia remained the ultimate tour for any aspiring MCC cricketer, South Africa with its superb climate, stunning scenery and sumptuous hospitality invariably proved the most enjoyable. Following the recommendations of manager and captain after the previous trip there in 1956/57, this one not only comprised a reduced itinerary, it also began in Rhodesia to avoid its wet season. The colony was in a state of political ferment over the refusal of Ian Smith's government to offer any constitutional guarantee of black majority rule, but, despite the Rhodesians' impasse with the mother country, their hospitality couldn't be faulted. The team quickly came together under Smith's benign leadership, their camaraderie helping them perform beyond expectation on the field, especially given the inexperience of their pace attack. They began with convincing wins against Matabeleland XI and Rhodesia, only then to struggle against South African Colts, a team strengthened by the inclusion of the young Barry Richards. The fact they avoided defeat was primarily down to Brearley. After scores of 26 and 19* against Matabeleland and 29 and 23 against Rhodesia, his promising first innings against the latter ended by a brilliant run out by Colin Bland, the world's finest outfielder, he top-scored in the first innings against the Colts with 68. According to Ron Roberts of the *Daily Telegraph*, 'Brearley's judgement, until beaten by a beautiful ball from Macaulay, the brisk left-hander, underlined the encouraging development he has shown on this tour.'[2]

He again impressed in the second innings by playing out the last 70 minutes to help stave off defeat, and then won glowing reviews for his century against Transvaal Colts, a non-first-class game like Matabeleland, adding 183 in 115 minutes with Smith. 'Brearley's century was another milestone in the career of a young man maturing with every innings,' wrote the *Daily Mail*'s Ian Wooldridge.[3] A week later, he again sang his praises after his composed 49 in MCC's innings win against Transvaal. 'Brearley, like Boycott, has played in all five matches and his haul to date is an impressive 341 runs at an average of more than 58. More important, his technique has improved with almost every innings.'[4] 'I am sure you will be particularly pleased to see that Mike Brearley has done so well,' the manager Donald Carr wrote to Billy Griffith, secretary of MCC. 'He has improved with almost every innings and might well find a place in the Tests.'[5]

No sooner had these words been written than Brearley's fortune began to wane with an indeterminate shot against Natal. All at sea against off-spinner Norman Crookes, he was eventually bowled by him for 7 as he made room to late-cut. 'How many runs would you have got if you'd played that shot exactly right?' his captain gently quizzed him afterwards, and when he replied 'one', Smith said, 'So was it worth it?' Only Brearley and Boycott missed out as their batting prospered, setting up a ten-wicket win. Opening for the first time in the next match against Eastern Province, Brearley failed yet again – bowled by Springbok all-rounder Eddie Barlow for 12 – while Boycott banished doubts about his pedigree with a painstaking 193*, adding 278 for the fourth wicket with Smith.

Boycott continued in similar vein against Western Province with another century, compared to Brearley who looked a mere novice as he repeatedly played and missed. When after an hour he was caught at slip for nine, the error surprised nobody, reported *The Guardian*'s Denys Rowbotham. He restored some confidence with 64 in the second innings, helped by the encouragement of his partner, Ken Barrington, but it took the best part of four hours and was marred by technical defects. According to Woodcock, he 'found the art of batting more elusive than the mastery of moral sciences'.[6] His stance became increasingly open and the predominance of his bottom hand not only hampered his timing, it also restricted his off-side strokes, especially on the front foot. Others noticed his flaws. During the first Test at Durban, he was floundering in the nets batting against David Brown and Robin Hobbs when he became aware of an elderly man standing behind the net. He was wearing a trilby hat and looked a bit yellow; he obviously wasn't well. On finishing his net, Brearley was approached by the man who asked him if he might make a comment on his batting, and when Brearley agreed, he told him that he had to relax; his hands were too tight on the bat, especially his left hand. Brearley listened politely and did nothing about it.

'At some point I was told that this sallow man … was none other than Wally Hammond, one of England's most successful batsmen, and one of the greatest stylists of all time,' Brearley later wrote. 'Despite knowing this, I did not properly take on board what he had said.'[7] He called it his lowest point. 'I was arrogant not to take any tip from Hammond seriously. I was also insecure, not solidly in my own self. I was both eager to please and unwilling to buckle down in order to reflect on what was said, and work to strengthen my technique.'[8] It didn't help that he was given endless advice – much of it conflicting – from scores of different people, some suggesting a change of grip, others a different pick-up.

With Boycott and Barber, England's established opening pair, scoring heavily in the team's innings victory in the first

Test, Brearley was destined for a life in the shadows. The tour began to lose some of its lustre, he wrote from Durban. 'Very quickly one gets used to the chauffeur-driven cars, the packing and unpacking, the press and the official welcomes. I can now better appreciate Wes Hall's remarks the first time I met him as he mechanically tore a telephone directory to pieces in his hands, to the effect, that "Man, was he tired of living out of a suit-case".

'Wes … would find himself *persona non grata* in this country, of course. But this whole subject is very *non grata*. It is very unfortunate for cricketers and for cricket lovers here that they can never see him and the other West Indians. There would certainly be some attractive cricket then.'[9]

Running himself out for 11 in the next match against South African Universities, he found some form against North Eastern Transvaal with 45, his last match for nearly three weeks to accommodate back-to-back Tests at Johannesburg and Cape Town – both drawn. The break did nothing for him as scores of 0 and 5 against Border and 0 and 2* against Orange Free State – and that was an edge to win the match in the final over – would testify. 'I was immature when I went to South Africa,' he later confessed. 'I got tense batting, flaws into my technique, and I got very bored with having to watch the cricket all the time and having no role I fooled around, stayed out too much, went to parties. And I played worse and worse.'[10]

An injury to Barber in the fourth Test which finished his tour gave the reserve opener a golden opportunity to stake a claim for the final Test, but even this inducement did little to raise his stock. Against Griqualand West, one of the weakest provincial sides, he opened with reserve wicketkeeper John Murray and made 43 but unable to establish any fluency it took him nearly three hours. Given one final opportunity to impress, against a South African Invitation XI, he failed in both innings with 0 and

5 and lost out to Murray, whose transition from the lower-middle order to opener had yielded a mere 35 runs in four innings. 'This morning, at practice, it was sad to see Brearley, whom everyone likes so much, neglected and forgotten as a batsman,' noted Woodcock.[11]

Reduced once again to a passive role in the Port Elizabeth Test, Brearley was appalled and embarrassed to watch England bowl 29 overs in one two-hour session as, forced to field first with a makeshift attack, they resorted to defensive tactics to preserve their 1-0 series lead. Thanks to a first-innings century by Boycott and bad weather bringing a premature end to the game, they achieved this even though the tedium of much of the cricket somewhat sullied their triumph.

With three ducks in his final eight innings and only two first-class half-centuries from 19 innings, Brearley's tour average of 25.37 paled compared with his team-mates. 'Brearley was bitterly disappointing for himself as much as for everyone else,' wrote Basil Easterbrook in *Wisden*. 'This personable young man who conducted himself well in adversity should also draw comfort from the fact that many distinguished cricketers made a hash of their first tour.'[12] Describing the second half of the tour as 'a complete disaster for him', the BBC cricket correspondent Brian Johnston thought Brearley acquitted himself remarkably well. 'I never once heard him complain, and throughout he played his part in supporting Mike Smith and the team in every possible way.' Making up a four for bridge with Brearley, David Brown and Charles Fortune, the South African sports broadcaster, Johnston voted him by some way the best player. 'I'm bound to say that it didn't matter what Brearlers had in his hand. He always seemed to win.'[13]

Such positive assessments of Brearley chimed with those in official circles. In his end-of-tour captain's report, Smith wrote:

After a good start he had a most disappointing tour with the bat. Fortunately, he was able to accept his failures where someone else less sensible might have caused embarrassment. I do not think it is sufficiently appreciated how much the standard of University cricket is below Championship – particularly University batsmen can show up favourably. Once he hit a bad patch, he had no experience to fall back on, or a proven technique. Sound in the field and a safe catcher.'[14]

Looking back over half a century later, Smith declared that those who fail on tour miss out quite a bit. 'That's life. It has happened to plenty of others over the years. There's only one way to resolve it – get some runs. Mike was a good player but, unfortunately, didn't make the most of it.[15]

Responding to a complaint by an MCC member that Brearley had been treated shabbily, a bizarre allegation considering that he'd played in every game outside the Tests, manager Donald Carr had this to say:

I can assure you all the Selectors would have been only too delighted if Brearley had had some success, but unfortunately following some good form in the early matches, he failed to do himself justice. When a player is not selected for Test matches on the tour it is bound to be somewhat difficult for him to regain his form and confidence, since he may go for a week or two without an innings in the middle, but I am afraid this is one of the hazards of touring and there have been several similar instances in the past. Brearley is, of course, a delightful person and a fine cricketer, and I sincerely trust that any disappointment which he may have had in South Africa will not affect his views regarding playing first-class cricket for a number of years.[16]

While disillusioned by his failures and chronically unsure of himself, the tour gave Brearley an opportunity to broaden his political horizons. Prior to departure, his views on apartheid weren't fully formed but once out there he had his eyes opened.

'I suppose I was distantly disturbed about apartheid before I went to South Africa. All we had been told about apartheid was that we should keep out of it. Very much par for the course. I knew that people like David Sheppard had called for tours to be cancelled but it was a bit distant from me ...

'During the tour I had quite a lot of time off and I spent Christmas Eve in one of the townships near Johannesburg with a bloke who worked at our hotel. He was of Indian origin and he took me to his home. I was only 22 but I was a young 22 and for the first time I came across an Indian family in which the woman served me and then retired behind a screen. So there was a cultural bit of learning in addition to the township with the dogs barking and my being a bit afraid and not really sure I was supposed to be there. I was outside my comfort zone.'[17]

He spent Christmas Day with his Cambridge friend Ray White and his family, including his sister Jill and her barrister husband who were both left-wing activists strongly opposed to apartheid. According to fellow tourist Robin Hobbs, Brearley was more interested in talking with the Cape Coloureds and his local friends than mixing with the cricketers in the evening, but he did gravitate towards the Warwickshire pair of Cartwright and Barber, another Cambridge graduate with liberal sympathies. Although the team had been warned off politics at the beginning of the tour, the three of them tried to probe behind the veneer of apartheid to discern its reality. 'Mike Brearley was very conscious of the politics,' recalled Barber, 'and on two occasions, once in Cape Town and once in Durban, we got one of the black drivers of the Rothmans' cars to take us into townships at night. It was dangerous. You could end up in prison for doing that sort of thing. I suspect the instigation came from Brearley. Mike and I said to the driver, "Stop the car!" We got out and knocked on someone's door and asked to come in. Very nosey but everyone was very polite.'[18]

Brearley's closest companion on tour was Cartwright, a car-worker's son from Nuneaton, whom he called 'decent, honest and thoughtful' with a great commitment to the underdog. Cartwright, in turn, admired Brearley for his humility and found him engaging company. 'Michael was always very keen to learn. He was younger than me, but I felt comfortable with him except I used to say to him, "Don't start analysing me." He found it very difficult not to do that. It's very disconcerting when you're talking to somebody and you know they're analysing you.'[19] On one occasion Brearley asked Cartwright if he would go around a Ford Motor company plant in Port Elizabeth with him. Escorted by the local manager, Brearley went further than Cartwright thought wise. 'But Michael got this notebook out and he kept asking these questions – questions that I was hoping he wouldn't. He was asking what they were paid – the coloureds, the blacks – and he turned to me, "What would they get paid in Coventry at Rootes, Tom?" Then he'd write it down.'[20]

During the tour Brearley met up with Sir Cyril Hawker, chairman of Standard Bank and an Old Citizen, who believed that British business would open up South Africa and help pave their way to democracy. Discovering that Brearley didn't share his optimism, he placed a car and driver at his disposal at the end of the tour, giving him the opportunity to go wherever he wanted and to meet whomever he pleased, confident that he would come around to his thinking. He went to Swaziland and the Transkei, visited a township and met politicians of all persuasions. At Pietermaritzburg, he lunched with Alan Paton, the renowned writer and anti-apartheid activist, whose novel *Cry, the Beloved Country* was a searing account of social and racial injustice in South Africa. When he expressed concern about the perils of social upheaval, Paton told him that sometimes it was necessary simply to do what was right. 'I came to realise that though it was hard to be sure that a sporting boycott would be effective, even in that sports-mad country,' Brearley later recalled, 'it felt intrinsically wrong to carry on sporting contacts, and I spoke out against such tours in 1968 and subsequently.'[21]

Chapter 4

The Wilderness Years

AFTER his travails in South Africa, it was gratifying for Brearley to regain his touch in the traditional opening fixture between MCC and Yorkshire. He began imperiously, hooking Trueman for three successive fours and looked the young Lochinvar of old as he carried his bat for 90. Unfortunately, his innings proved something of a false dawn since, in a wet summer, he struggled against the moving ball, and after a wretched run of 222 runs in 15 innings he was dropped. His return at number six brought little improvement till he was restored as opener. A watchful 89 against Northamptonshire was the prelude to a fluent 71* against Sussex, which helped Middlesex to a nine-wicket victory, but aside from 73 against Glamorgan there was little else of note. A county average of 20.07 signalled a highly inauspicious season and helped shape Brearley's subsequent destiny.

Unlike the vast majority of professional cricketers, Brearley, despite his love of the game, wasn't completely in thrall to it. In an article in *Varsity* during his final year at Cambridge, he declared that total commitment to an activity tended to diminish other sensibilities. 'In a sense it is a relief to lose, for a while, the almost servile relationship to the Master. I am still unable to achieve the ideal of the sportsman, relaxed concentration.'[1] He felt that it was about time that he got rid of this nervous tension which afflicted him on occasions, and the irritability and lack of tolerance which accompanied it. In a subsequent interview with *The Cricketer*, he thought playing six days a week, month in and month out, rather daunting. 'Cricket is very different at the University. We really only play half a season, and for the past two years I have had the mental stimulus of captaining the side.'[2] Without the captaincy, cricket became less enticing, especially in the fractious Middlesex team where his face didn't quite fit. 'When I went into the Middlesex dressing room as a young undergraduate, I realised it wasn't like being in the Cambridge dressing room. I realised I had to earn my place. Sometimes I felt out on a limb but not really lonely.'[3] Less forthcoming in this company, he kept his distance off the field and even some of his friends felt wary of being analysed by him.

His failures in 1965 left him further isolated and demoralised. 'Cricket is not a good game if you're not good at it,' he wrote. 'If you're out for nought, you've done nothing all day, then you're not much good in the evening either. It's hard to separate bad play from your own self; you begin to feel feeble.'[4] 'After leaving Cambridge I had a lean time with Middlesex and I failed in the MCC's tour of South Africa. I just didn't think I was good enough for first-class cricket,' he told the *Daily Mail* in February 1967.[5] With success less assured and boredom creeping in, he sought a career in academia, 'with a high-minded (and probably snobbish) idea that becoming a philosopher would be intrinsically more valuable or estimable than becoming a cricketer'.[6]

In October 1965 he returned to Cambridge to undertake research in philosophy at his old college, St John's, and was asked by university captain Deryck Murray the following May to play against Yorkshire to provide support for the less experienced batsmen. After a duck in the first innings he proved his worth with a second-innings century as his team lost by eight wickets. He then played for Cambridge against Gary Sobers's West Indians but made only 9 and 4, bowled by the leg-spinner David Holford in both innings.

He also helped St John's win Cuppers for the first time, beating Jesus in the final over, and played for Cambridgeshire in the Minor Counties championship as wicketkeeper-batsman with beneficial results. According to *Wisden*, 'Cambridgeshire, who rose fourteen places and finished fourth, were fortunate in having the services of J.M. Brearley; he kept wicket ably and opened the innings consistently well.'[7]

Opening the innings with Tony Shippey, a good enough player to score 94* against the 1969 West Indians, he averaged 30.35 from 19 innings with a top score of 85 against Hertfordshire. 'Mike was a stylish batsman – very circumspect and correct. He didn't believe in bludgeoning the bowling,' recalled fast bowler Derek Wing, a stalwart of the county for over 20 years. When asked whether he should have done better, Wing replied that the Minor Counties had some decent cricketers and that the wickets were generally of poor quality, especially compared to Fenner's.

A fascinating pastime for Brearley was keeping wicket to Johnny Wardle, the former Yorkshire and England left-arm spinner, who took 69 wickets at 12.50 that season with his chinamen and googlies, many a victim being caught at the wicket or stumped. 'Mike could read him,' recalled Wing. 'A lot couldn't.'

Beyond that, the team, comprising a number of farmers, looked back on Brearley with respect. 'For us to have him in the side was a privilege,' commented Wing. 'He didn't attempt to lord it over us and was a thoroughly good companion.'[8]

In September 1966 Brearley had the opportunity to pursue research in philosophy and psychoanalysis at the University of California, Irvine, in Orange County, one of its ten campuses, a vigorous year which he greatly enjoyed. His bat and ball were objects of curiosity to his fellow students brought up on baseball and American football. Before he departed for the USA, he was invited to lead an MCC under-25 tour to Pakistan in January/February 1967, a surprise given his lack of first-class cricket over the previous year. Enthused by the prospect of leading a strong side that contained the likes of Dennis Amiss, David Brown, Keith Fletcher, Alan Knott, Pat Pocock and Derek Underwood, he couldn't formally accept till he'd cleared it with the authorities at the University of California. Fortunately, the dean of humanities, Samuel McCulloch, an Australian by birth, was a cricket buff and permission was readily granted.

Having kept himself fit in California by playing squash, Brearley returned to England for two weeks' practice before the team's departure in mid-January for an arduous six-week tour of non-stop cricket. Before they left, they received a briefing from the Commonwealth Relations Office about the volatile nature of Pakistan and the potential obstacles to overcome. Given the vagaries of the local climate, food and accommodation, the manager Les Ames, the former England wicketkeeper and secretary-manager of Kent, went well stocked with preventative medicine and tins of bully beef for sandwiches on long journeys. After endless meals of curry, Brearley amazed his team-mates one lunch by ordering steak and kidney pie, roast potatoes and cauliflower, followed by apple tart and thick custard, from the waiter, all of which arrived within a few minutes.

Following four days of practice in Karachi, MCC began with convincing wins over South Zone and Central Zone. The latter game, however, was tainted by the running out of Geoff Arnold for backing up too far, without receiving the customary warning by the bowler, Saeed Ahmed. The tough, uncompromising nature of Pakistan's cricket surprised the tourists, but it helped them forge a healthy team spirit. On those dead wickets and against opposition of the calibre of Asif Iqbal, Majid Jahangir Khan, Mushtaq Mohammad, Sadiq Mohammad and Wasim Bari, MCC would need something special to secure victory in the three-match series.

Fielding first on a lifeless wicket in the first Representative Match at Lahore, they made an encouraging start when Pocock quickly dismissed both openers, which brought in Mushtaq, the most experienced batsman on either side. Knowing that he tended to stab at the ball early in his innings, Brearley wanted Pocock to have a short leg in case he did this to the turning ball, but Pocock wasn't keen on the idea and his way prevailed. A few deliveries later, Mushtaq pushed forward and the ball lobbed gently off bat and pad to where short leg would have been. He didn't give another chance in his innings of 120.

Facing a total of 429/6 declared – an innings marred by crowd trouble after the police attacked spectators who rushed on to the field to congratulate Mushtaq when he reached his century – MCC soon lost Brearley for 4. Attempting to glance Majid, he looked startled to be given out caught down the leg side off his pads. Later the umpire concerned approached him to apologise for his decision, explaining that he'd felt his arm going up and couldn't stop it.

With 124 from Fletcher, 99 from Amiss and 50 from Knott, MCC gained a narrow lead in a match that drifted aimlessly to a draw.

Brearley's fortune turned days later at Peshawar where, in ideal batting conditions, he pulverised North Zone for 312*, becoming only the second Englishman to score 300 in a day.

(The first, ironically, was his childhood idol, Jack Robertson.) Opening with Knott, who hit his maiden first-class century, he reached a chanceless hundred, before he threw caution to the winds with an aggressive display of indiscriminate hitting against the pedestrian attack. The first of his three sixes nearly sent Radio Pakistan off the air since it missed the commentator's microphone by inches and the second dropped in the Ladies' Stand, causing many of its occupants to scurry for safety. By the time of the third, the scorer is said to have thrown his pen away overwhelmed, and walked off towards the Khyber Pass. According to *The Times*'s correspondent, 'The MCC captain batted with the grace of a master, excelling with cover-drives, lofted pulls, and square cuts.'[9]

Buoyed by handsome wins over both North Zone and the President's XI, MCC entered the second Representative Match at Dacca in confident vein. Batting first, they overcame the loss of Knott for nought as Brearley, in company with Amiss, took control. In a scintillating innings far superior to his 312, he constantly pierced the defensive fields with effortless drives, pulls and square cuts. From 187* overnight, he continued his chanceless knock the next morning till he was out driving for 223. He'd batted six hours and 40 minutes, hit 40 fours and outshone Amiss in their second-wicket stand of 356. According to Alex Bannister, he could have scarcely batted better. 'Brearley played so remarkably well that any partner could have been no more than subservient to him.'[10]

Although MCC lost their last seven wickets for 64, they made 474 before their bowlers began chipping away at the Pakistan batting. When a brief shower on the third morning halted progress, the long delay seemed out of all proportion to the conditions. Brearley and Les Ames tried to hurry the umpires along but they weren't for turning, much to their frustration.

Although they enforced the follow-on, their lacklustre bowling on a flat wicket and a dashing century by Asif Iqbal enabled the home side to escape with a draw.

The third Representative Match at Karachi saw the bowlers assume greater control but not enough to break the stalemate. After dismissing MCC for 183 to gain a first-innings lead of 37, Pakistan challenged them to score 255 to win at 68 an hour. With no regulation new ball available at the beginning of their innings and Brearley refusing to play with the old one, play was halted till after lunch by which time a new ball had been found. They soon lost makeshift opener Mike Bissex but Brearley and Amiss comfortably played out time, the former surpassing his first-innings 58 with 79*. Considering his team's onerous schedule and their misfortunes with injury, their tour record of four wins from seven first-class matches and no defeats was an admirable one.

While Knott, Amiss, Fletcher, Hobbs and Pocock had enhanced their reputations, their accomplishments paled in comparison to Brearley's, who finished with 793 runs at an average of 132. 'As for myself I could hardly put a foot wrong,' he wrote in his tour report in *The Cricketer*. 'Even Cyril Coote, our Cambridge mentor, would have been pleased with my cover-drives at Dacca.'[11] Knott, recalling how Brearley's exploits earned him the sobriquet of 'The King' in the local press, thought him perfectly at home on the subcontinent. 'A magnificent driver of the ball, Mike could play off the front foot in complete safety in these conditions. He was never afraid to hit on the up and, being very quick on his feet, he danced down the wicket to the spinners.'[12] According to Peter Smith of the *Daily Sketch*, Brearley showed all the fluency in his stroke-making which marked his progress during his time at Cambridge. The feature which impressed onlookers most was the manner of his scores, made at a time when he knew he could not afford to fail because the batting behind him, Amiss and Fletcher excepted, was not equal to the situation, even on Pakistan wickets. 'Only in captaincy did Brearley falter. Some of his field placings were both immature and ambitious. For example, he allowed Brown an umbrella field on wickets where the ball neither moved off the seam or through the air. This, one felt, was carrying psychology too far.'[13]

Nevertheless, his influence on the team was considerable at the various stages when feelings were running high caused by some raucous appealing and debatable umpiring. He accepted that there were going to be contentious decisions and for the most part he managed to keep emotions in check. 'The chances are that in an under-25 side you won't have a very good captain,' recalled Pocock. 'We didn't realise how lucky we were to have a captain like Brearley. He did a great job. The great thing about him was the way he communicated so well with everyone. He seemed to get inside everyone's head in a very positive way.' While explicit in what he wanted from each player, Pocock liked the way he gave everyone the opportunity to have their say.[14]

'We were a good young team,' wrote Hobbs. 'Brearley was brilliant, he let you set your own fields but if he wanted to change it he did, but he was a very astute captain, a very nice guy.'[15] Not only did he establish a close rapport with manager Les Ames, he spent much time with the team and entered into the fun with his lovely smile. Knott noted that while Brearley could be moody, he took an interest in everyone and captained brilliantly. His view was endorsed by Underwood, who depressed by his lack of wickets and the poor accommodation, found him sympathetic. 'He left a lasting impression on me both as a captain of remarkable maturity for someone so young and as a batsman who was in his element on the slower paced wickets.'[16]

While Brearley's future in the game remained uncertain, the legacy of his success in Pakistan stood him in good stead, since even during his wilderness years he remained the 'king across the water', ready to claim his inheritance when time permitted.

On returning to America, he played cricket for Pasadena, the leading team in South California, under the leadership of Jim Reid, a former Lancashire League player who'd become an active member of the cricket community in Los Angeles after emigrating there in 1957. In 1966 he'd won renown by captaining the USA to their first victory in the annual match against Canada since 1912 and, having served under Horace Brearley in the Royal Navy during the Second World War, he was delighted to have Mike at Pasadena, especially given his positive contribution during his time there. 'I don't remember a great deal about cricket at Pasadena,' Brearley later recalled, 'except that the matting was put down on matt grass and the outfield was extremely slow. So I thought this counted against playing proper strokes, and put emphasis on strength and hitting. But it was fun.'[17]

Brearley also gave his first paper at the University of Oregon and gained himself a wife. According to his Middlesex team-mate Mike Smith, he had a well-developed sense of female beauty and enjoyed the company of women in the same way that he loved good food and wine. With his handsome dark features, his impeccable manners and refined intellect he made an alluring catch and he soon became involved with Virginia Hjelmaa, a popular academic with an eccentric dress sense, from Tukwila, near Seattle. They were married there at the end of August before they returned to England, enabling Brearley to resume his research at Cambridge.

During 1968 he played three times for the university, in addition to representing the Combined Oxford/Cambridge XI against the Australians, with little success. His star beamed no brighter when he played for Middlesex in the second part of the season. Aside from 55 against Northamptonshire and 82* against Sussex in the penultimate match, there was little to cheer about. In 16 first-class innings at Lord's, his top score was 35 and his county average of 24.27 from 21 innings paled in contrast with his feats in Pakistan 18 months earlier.

At the end of that summer the cricket world descended into uproar when Basil D'Oliveira, England's popular Cape Coloured all-rounder, was omitted from the MCC tour to South Africa, apparently on political grounds, a decision with far-reaching ramifications.

Knowing relatively little about apartheid before touring South Africa in 1964/65, Brearley had found it to be much worse than he'd imagined. His hostility was exacerbated by MCC's treatment of D'Oliveira and the refusal of the South African government to admit him following his belated selection. Like the majority of cricket lovers, Brearley found D'Oliveira's exclusion on cricketing grounds baffling, especially after he'd scored 158 against Australia on his recall to the England side days earlier. In his book, *On Cricket*, he gives some credence to a recent explanation for his omission, supposedly emanating from Doug Insole, the then chairman of selectors, namely that he was picked for the tour only for his name to be vetoed by the MCC committee. From my own research on the subject, which included interviewing Insole for my biography of Colin Cowdrey, I remain unconvinced by this claim, however logical it might appear. The truth is that both the manager, Ames, and the captain, Cowdrey, having encountered problems with D'Oliveira's colourful lifestyle on the previous tour to the West Indies, were reluctant to take him to South Africa and, with no other selector fully supportive of him, he narrowly missed out. In fairness to the selectors, their decision found a fair degree of support among the leading cricket writers, but given the turbulent political currents swirling around D'Oliveira, both the selectors and MCC should have given a much clearer explanation for his exclusion.

Disillusioned with MCC's bungling approach, a small group of members, under the leadership of David Sheppard, the former England batsman and staunch opponent of apartheid, called for a special general meeting of the club. They were soon joined by Brearley and he seconded Sheppard's two resolutions: the first censuring MCC for their mishandling of the affair and the second proposing no further cricketing contact with South Africa till genuine progress had been made towards non-racial cricket.

Keen to avoid an embarrassing public rift, MCC invited Sheppard and Brearley to what they thought was a small informal meeting only then to be confronted with the whole committee. Their spokesman was Sir Alec Douglas-Home, the former prime minister and president of MCC, who'd talked to the South African prime minister John Vorster about D'Oliveira earlier that year. He took issue with Sheppard's contention that MCC should have sought an assurance from the South African government that they could pick the team they wanted, stressing that one couldn't ask it hypothetical questions, but Sheppard stood his ground. From conversations he'd held with Lord Cobham, an MCC grandee, who'd met the South African prime minister weeks after Douglas-Home, he knew that the crucial question had been asked and answered in the negative, although he felt honour-bound to keep this information private.

Before the special general meeting, attended by some 1,000 members at Church House, Westminster on 5 December, Sheppard and Brearley agreed that they wouldn't resort to personal attacks, but their opponents weren't so charitable. In an acrimonious meeting, the most fraught Sheppard had ever encountered, they heaped abuse on him. At one point, Brearley, who was sitting next to him, turned his body to protect him. He supported Sheppard, somewhat nervously, according to John Arlott, asking whether the continuation of the tour was of greater importance than the other issues at stake. He was even less confident than previously that liberal influences in South Africa could be spread by visiting cricketers. The resolutions they submitted attracted considerable support in the hall but they were decisively defeated by a postal vote of the membership.

Keen to mend fences, the campaign group invited a number of their opponents to meet with them in private. Billy Griffith, the MCC secretary and a good friend of Sheppard's, was one such person to take up the olive branch. He repeated the argument that continued sporting contact with South Africa would usher in change, but he was brought up short by Brearley. He reminded Griffith that at the first meeting of the 1964/65 tour party he recalled him warning them to stay off politics. How then were they to help change attitudes if they weren't able to discuss them?

Although MCC were determined that South Africa's 1970 tour of England should go ahead, and the South Africa Cricket Association spoke of their commitment to multiracial cricket, they weren't helped by their government's refusal to reform the apartheid system. In November 1969 Brearley made his position clear in the *Sunday Times*. 'I feel little is gained by a stop in sporting contacts between England and South Africa. I also feel we should bring pressures to bear on the South Africa Cricket Association to do all they can to promote multi-racial cricket. I would regard progress in this direction as a justification for our going ahead with the 1970 tour. But what constitutes progress? ...

'If the SACA were to state that they are working in the direction of multi-racial cricket, especially if the coloured cricket board supported the statement, this would be progress. If the

SACA proposed an unofficial mixed-race team to tour England in 1970, this would be progress. Such things are unlikely. Only if they are offered should MCC uphold their 1970 invitation. Otherwise I do not think I would be prepared to play against the South Africans.'[18]

With South Africa's rugby team on tour of Britain that autumn, the Stop the Seventy Tour (STST) was formed in September 1969 under the 19-year-old Peter Hain, an articulate white South African exile who later became a leading minister in the Blair government. Drawing on a host of support from students to the churches, the trade unions and the Labour Party, the pressure group was committed to direct action in pursuit of their aims. Its mass demonstrations, including pitch invasions, harassed the South African rugby team wherever they went, and with the policing of cricket a far more onerous task than for rugby, the South African cricket tour would be highly vulnerable to mass disruption. Although no supporter of direct action, concerned that the protests could descend into violence, Brearley won Hain's admiration for speaking at STST's national conference. His stance placed him at odds with the vast majority of his fellow cricketers who remained supportive of cricket links with South Africa, especially those who coached out there, but the political tide was flowing in his direction. With the threat of civic disorder looming ever greater, the Cricket Council, the governing body of English cricket, reluctantly bowed to the wishes of the Labour government in May 1970 to call off the tour.

As Brearley completed his research, he decided his future lay in academia and in 1968 he was shortlisted for a job as lecturer in philosophy at Newcastle University. On being asked a complicated question at interview by the professor of law, Brearley was groping his way towards an answer when the professor contradicted him. At which point the professor of philosophy, Karl Britton, cut across his colleague and insisted that Brearley should be permitted to finish. Britton's intervention gave him confidence to formulate a convincing answer and he performed well enough to be given the job.

Founded in 1834 as the School of Medicine and Surgery and later attached to the University of Durham, Newcastle University achieved its independence in 1963. From humble origins, the philosophy department, under Britton's genial leadership, expanded as student numbers burgeoned, helped by the quality of its teaching. Particularly prominent were Geoff Midgley, an engaging teacher who inspired several generations of students, and his wife Mary, one of Britain's most renowned moral philosophers, whose prodigious literary output continued right up to her death in 2018, aged 99. A generous hostess at the family home in Jesmond, she took a liking to Brearley, deeming him to be a lively philosopher and respected teacher, a view shared by their colleague Michael Bavidge, who bought Brearley's house at Kenton Bar, a modern housing estate on the northern edge of the city, when he left.

Although his lecturing left little time for his PhD, Brearley greatly enjoyed it and he found he had a talent for explaining complex ideas clearly. In common with many academics of that era, he grew his hair long, dressed scruffily and supported liberal causes. He also derived pleasure from a rewarding social and cultural life. One evening he went to listen to the American singer-songwriter Ray Charles, the man responsible for the development of soul music. Enchanted by his sheer vivacity and exuberance, he later told Roy Plomley on *Desert Island Discs* that he'd never enjoyed himself more.

He played hockey for the Tynedale club and Northumberland, his game all the more creative and versatile for having played alongside the Dutch A international, Aard Moolenberg, at Richmond Hockey Club in the London League.

He also played cricket for Percy Main, a former mining village close to North Shields, which had won the Northumbrian League the year before. Blending into this homely environment, he mixed easily with players and supporters alike, and gave a helping hand to the youngsters. Playing as an amateur, his presence helped the side win their first six matches of the 1969 season. Beginning with a century against Ashington, putting on 194 for the first wicket with Tom Watson, he followed this with 56 against Morpeth and 107* and 3-16 against Tynemouth; then, after two relative failures, he returned to form with 115 against South Northumberland, his last game before returning south at the end of June.

Surplus to Middlesex's requirements till mid-August, he turned out for Brentham alongside his father, still a first-team stalwart at the age of 56, scoring 508 runs in eight innings. He marked his return to the county championship with a cultured 72 against Surrey; otherwise he supplemented his meagre rations with something more substantial against Hampshire, a steadfast 75 which saved his side from embarrassment.

He was back at Percy Main for their league decider against Northumberland County Club and their professional, Jack van Geloven, the ex-Leicestershire all-rounder. Percy Main went into the match leading the table, but batting first on a damp wicket at Jesmond they were skittled for 75, their lowest score of the season, and defeat by eight wickets robbed them of the championship. Brearley could only manage 8 before he was brilliantly caught at leg slip off van Geloven, who finished with 7-21.

Having headed the league averages for 1969, Brearley's contribution the following year wasn't quite so spectacular, but he still managed four half-centuries in nine innings including

97* against South Northumberland, 91 against Benwell and 82 against Northumberland County Club. He also scored a brilliant century for the Northumbrian League XI against the Saddleworth League XI in the Rothman Cup, winning the admiration of his captain, Mike Crawhall. He recalls Brearley's class as a batsman and the affection he generated at Percy Main.

After his disappointing first-class record in 1969, 1970 brought a modest upturn in fortune. Beginning with two centuries for Derrick Robins' XI against Cambridge (the match wasn't first-class), he showed his pedigree with a breezy 82 against Northamptonshire in his second match back for Middlesex. He accomplished little in the next three matches, but 67* against Yorkshire and 75 and 85 against Surrey, along with several telling contributions in the 40-over John Player League (JPL), recalled happier times. In a depressing season, in which Middlesex slipped to 16th in the championship, Brearley's gradual rehabilitation constituted a ray of light in the darkness which was to have profound consequences. 'Brearley wasn't even in the side full-time in 1970, but we all knew him,' one of his contemporaries told Christopher Sandford, the biographer of John Murray. 'He did speak beautifully, Mike, lovely manners, soft voice, very refined, didn't like to hear anyone swearing around him.'[19]

For a side that contained five Test cricketers – six in 1968/69 when Alan Connolly, the Australian pace bowler joined as their overseas player – Middlesex constantly underperformed throughout the 1960s. 'Middlesex weren't together enough as a team,' recalled fast bowler John Price. 'We should have been better. I opened with all sorts of people and never had a regular partner for more than a couple of seasons.'[20] It is true that their bowling relied unduly on himself and Titmus, but, that said, their unimaginative cricket, especially their lack of batting bonus points, and dressing room rifts didn't help.

Part of the problem stemmed from a lack of leadership. When Titmus became the county's first professional captain in 1965, he made it clear to his players that he was no democrat. Brought up in the hierarchical world of National Service and post-war county cricket, he, like Murray, began his time at Middlesex on the ground staff, selling scorecards, sweeping the stands and transporting the team kit to away matches. Convinced that such a tough apprenticeship had done them no harm, he saw no reason why the old order should be toppled when it was their turn to enjoy its privileges. Consequently, the team divided very much between the England players and the rest, although Parfitt maintains that dressing room harmony compared favourably with both Surrey and Yorkshire.

As the enterprising spirit of the amateur gave way to the risk-averse ethos of the professional, so cricket lost much of its lustre as crowds rapidly dwindled and the membership became increasingly disaffected. This was particularly the case at Middlesex. Like a number of his contemporaries, Titmus, raised in the hard school of wickets, averages and contracts, felt unable to shed the habits of a lifetime. 'Fred was very stubborn, he didn't want to change,' declared spinner John Emburey. He recalls him saying that a bowler's job was to stop the batsman scoring runs as opposed to taking wickets. [21]

At a time when the championship points system placed a premium on teams securing a first-innings lead, his captaincy proved equally defensive and his flaws in man-management grew more glaring as he wrestled with an unhappy first marriage. He resigned in August 1968 to be replaced by the affable Peter Parfitt. His more relaxed style brought immediate success but, with little support from the committee, the improvement didn't last and after Middlesex's slump in 1970 he was unceremoniously dismissed that November. During the latter part of that season when Brearley became available, Gubby Allen, the treasurer of MCC and a formidable powerbroker, was so keen to get him back full-time that he told Parfitt that he had to play, even if that meant dropping the consistent Clive Radley. Always a great admirer of Brearley, Allen had selected him to captain his President's XI against the 1964 Australians and he would have liked him to have succeeded Colin Drybrough as captain of Middlesex in 1965.

After Titmus resigned in 1968, Brearley, about to start at Newcastle, ruled himself out as a possible successor, but Allen wasn't giving up on his man. His intentions chimed with the rest of the Middlesex committee when word reached them at the end of the 1970 season that Brearley had been approached by Warwickshire and Worcestershire with a view to taking over the captaincy. Unable to persuade him to return full-time in just a playing capacity, the committee, led by former players Charles Robins and Mike Murray, threw in the captaincy as a further incentive, a decision which sealed Parfitt's fate. John Murray recalls Allen taking the senior professionals up to the dressing room and telling them that the committee couldn't let Brearley leave Middlesex, 'and you boys are going to have to put up with it'.

When Brearley embarked on an academic career, it appeared to be the end of his cricket one, a few appearances in the vacation for Middlesex notwithstanding when he seemed something of an impostor. 'At that time if you came in and took a professional's place for a few weeks, either if you were a teacher or studying, it didn't make you the most popular person,' he recalled. [22] Previous attempts to lure him back full-time had failed, not least because of patchy form and a reduction in salary, but the captaincy was something different. 'It was the idea of captaincy that led me back to Middlesex,' he later wrote. 'I like to be bossy.

I hate to get bored. I want to be doing something all the time, and the tactics of the game fascinate me. I liked the idea of the inter-relation with people, and, above all, I like trying to get the best out of people.'[23]

His decision was made easier by his lack of fulfilment in philosophy as an academic profession, his failure to complete his PhD topic and his uncertain future as a leading light in this most competitive of disciplines. 'I liked the students and I liked the teaching but I wasn't ever going to write masterpieces in philosophy,' he recalled.[24] His ex-supervisor, Renford Bambrough, wrote him a letter of encouragement: 'This is one of those occasions when what one ought to do coincides precisely with what one wants to do.'[25]

His departure was a source of regret at Newcastle. 'We were all very sad to lose Mike,' wrote Mary Midgley in her memoir. 'But we knew for some time he had been torn, as people are who are very good at two things, trying to divide his life between them. Eventually cricket had won. I recall a lecturer in another department being much shocked that any academic should make such a choice, but certainly none of his immediate colleagues felt like that about it. We saw his point entirely.'[26]

It was in recognition of his legacy there, as well as his subsequent accomplishments as England cricket captain, that Newcastle awarded him an honorary degree in May 1984. 'In conferring this honour on him, the University aims to honour Mike Brearley,' commented its student newspaper, *The Courier*. 'His acceptance honours us much more.'[27]

Bambrough's advice to Brearley proved prescient, since his return to full-time cricket not only fulfilled his latent ambition of playing for his country, it sowed the seeds of his future triumphs for both Middlesex and England, even though it proved something of a slog at first.

Chapter 5

New Wine in Old Bottles

WHEN Brearley took over the Middlesex captaincy, their opening batsman Mike Smith told him, 'That's not a crown on your head but a coconut.' His accession was greeted with wariness by the senior professionals. Not only did they resent the ousting of Parfitt and his replacement by an inferior player who, they thought, was using the club for his own purpose, they disliked the new culture he was trying to promote. 'The club had been fairly snobbish,' Brearley recalled. 'There was quite a class distinction. There was a lot of humour, some of it quite sharp. It wasn't a kindly set up. There wasn't much sense that your opinion was welcomed until you'd played ten years as a capped player or played 20 or 30 times for England. It wasn't conducive to good team spirit. When I was made captain I did try to change that attitude in the dressing room and I had some sympathy with the younger players, which meant I probably didn't have sympathy with the older players. They were suspicious of me, with some cause.' He struggled to get the best out of them. 'I think I was tactically experimental compared with what was customary. I had always been interested in tactics and was always willing to try things that were different from the norm. I'm not sure everyone agreed with the way I was going, but I had a fundamental belief that this was the right way.'[1]

The older players voiced criticism about these tactics, especially his tendency to place fielders in unorthodox positions. Titmus wrote:

> Mike Brearley had not been captain for long, but he had already developed an irritating habit of trying to set my field for me when I was bowling. I never minded advice, so long as it coincided closely with my own views, but I thought that Mike had some daft ideas. I was bowling to Geoff Boycott and Brearley insisted on fielding at forward short leg. It inhibited the way I wanted to bowl, so I asked him to move and he wouldn't. Boycott duly crashed the ball and almost hit Brearley. Brearley complained that Boycott had tried to hit him. Boycott observed that if he had wanted to hit him, he would have done. I found it hard to sympathise too much with our captain.[2]

Resistance to his cerebral approach manifested itself in other ways. In his first year as captain, he recalls them playing a ten-over JPL game against Glamorgan at Ebbw Vale. 'As we fetched our bags from the cars (the rain had unexpectedly stopped at about tea-time) I said excitedly, "We'll have to think about this!" The senior players found this hilarious: *think* about a ten-over match! About a sheer slog! I can see their point; in those days I did have too much confidence in the power of thought in predicting or controlling events.'[3]

Outside the dressing room, Brearley's appointment was greeted with anticipation. Reviewing the prospects for the 1971 season, Woodcock wrote that it could have far-reaching consequences. 'It will be no surprise to me if he captains England within the next two or three years.'[4] He immediately put his pledge to play purposeful cricket into effect, declaring twice in Middlesex's opening match against Derbyshire and bowling the leg-spinner Harry Latchman for long periods as he took his team to the brink of victory. According to Woodcock's colleague Richard Streeton, 'Brearley, who straight away on his return to the first-class fold, has shown in this game that his instinctive flair for cricket leadership remains, setting Derbyshire 252 to win in three hours.'[5]

His enterprise was again in evidence in the next match against Nottinghamshire when Middlesex just failed to score 162 to win in 105 minutes. A fluent 77 from Eric Russell led the victory charge before a middle-order collapse compelled them to settle for a draw, five runs short with two wickets left.

A ten-wicket haul for Price against Leicestershire gave them their first win and, following a draw against Gloucestershire, they suffered their first reverse against Yorkshire. A generous declaration on an easy-paced Headingley wicket inspired Boycott to one of his finest efforts and his unbeaten 112 saw Yorkshire home by eight wickets with nearly six overs to spare. 'Boycott had tears in his eyes as he thanked me for the game,' Brearley later wrote. "If ever we have a chance to make a game of it with you, Mike, we will." In the next ten years, Yorkshire never risked anything in a declaration against us.'[6]

Middlesex returned to winning ways against Sussex and Northamptonshire, drew with Worcestershire and Glamorgan, and compensated for defeat by Kent with exciting last-minute wins over Gloucestershire and Hampshire.

Crucial to their success had been Brearley's consistency with the bat, which had yielded eight half-centuries to date. A strained back getting out of a chair in the dressing room indisposed him for three weeks and Titmus, the official vice-captain, took over the captaincy. He led Middlesex to victory against Surrey, which restored them to the top of the table in mid-July, before the tide turned with a vengeance. A heavy defeat against Nottinghamshire was the prelude to four successive draws, a win and three losses in their final eight matches. Not even Brearley's return could paper over the cracks in their batting. Their late-season slump saw them slip to sixth place in the championship, but in both style and substance their performance compared favourably with the previous year. According to *Wisden*, 'Brearley's enthusiastic leadership, and specifically his ability to persuade the best out of each member of his team, proved the basis of this most encouraging season.'[7]

His imagination appealed to Latchman. He wrote: 'He'll try something different. Against Nottingham last season their wicketkeeper, Pullan, was playing dead-bat to everything and we had everyone up round the wicket. Nothing was happening. I said to Mike ,"Why don't you put them all back and let me toss it at him."

'"Leave it an over," he said. Next over he put me on, put the field back and bang the batsman has a smash and is caught.

'In another match I actually bowled the fourth over of the innings. Don't ask me why. He took Bob Herman off and put me on. He just wanted to try something different.'[8]

Brearley brought off another enterprising ruse when Middlesex played Sussex. He wrote:

> Jim Parks was batting at the Pavilion end at Lord's against Harry Latchman's leg-breaks. I got this feeling that, driving freely in his inside-out style, he might get a thick outside edge so I put in a deep gully. They'd think, 'That's not a proper position!' But he was caught there. That did please me.[9]

After their progress in 1971, Brearley looked forward to 1972 with high hopes. Another promising start saw his team stand fourth in the championship and top of the JPL on 10 June, but the good times couldn't last. A first-innings lead of 106 against Hampshire was meekly surrendered with a feeble second innings of 86, which resulted in a five-wicket defeat. They weren't to win again for another month. A late rally brought them three wins in their last five matches and a position of eighth in the championship, but successive losses in their final three JPL matches put them out of contention for honours. With Illingworth unavailable to lead MCC in India and Pakistan that winter, Brearley was a strong contender to fill the vacancy. In the end he missed out to Tony Lewis, primarily because his batting, still without a championship hundred, lacked the necessary class.

Dressing room schisms continued to dog Brearley's second year in charge when he informed the rest of the team that he'd been awarded a rise in salary as captain. His disclosure prompted the five Test players to write to the committee to express dissatisfaction with the differentials between their salary and that of Brearley's. At the end of that season three of those five players retired: Price, although he continued to play part-time for the next three years, Russell after a disappointing season which led to him being dropped and Parfitt, despite heading the county batting averages and regaining his England place. (Bizarrely, he was omitted for Middlesex's vital JPL match against Warwickshire, which they lost by two runs.) 'I quite liked Peter Parfitt but I'm not sure he liked me very much,' Brearley later said, but Parfitt, it should be stressed, bears Brearley no animosity.[10] He retired because he thought it time to move on and safeguard his future by purchasing a pub in Yorkshire. When asked to tour East Africa under Brearley 18 months later, he recalls Brearley coming up to him at the airport and saying,

NEW WINE IN OLD BOTTLES

'We are not going to have a problem are we?' to which Parfitt replied, 'Of course not, Mike.'

Titmus, in contrast, was less forgiving. Although an old-school professional brought up in a more class-conscious era, his personal relationship with Brearley had been civil. As senior professional and then captain, he'd gone out of his way to encourage him when he was struggling and he amused him with his sense of humour. Brearley wrote:

> I remember when I first played a match for Middlesex, I fielded at deep square leg and Fred Titmus was bowling off-breaks. Somebody swept the ball and not only did I drop the catch, it went through my hands for six! And I thought he'll be quite mad at me. Actually, he[Titmus] took it quite philosophically. What he said was, 'Wasn't so much you missed the catch but palming it on for six[laughs].' In other words, he was very nice about it.[11]

Brearley, for his part, greatly respected his all-round prowess, professional work ethic and tactical nous, ranking him one of the best captains he played under, not that he considered any of them particularly outstanding. On becoming captain in 1971, he appointed Titmus his vice-captain for two years and continued to draw on his advice thereafter. Despite acknowledging some differences, he always spoke highly of him, and when he asked him to play for Middlesex against Surrey in August 1982, Brearley's own swansong at Lord's, the wheel had come full circle, since Titmus had played alongside his father on his debut in 1949.

Given Brearley's generosity towards him, it seems rather strange that Titmus should write so disparagingly about him in his autobiography, *My Life in Cricket*, published in 2005 when, admittedly, he wasn't in the best of health. Yet according to the cricket writer Stephen Chalke, their fluctuating relationship concealed a deep affection at the core born of a shared love of cricket and Middlesex. It was an affection that Titmus's widow Stephanie expressed to Brearley when she put her arms around him after her husband's funeral in 2011. 'He loved you, you know,' to which Brearley replied, 'And I loved him too.'

What aggrieved Titmus was the feeling that he and his contemporaries hadn't been accorded the same respect that they had shown to the senior players when they were young professionals. 'I don't think Mike treated us in the same way when he was coming up. I certainly feel that Brearley hurried the departure of nearly all of our senior pros. He just came in and instantly wanted his own way.'[12]

Whosever fault it was these were difficult times for Brearley. He didn't feel wanted, his confidence was low and his future in the game remained far from assured as he weighed the importance of playing cricket against that of other pursuits. 'There were times during those Middlesex years when I felt like giving up,' Brearley later admitted. 'One of the reasons I didn't was that some people valued what I did and so my confidence wasn't totally shattered.'[13]

The county's erratic form was manifest once again in 1973 when the loss of Russell, Parfitt and Price, for all but eight matches, was truly felt. In contrast to their flying start in the JPL, they struggled badly in the championship and by mid-July they propped up the table, still without a win. The tide began to turn at Dover in mid-July when the return of Price and Phil Edmonds, their talented slow left-arm spinner, from Cambridge, helped Middlesex beat Kent by ten wickets, Kent's first defeat of the season. On an uneven wicket, Brearley, who the week before had been at his best when scoring 87 and 70* against the West

Indians, impressed with a stylish 82. 'When he plays like this his failure to make runs more regularly is not easily accountable,' commented Woodcock. 'Perhaps he lacks a middle gear, in which to avoid being pinned down by accurate but not hostile bowling; it may be that, in becoming a more precise technician, he has forfeited a certain freedom.'[14]

Bolstered by these performances, he began to bat with greater assertiveness and, against Yorkshire in Middlesex's last home match of the season, he recorded his first championship century. Two more half-centuries in the final two matches followed, including 83 in the tie against Yorkshire at Bradford, and with the demise of Illingworth as England's captain after their trouncing by the West Indies, he once again appeared a candidate for the succession. 'If only because of the new frontier, which is so important, I would take a chance with Brearley,' wrote Woodcock. 'He is a great enthusiast, and in spite of a disappointing county record a good enough player to get runs for England. As well as being a crisis of confidence this is one of leadership, a quality which Brearley has been shown to possess.'[15] Others supported his claim, but the prize went to Mike Denness, the captain of Kent who'd been Lewis's vice-captain in India and Pakistan the previous winter. Brearley, however, could look back on a season of progress in terms of team spirit. He wrote in *The Cricketer* that Middlesex had enjoyed their cricket and he himself was gaining in experience. According to Murray, 'He was a very good thinker about the game. Once he found a team of bowlers, I could see him doing a very good job. The young boys felt Brearley was interested in what they had to say. He always played the listener.' At the same time, he had a mind of his own and he could prove a tad stubborn. During Middlesex's end-of-season fixture against Sussex at Hove, Brearley had tried to persuade Murray to let Nigel Ross, their young wicketkeeper-batsman, keep wicket in the second innings, but with the ball turning sharply, Murray refused. 'Just as well I did,' he later recalled as he stumped four of the top five Sussex batsmen in Middlesex's convincing win.[16]

While most county cricketers spent their winters coaching or doing odd jobs in the locality, Brearley cast his gaze further afield. In 1971/72 he wintered in the USA and Canada, staying with his wife's family near Seattle and with friends in New York, Boston and Calgary, an experience not altogether to his liking since he found the USA to be vast and violent. The following winter he lectured in adult education and taught geography for a term at University College School, where his inability to draw on the blackboard left a lasting impression on the future author Simon Garfield. He also covered two Tests of MCC's tour of India for *The Guardian* and *The Observer*, shouting his copy down dodgy phone trunk lines in Calcutta. He found cricket watching enhanced by journalistic duty, since it sharpened his concentration and he liked having to formulate his response to the day's play. 'By the end of my stay in India I was reluctant to leave. I had had just a taste of the sights and exotica of the East,' he wrote in *The Cricketer*. 'I had spent a good deal of time with the MCC team, enough to see how excellent their team spirit was, and how uncynical about a strange place and culture.'[17]

He then guested for Kent on their 18-day tour of the West Indies, a reward for them winning the JPL the previous year. Sleeping everywhere on a plank because of a bad back, he nevertheless contributed several useful innings, the most notable of which was 82 against Antigua on a pitch prepared by the local convicts. The opposition reply was centred around a cameo half-century from a promising young player called Viv Richards who smacked them all over the ground. Brearley wrote in *The Cricketer* that he was 'a batsman of sound technique and bold method'. He mentioned Colin Cowdrey's prediction that he would be playing for the West Indies soon, a prediction seen by Somerset's vice-chairman, Len Creed, who was about to visit Antigua with a touring side. No sooner had he arrived than he arranged to meet Richards and offered him a trial with Somerset, marking an important stage on his road to world eminence.

As with India, Brearley found a great enthusiasm for cricket in the Caribbean and the same generous hospitality, especially on the smaller islands. 'Most of us were closer to 1,000 rums than 1,000 runs in January.'[18]

In November 1973 Brearley played for a Rest of the World XI under Clive Lloyd against Pakistan in two matches in aid of flood relief in that country, scoring a century in the first match and a half-century in the second. During his century, he recalled being repeatedly refreshed by their 12th man, Salahuddin, the former Pakistan all-rounder. 'I was just on 50 when he brought the first lot out. "Well played Mr Brearley," he said. "You are Rock of Gibraltar." At the next drinks interval, I had got about 80 and Salahuddin approached again. "Very well played Mr Brearley. You are all Great Wall of China." After I had well passed my century I was "Great Barrier Reef".' [19]

At some stage during the afternoon, Sarfraz Nawaz, Pakistan's opening bowler, came back for a second or third spell with the old ball. 'Suddenly, it started to dart in from the off in the air. I remember looking up and seeing Sarfraz grinning at me,' Brearley later recalled. '"Where did that come from?" I wanted to know. He simply went on grinning.

'In retrospect, I realised this was my first experience of reverse swing.'[20]

Brearley then captained a strong MCC side of past and present players on a four-week trip to East Africa at the turn of the year. Beginning with two two-day games in Zambia, they proceeded via Tanzania to Kenya, where they concluded their tour with a three-day match against East Africa at Nairobi. Overcoming the heat, the inefficiencies of East African Airways and the excessive socialising, they remained unbeaten in their eight matches against opposition, mainly Asian, which bordered on the first-class. Led by the Gloucestershire all-rounder Roger Knight, Parfitt and Barber, the batting proved solid and while the bowling lacked penetration with the new ball, the efforts of Brearley's friend Cartwright did much to compensate, his ten-wicket haul against East Africa crucial to MCC's decisive victory. When Brearley asked him to bowl a few overs into the wind, Cartwright replied, 'Michael, if you want me to float up a few half-volleys, of course I'll bowl into the wind. But if you want me to bowl properly, and keep going for you, you'd better give me the other end.' 'He took one wicket, rather against his better judgement, bowling into the wind,' Brearley recalled, 'then I gave him the end he wanted, and he finished up with five.'[21]

Although 17 formal cocktail parties took its toll on the players, the trip was immensely enjoyable and Brearley appreciated captaining a side notable for its general willingness. According to the manager Jack Bailey, the assistant secretary of MCC, it was a role he performed with distinction. Any small points of difference between them were sorted out quickly and amicably, and he was always prepared to recognise the demands this particular type of tour placed on the individual. 'He led the team very well on the field and was popular off it. He also showed a very real concern for his players. In my book, he would be a very good captain to take anywhere.'[22]

Looking back on the tour, Brearley feared for the long-term prospects of cricket in East Africa, given the likely exodus of Asians from there over the course of the next decade. 'The vast majority of good players are Asians,' he wrote in *The Cricketer*.

'We played a few Europeans and one African in Zambia. Uganda sent six Africans to play in a combined team against us in Nairobi. Perhaps the best long-term hopes for cricket in this area lies within the sphere of General Amin,' a rather ironical comment in light of subsequent events.[23]

Brearley also concerned himself with the affairs of the Cricketers' Association. Founded in 1967 by the Somerset fast bowler Fred Rumsey, it represented the interests of professional cricketers at a time when they lacked a voice. Firmly committed to improving the lot of his fellow professionals, Brearley served on its executive alongside the chairman, Mike Edwards, the Surrey opening batsman, and the secretary, Jack Bannister, the Warwickshire seamer. In April 1973 Edwards resigned because of a major decision to accept a donation from the Transvaal following a private tour of South Africa organised by sports promoter Derrick Robins, expressing disappointment that Brearley didn't resign too. Brearley, however, was deep in lengthy negotiations with the Test and County Cricket Board (TCCB) regarding the right of the Cricketers' Association to a share of broadcasting and television revenue. Their threat to disrupt Sunday matches persuaded Lord's to give ground and Brearley, along with new chairman Peter Walker, Bannister and financial adviser Harold Goldblatt, negotiated a satisfactory settlement – some £3,500 a year for four years – to provide a proper injury insurance for their members and a non-contributory pension scheme. Later, further concessions were achieved such as the minimum wage by which time Brearley had moved on.

After finishing the previous season 13th in the championship, seven places lower than in his first year as captain, Brearley hoped for better things in 1974. A convincing win in their opening match against the county champions Hampshire augured well, while their next championship match against Warwickshire at Edgbaston proved something of a watershed for Brearley's batting. After making a laboured 78 in the first innings, he sought the advice of Tiger Smith, the respected former Warwickshire wicketkeeper-batsman and coach. The 89-year-old Smith, who'd watched him bat, told him to stand facing him with Smith's walking stick as his bat and play a few shots. 'He showed me how tense I was in face, hands and arms. Using his walking stick as a bat, I came to see how easier it is to swing it if the body relaxes.' He offered him only one piece of technical advice: that he should stand up more, to enable the bat to swing straight down close to his body like a pendulum.

'Until 1974 I had been a moderate county batsman, averaging in the late 20s or early 30s,' Brearley later wrote. 'From 1974 on – apart from one disastrous season in 1978 – I regularly averaged 40 or above in county cricket. Smith's advice – of which the technical point was probably the least important – was integral to my progress.'[24] In the next three championship games he scored half-centuries and then, against Essex at Ilford, he made 79 and 78. He hit a majestic 98 against Surrey at The Oval and any regrets at missing out on a second championship century were soon erased by scores of 173* against Glamorgan, one of his finest innings, and 163* against Yorkshire in successive matches. Despite a barren end to the summer, he topped the county averages with 44.55 as Middlesex rose to sixth place in the championship and dropped to eighth in the JPL.

He continued to make strides in 1975 with his batting, this time averaging 53.41. Commendably consistent throughout, he scored four centuries and moved up from number three to form an effective opening partnership with his friend Mike Smith. According to *Wisden*, 'He adapted to pitches of unreliable quality so resourcefully that he finished sixth in the averages, and was the second-highest Englishman. He has the skill to bat anywhere in the order and is, simply, playing better than at any time in his career.'[25]

In contrast to their mediocrity in the championship where they finished a disappointing 11th, Middlesex won kudos by appearing in the two one-day finals at Lord's. Fortunate to qualify for the quarter-final of the Benson and Hedges Cup, they beat Yorkshire by four wickets then Warwickshire by three wickets in the semi-final. Their reward was a final against Leicestershire, but, on a humid morning and on an uneven pitch, they contracted stage fright. Only Smith with 83 suggested permanence as they were shot out for 146, giving Leicestershire victory by five wickets.

In the Gillette Cup they made stately progress, easily disposing of Buckinghamshire, Warwickshire and Worcestershire and beating Derbyshire by 24 runs in the semi-final. Back at Lord's, they faced the Gillette specialists Lancashire in the final, and inserted on a damp wicket they struggled to break their stranglehold. All they could manage off their 60 overs was 180/8 and although they fought hard in the field, a powerful 73* from Clive Lloyd guided Lancashire to a seven-wicket victory with three overs to spare.

The match marked the retirement of Murray after 24 years' loyal and distinguished service to Middlesex. Brearley paid generous tribute to him in *Wisden* but with only Titmus left of the old guard he was close to fulfilling his ambition of having his own team.

Chapter 6

Stepping Up

AFTER five years of Brearley's leadership, Middlesex's progress in the championship remained infuriatingly inconsistent, chiefly because both their batting and their bowling lacked depth, but far out west the land looked brighter. Working with a young, forward-looking committee, three of whom were to play for the county in 1976, Brearley brought players and administrators closer together. Pay and working conditions were improved, standards of dress were relaxed, and better levels of fitness were instituted. Playing at Lord's wasn't always ideal, since Middlesex, as tenants, had no say in the preparation of wickets, much to their disadvantage when their spin attack had to bowl on ludicrously short boundaries, but following the fiasco of a dangerous pitch against Leicestershire in 1974, MCC began to consult them more frequently.

Equally important, Brearley forged a healthy relationship with his former team-mates, Bob Gale, the chairman of selectors, and Don Bennett, the highly respected coach. 'I don't want you to agree with me the whole time, Don,' he used to say to him, acknowledging that he wasn't always right. 'I want some different solutions.' The growth of colts' cricket at club level in the late

1960s and the formation of the competitive Middlesex League had yielded a rich haul of talent for the county's sophisticated scout system under Bennett. They won the new under-25 competition three years running, along with the 2nd XI championship in 1974, and by 1976 this new generation comprising Graham Barlow, Roland Butcher, John Emburey and Mike Gatting was ready to earn their stripes by responding to Brearley's clarion call that they assert themselves more. 'Under Brearley more aggression, confidence, cockiness even, were introduced and grafted on to the existing qualities of experience,' recalled Emburey. 'There was a more flexible attitude, the willingness to try things, all part of a changing style which was evolving at about the time that I established myself in the team.'[1]

Since becoming captain Brearley had gone out of his way to lure established players reputedly looking for a fresh start to Middlesex, such as Northamptonshire's Mushtaq Mohammad and Bob Cottam, but the high living costs of the capital deterred them from moving. In 1976 his luck changed when he was able to persuade Allan Jones, the former Sussex and Somerset fast bowler, who was on the brink of emigrating to New Zealand, to sign for Middlesex. It proved a shrewd move. Something of a loose cannon, Jones's quirky personality and outlandish fielding had made him a figure of fun at his previous counties, but keen to boost his self-confidence, Brearley encouraged him to take himself more seriously. It proved astute psychology as Jones repaid his captain's faith in him by greatly improving his fielding and becoming the county's leading wicket taker for 1976.

By the time Brearley celebrated his 34th birthday that April, his chances of playing Test cricket appeared to have receded. His Cambridge friend Michael Silk recalls making that point to him and getting a pained look back as well as a non-committal answer. Silk hadn't realised how ambitious he was – he seemed so relaxed – but with Boycott still in self-imposed exile, a vacancy existed at the top of the England order. Given an opportunity to stake a claim for MCC in the traditional opening fixture against the champions, Leicestershire, Brearley seized it with alacrity. Set 325 to win, he and Amiss made victory all but certain by putting on 301 for the first wicket, his contribution being 137*. He followed this up with an elegant 153 against Kent, which greatly impressed Test selector Ken Barrington and earned him a late call-up for MCC against the West Indians, because of an injury to Yorkshire opener Richard Lumb.

After being thrashed 5-1 by Australia the previous winter, the West Indies had regrouped with a 2-1 home win against India, and, under Clive Lloyd's leadership, they would prove formidable opposition to an England side low on confidence. While batsmen such as Viv Richards, Alvin Kallicharran and Lloyd himself were renowned for their audacious stroke play, they possessed an intimidating pair of opening bowlers in Andy Roberts and Michael Holding. They demonstrated their raw pace during the closing overs of the first day of the MCC match as the home side replied to their 251/9 declared. Brearley called it the quickest bowling he'd ever seen and Fred Trueman, watching Holding for the first time, reckoned they would be drawing lots in the dressing room for the role of nightwatchman. His words were borne out minutes later when Amiss was struck a vicious blow on the head by Holding and had to be carried off. Because the deputed nightwatchman Pocock had found reason to leave the dressing room, the man chosen in his place was Yorkshire's Phil Carrick. 'As he approached the bloodied crease he looked pale,' Brearley wrote. 'I remembered the line from *Beyond the Fringe*, and greeted him with: "The time has come, Perkins, for a useless sacrifice."' [2] Carrick was in no mood for witty repartee, but the pair survived to the close and on the second day Brearley's 36 in the best part of three hours was testament to his composure and willingness to get behind the line of the ball. According to Woodcock, he'd grown a little in stature.

Fifty-four ahead on first innings, the West Indians, with centuries by Richards and Larry Gomes, took control, dismissing their opponents for 83 in their second innings, an early warning of the storm to come.

Brearley remained in the selectors' thoughts when asked to captain The Rest against England in the Test trial match at Bristol. The evening before the game he discussed tactics with his seam bowlers and upset Yorkshire's Chris Old by deciding to give the new ball to Glamorgan's Malcolm Nash, figuring that he would get more movement early on. When Nash duly delivered the next morning by getting Amiss caught at short leg in the opening over, Brearley turned to Old in the slips and smiled.

Although Amiss redeemed himself with a second-innings century, the selectors, concerned by his weakness against the short-pitched ball, were loath to subject him again to the pace of Roberts and Holding. They chose Brearley to partner Edrich in the first Test at Trent Bridge and recalled the 45-year-old Brian Close after an interval of nine years. 'One of our "younger selections" is Mike Brearley, 34, again chosen for solid courage against fast bowling, which he demonstrated in the MCC match against the tourists last week,' commented Tony Lewis, the cricket correspondent of the *Sunday Telegraph*. 'If we are simply going to be satisfied with parrying the blows, are we ever going to get to a position of winning the match?

'In fairness to Close and Brearley, both can play shots and both are in good form. Yet it will need a lot of luck for them to express that form in the face of the fastest bowling, the screaming media, and the millions watching on TV. But good luck to them.'[3]

England's defensive tone was set from the opening overs by captain Tony Greig's run-saving field, but up against the brilliance of Richards it made little difference. His 232 and Kallicharran's 97 formed the nucleus of the West Indies's 494. Bad light restricted England's reply to one over on the second evening, safely negotiated by Edrich, but Brearley's reprieve was all too brief. The next morning, he was out in the first over caught by Richards at third slip off Bernard Julien for 0, playing at a rising ball he could have left alone.

Thanks to a dogged 106 from David Steele and a painstaking 82 from Bob Woolmer, England saved the follow-on and kept their opponents in the field till well into the fourth day. Challenged to score 339 in just over five hours, Edrich and Brearley began steadily before Brearley was caught behind off Vanburn Holder for 17. Steele didn't last long but Edrich and Close dropped anchor to ensure an honourable draw.

With Edrich out of the Lord's Test because of injury, Lancashire's Barry Wood was drafted in to open with Brearley. In testing conditions, he and Steele were soon out and Brearley had to be at his most tenacious to survive. Gradually, he grew in authority in a third-wicket stand of 84 with Close and it took a good ball by Roberts to bowl him for 40. England made 250 and with Snow and Underwood dismissing the West Indies for 182, they ended the second day in the ascendancy. After a wash-out on the Saturday, neither side displayed much enterprise on the Monday. Brearley soon departed, yorked by Holding for 13, and although Steele and Close batted solidly they weren't able to lift the tempo sufficiently to allow Greig to declare that evening. Content to bat on till they were all out the next morning, the England captain might well have rued his caution, since the West Indies survived a late collapse to secure a draw.

Brearley's productive county form wasn't enough to save his Test place for Old Trafford, the selectors deciding to open with Edrich and Close. 'Brearley can consider himself unlucky to be left out,' wrote Woodcock. 'He played better in the second Test at Lord's than in the first Test at Trent Bridge and he has made runs for Middlesex since ... What is so bad for the future is that the England innings will be opened by two men whose combined ages come to 84.'[4] It was indeed a bizarre decision to subject these two aged titans to the full ferocity of the West Indian quicks on a terrible Old Trafford wicket. England were thrashed and neither man played for his country again. For the fourth Test, Steele was chosen to open with Woolmer and after the former failed in that position Amiss was recalled at The Oval. On an easy-paced wicket and with a new technique, he marked his return with a double hundred, but with Woolmer once again failing in this unfamiliar position at least one opening slot would be available for the winter tour to India and Australia.

Brearley's omission from the Test side meant he could fully concentrate at Middlesex's tilt at the championship. After a quiet May, they came to the fore in June as Barlow, Selvey and Jones emerged from the wings to take centre stage. Comprehensive wins against Essex, Sussex, Somerset and Gloucestershire gave them a 26-point lead by 18 June. Thereafter their form fluctuated somewhat despite their captain's sterling efforts. He scored 79 and 128* in the six-wicket defeat by Hampshire at Lord's and he followed up with another century in their innings victory against Sussex. Defeat then by Yorkshire led to the omission of Titmus in favour of the young off-spinner John Emburey.

The previous winter Titmus had been shocked to receive two letters from Brearley, which spoke of his 'fading drive and ambition' and that 'his withdrawal and bitterness was a real difficulty for the team'.[5] Irked by the criticism which he thought very unfair, and concerned about his future, Titmus's relationship with Brearley remained tense. In July he suffered a loss of form and with Emburey impressing all and sundry, Brearley was placed in an awkward dilemma. As he pondered the enormity of dropping one of Middlesex's all-time greats, he was strengthened in his conviction by the support of his chairman of selectors, Bob Gale. 'Without his influence I doubt whether we players – who had not only played with Titmus for years, but had grown up as cricketers when he was in his prime – would have brought ourselves to make the change.'[6] He was omitted for the games against Nottinghamshire and Kent.

Two excellent innings by Roland Butcher helped Middlesex to a four-wicket victory against the former with two balls in hand, before they lost to the latter at Dartford. Batting first, Smith and Brearley gave them the perfect start with an opening stand of 106, Brearley making a stylish 87, and their total of 305/5 appeared more than adequate as Kent could manage only 151 in reply. Forced to follow on, their batsmen showed a greater resolve, and half-centuries from Woolmer, Alan Ealham and John Shepherd brought them back into the game. Left 195 to win in three hours, Middlesex flickered briefly but once Brearley and Featherstone were both out for 32, the rest of the batting succumbed to the Kent spinners Underwood and Graham Johnson. They lost by 57 runs. It was their last reverse of the season as the hot summer and worn wickets increasingly favoured their spinners.

Middlesex returned to winning ways against the West Indians, inflicting on them their first defeat of the tour. Titmus, restored to favour, took 5-41 in their first innings of 222 and he dismissed Fredericks and Richards in the second innings just when they threated to run amok. Needing 274 to win, Smith and Brearley opened with a stand of 131, the former's 108 being primarily responsible for his side's four-wicket victory, their first over a touring team since 1936.

Against Derbyshire, Smith and Brearley again provided a sure foundation and Barlow built upon their start with a muscular 160*. Their total of 369/9 proved a match-winning score, since, on a turning wicket, Titmus was in his element, his match figures of 12-135 the catalyst for his side's convincing victory.

Having survived a spirited run chase by Essex on the final afternoon, Middlesex triumphed at Chelmsford by 36 runs before they overwhelmed Glamorgan at Swansea. Brearley was to the fore against Lancashire with scores of 45 and 73, but, despite dominating throughout, his team ultimately had to settle for a draw.

A rain-ruined Bank Holiday fixture against Worcestershire, which netted Middlesex a solitary point, left them needing five points from their final match against Surrey at The Oval. On an abbreviated first day, an obdurate century from Edrich, the 99th of his career, in Surrey's 233/5 kept the champagne on ice. Gloucestershire's failure to bowl out Derbyshire reduced Middlesex's target on the second day from three points to two, one of which they soon secured when Jones took two quick Surrey wickets. Needing 150 to put themselves clear of their remaining challengers, they soon lost Smith and Brearley for 29, but Barlow with 61 and Radley 70 steadied nerves, and after the former was out, the latter, in company with Norman Featherstone, saw them through to the championship. It was their first outright one since 1947, the seventh in their history and one greeted with enthusiasm around the circuit. 'Most important of all, Mike Brearley's captaincy was accepted by other counties as being fair and reasonable,' wrote Tony Lewis. 'Everyone was inclined to play cricket with Middlesex. There were no longer the grudge drawn games, as there were against the club in the late 50s and early 60s.'[7] Even Boycott admitted they merited their win because they made their own luck.

Aside from their excellent team spirit, the key to their success had been their ability to bowl sides out. Six of their bowlers finished among the top 21 places in the national bowling averages including Featherstone, a part-time spinner. They were also indebted to the rapid emergence of Barlow as an attacking batsman and the consistency of Radley. 'But for gathering the threads together no one deserves greater credit than Brearley,' wrote Woodcock. 'He and Smith have made a reliable opening pair, he himself a sagacious captain.'[8] 'The Middlesex players, committee and supporters owe much to their captain, especially when they contrast his term as leader with the dark days,' declared *Wisden* on making Brearley one of their five cricketers of the year.[9] He in turn complimented Smith, Radley and Titmus in particular for their tactical guidance, while stressing that everyone was entitled to their opinion, a change that even Titmus came to accept. He remarked approvingly that 'there was a lot more genuine debate, and a better atmosphere as a whole, than when Murray, Parfitt and I ran things. A lightbulb went off for some of us in the mid-1970s: What we did to be good before wasn't good enough anymore.'[10]

There were further triumphs to come. First, Brearley captained T.N. Pearce's XI to a two-wicket victory over the West Indians at Scarborough, the second defeat he inflicted on the tourists – no one else managed it once – and second, he was appointed vice-captain to Greig on MCC's tour to India and Australia that winter. At 34 and the eldest man in the party, he could count himself fortunate to have been selected in preference to Steele, who'd batted heroically against Australia the previous year, and Peter Willey, who'd shown a refreshing enterprise in the final two Tests against the West Indies. Even his renowned reputation for leadership didn't seem to justify the vice-captaincy once Boycott had declined it, since Fletcher, an astute captain of Essex and experienced Test match batsman, was also in the party. While Woodcock shared these misgivings, he sensed the selectors' reservations about Greig, who'd been below his best all summer. 'Although Brearley could be going for the wrong reason [that is in case Greig falls down on the job and another captain is needed against Australia next season] he could, as an opening batsman, make as many runs as anyone.'[11]

Others wrote in a similar vein. 'By naming a positive deputy and not merely a figurehead,' wrote Alex Bannister, 'Lord's have given Greig a simple message – you cannot take the captaincy in the home series against Australia for granted,' an ironic statement in light of future events.[12]

Chapter 7

The Lure of the Orient

A FTER a turbulent two years during which England registered only two wins in their previous 20 Tests, MCC travelled to India keen to restore their bearings. While the bowling led by Willis, Old and Underwood looked to be in good hands, the batting appeared vulnerable with much resting on Greig, one of the few successes from the previous tour there. The captain immediately re-established his rapport with India by saying all the right things on arrival, not least his flattering references to the quality of their umpires, recently the bane of the touring New Zealanders. He was the charismatic maestro who captivated his audiences on every stage while Brearley slipped unobtrusively into his role as understudy. Quieter and less flamboyant than Greig, the two weren't natural soulmates. Back in 1973, Brearley had objected to him sledging his Middlesex team-mate Larry Gomes and when Greig, prior to the West Indies series, stated it was his intention to make his opponents grovel, Brearley declared that his words 'carried an especially tasteless and derogatory overtone'. Given his inexperience at Test level, and Greig's initial tendency to seek advice primarily from Fletcher and Knott, both seasoned tourists and shrewd observers of the game, he had to be patient and earn his captain's trust.

After several days of practice in Bombay, MCC journeyed to Poona to play West Zone. Although unable to force a win, the game boosted their morale as the batsmen engaged in a run glut. Replying to the home team's total of 257, Brearley began cautiously but after completing his fifty he cut loose with a dazzling array of strokes which reminded Alex Bannister of his 312 at Peshawar a decade earlier. Having added 292 for the second wicket with Fletcher, he reached his double century, before sacrificing his wicket to give others a bat.

He followed up his double century with 59 against the Board President's XI and 65 against North Zone, guaranteeing his opening slot in the first Test at Delhi. Although MCC had drawn their four matches to date, they had settled in well under Greig's leadership and approached the Tests with confidence. As ever, the fabled Indian spinners, Bishan Bedi, Erapalli Prasanna and Bhagwat Chandrasekhar, posed a real threat, but their batting, Sunil Gavaskar and Gundappa Viswanath aside, looked vulnerable.

Batting first on a flat pitch, England lost the opening salvoes and at one stage were 65/4. Brearley began uncertainly before he was run out by Brijesh Patel for 5 as he attempted a quick single towards cover. He called it a 'moment of madness' which spoiled his whole tour. Greig later told him that he could have cried when he saw him self-destruct. Their recovery to 381 all out was built around a marathon innings of 179 by Amiss with Knott's 75 and John Lever's 53 offering valuable support. The debutant Lever then followed up his batting with a devastating spell of swing bowling that decimated the home side. All out for 122, they provided stiffer resistance in their second innings, but once Gavaskar was out for 71 no one stayed long enough to stave off an innings defeat.

England continued their dominance in the second Test at Calcutta. Losing the toss, they had the best of all starts by dismissing Gavaskar in the opening over, caught at slip off Willis. Deprived of their talisman, the Indian batting once again looked brittle against pace and were all out for 155. On the second morning, it was England who struggled, losing Barlow for 4 and Brearley, batting at number three, for 5, caught at short leg off Bedi. When Amiss was out at 90/4 the match seemed delicately poised but a fifth-wicket stand of 142 between reserve wicketkeeper Tolchard and Greig turned it very much in England's favour. Greig's 103 was a true captain's innings, given that he was battling a severe temperature, and it gave his team a vital 166-run lead. With Gavaskar failing once again, no one else stepped up until a dazzling 50 from Patel in the dying stages showed what might have been. All out for 181, India lost by ten wickets, their first defeat at Eden Gardens. The 80,000 crowd, forgetting their disappointment, gave the England team a generous reception as Greig led them round the ground in a lap of honour.

With Greig taking a well-earned rest, Brearley captained the side against Combined Universities and Under-22 XI and contributed a commanding 76*. On another turning wicket, the spinners, Geoff Miller and Geoff Cope, proved too good for their opponents as MCC ran out easy winners, only their second victory in a three-day game on their last three tours of India.

For the third Test at Madras, England recalled Woolmer to open with Amiss and kept Brearley at number three. Winning the toss again, they endured their habitual poor start and with Tolchard retiring hurt with an injured hand, Greig found himself coming to the wicket at 31/3. Both he and Brearley batted with patience and skill against the spinners, putting on 109 for the fourth wicket. Greig made 54 and Brearley 59 before the latter was out in unfortunate circumstances. Aiming to sweep the off-spinner Prasanna, the ball hit the head of Mohinder Amarnath, fielding at short leg, before it lobbed gently back to the bowler. He could console himself with his first Test half-century made in testing conditions.

From 175/5 overnight, England were all out for 262, a total that looked all the more imposing when India slumped to 17/3. Gavaskar hinted at something better but once he went to a deft catch at slip by Brearley off Old, the rest quickly succumbed to Lever. He finished with 5-59 only then to find that his efforts had been traduced by the Indian captain Bedi, who accused him of greasing the ball with Vaseline. MCC didn't deny the strips of Vaseline-coated gauze but explained their use as an attempt to stop sweat seeping into the eyes of Lever and Willis. As the debate convulsed India, causing manager Ken Barrington much stress, Brearley, unlike most of his team-mates, remained more open-minded about England's motives. 'Was this cheating to aid swing? Or was the aim simply to divert the sweat? I have never known the answer to the question. I was not involved in the discussions but nor did I enquire too closely … I am inclined to think that the action was innocent but naïve, certainly the plan should have been cleared in advance with the umpires.'[1]

Batting again with a lead of 98, Amiss, Greig and Brearley all made useful contributions in their second innings of 185/9 declared. Left to make 284 to win, India faltered against Underwood, his dismissal of Viswanath aided by a brilliant low one-handed catch by Brearley at slip, one of five he took in the match, his best-ever tally for England. With Lever mopping up the tail, the home team were shot out for 83. By winning the series so comprehensively, Greig's team had far surpassed any of its predecessors in India. They chaired their captain from the field before setting off on a victory lap.

While Brearley was rested for the game against South Zone, Woolmer, a double failure at Madras, missed out again and made way for Fletcher for the fourth Test at Bangalore. So far, the mercurial Indian umpiring had slightly favoured England, but fortune's wheel now turned against them in a game plagued by controversial decisions. Batting first, India scored 253 before their spinners got to work. On a turning wicket and supported by a cluster of close catchers who appealed for everything, they re-established the mastery they had exerted over the England batsmen on their previous tour. Brearley, restored to opening, was the first to feel the wrath of the umpire's finger after playing Chandrasekhar to Viswanath at slip. Dismayed to be given out on the half-volley, he left the field with a reluctance, exchanging a few words with Viswanath. Others suffered the same fate, as only Amiss proved equal to the challenge. All out for 195, England surrendered a first-innings lead of 58 and when required to score 318 to win they once again succumbed to the spinners, losing by 140 runs.

With a double failure at Bangalore, Brearley regained his confidence with 79 in the drawn game against Bombay. For the fifth Test at Bombay, India continued their improvement in the previous Test with a first-innings total of 338. In reply, Amiss and Brearley began cautiously till Brearley broke his shackles by using his feet to the spinners and driving effortlessly through the covers. By stumps he'd advanced to 68 (11 boundaries) out of England's 99/0, their first decent start in the series.

The next day was the rest day and Brearley was invited to dinner by someone he barely knew. Assured that the dinner wouldn't be late, he found himself standing around in a hot, crowded room sipping whisky till dinner was served at 10.30pm. He gulped down his food and caught a taxi back to his hotel, irritated and depressed. Feeling somewhat lethargic the following morning, he never regained his previous fluency as he and Amiss increased their partnership to 146, England's first century opening partnership in 13 Tests. After Amiss was out for 50, Brearley became wracked with tension. He was dropped by Gavaskar on 87 and scored only four more runs in 80 minutes before he was lured out of his ground by Prasanna and stumped for 91. His dismissal had potentially profound consequences, as he reflected many years later. 'I still torment myself with the thought that had I scored a century against India at Bombay in 1977 in my seventh Test innings when I was stumped for 91, things might have been different. I might have walked taller at the crease, and scored one or two others.'[2]

After their encouraging start, England fell away and it needed a fine 76 from Greig to keep India's lead down to 21 on first innings. They then bowled out their opponents for 192 in their second innings, but their target of 214 in just over four hours became all the harder following the early dismissals of Amiss and Brearley, the latter given out at short leg off Prasanna. He clearly felt the ball had rebounded from his pads and he showed his displeasure as he departed to a chorus of boos. 'For the first and only time in his career,' reported Alex Bannister, 'Brearley let his feelings escape by angrily waving his bat in the direction of the barrackers.'[3]

On a wearing wicket, England found survival an exacting business, but they did it thanks to a flawless 58* from Fletcher. For all their success in India, weaknesses remained in their batting. Despite his scintillating double century against North Zone, Brearley was never able to play with the same abandon in the Tests aside from his 91 at Bombay. 'He is the most assiduous of run gatherers and he never resorts to the brutish or the unorthodox,' wrote the BBC's cricket correspondent Christopher Martin-Jenkins. 'Yet it is difficult to judge him as a player in the highest company.'[4]

For his part, Brearley found that the poor quality of the pitches made batting a perpetual struggle and sometimes a lottery. 'Test matches are long, grim games when you are foolish enough to run yourself out in the first morning, but batting well in front of a keen Indian crowd, against superb bowling, is as great a cricketing satisfaction as one could have.'[5]

He enjoyed the role of vice-captain and was struck by how simple it was compared to being captain. Besides admiring Greig for his all-round prowess on the field, he respected his refusal to tolerate dissent towards umpiring decisions and his ability to identify with his players, regardless of their personality, form or status.

As a tactician, he thought Greig veered too dramatically between attack and defence but learned from his propensity to intimidate the opposition lower order with relentless pace and compel Underwood to reset his field when he came under attack. In time, Greig came to value Brearley's advice highly enough to consult him frequently. 'As vice-captain he played an important part in a quiet way,' wrote *The Guardian*'s Henry Blofeld in his end-of-tour assessment. 'To a man, the other players liked or respected him.'[6]

Compared to some of his team-mates who struggled with its eccentricities, Brearley was fascinated by India. At one with its tempo, he liked the fact that he could stand and talk to someone without being hustled along. Whenever the opportunity beckoned, he would slip away from the main party to absorb the local culture or spend time helping out in homes for the underprivileged or those with learning difficulties. He studied Indian philosophy, befriended the natives – it was on this tour that he met his future wife Mana Sarabhai – and once shocked Derek Randall by wearing Indian dress. He thought the spirit of the Bengalis remarkable and declared that he'd never encountered such warmth and kindness in the face of great odds as in Calcutta; Indian hospitality to strangers put Britain to shame.

Besides his appreciation of India, Brearley also enjoyed the camaraderie of his team-mates, especially those evenings at up-country venues like Nagpur where the lack of local entertainment forced them back on their own resources. According to Fletcher, Brearley was always good company on these occasions.

After two weeks in Sri Lanka, MCC flew to Australia for the Centenary Test. 'Perth could not have been more different,' wrote Brearley. 'Instead of smog and smoke, there was clean air; instead of a shambles there was almost clinical sharpness of light and architecture.

'And in place of overt friendliness, deference, eagerness to carry one's bags, the first remarks at the customs immigration desk were abusive. "You've no chance, Pommies. Lillee'll get yer in two minutes ... And you can pick up your bag and bring it over here."' [7]

In their warm-up match against Western Australia, MCC had the worst of the draw but Brearley overcame a battering from Lillee and his opening partner Wayne Clark to make 61 and 58*, his second innings batting at number eight because of a finger injury.

He was passed fit for the Centenary Test, and played in front of large crowds and 200 retired players at Melbourne. Winning the toss, Greig inserted Australia and saw his bowlers dismiss them for 138, only for Lillee to return fire with precision, his 6-26 primarily responsible for England's paltry 95. In more benign conditions, the home side piled on the runs, declaring at noon on the fourth day and setting England 463 to win. They lost Woolmer cheaply but Brearley and Randall stood firm and, after Brearley was lbw to Lillee for 43, Randall continued in partnership with Amiss, batting at number four, till the close.

On the final day, Randall played the innings of his life, his 174 taking England to the brink of victory before Lillee, with another five wickets in the second innings, bowled Australia to victory by 45 runs, exactly the same result as in that inaugural Test 100 years earlier. As past and present players celebrated the enormity of the occasion, a revolution was brewing which was soon to turn the cricket world upside down. In this febrile situation it needed cool heads to come to the fore and in Mike Brearley the English authorities found their ideal man.

Chapter 8

'England Arise!'

O N 20 March 1977, days after the Centenary Test, Brearley was relaxing with Greig and Willis at the home of Arthur Jackson, a Sydney hypnotherapist, when Greig raised the prospect of lucrative contracts for leading cricketers. It was the first stirrings of the pending storm that would shake the foundations of the cricket world. Since time immemorial cricketers had been poorly remunerated and relations between them and their governing bodies remained frayed. Their cause was taken up by the media magnate Kerry Packer following the refusal of the Australian Cricket Board (ACB) to give the television rights of Test cricket to his Channel Nine network. Used to getting his own way, Packer retaliated by signing up 35 of the world's top players for his WSC enterprise by offering them salaries far in excess of anything they had previously earned.

When the news broke on 8 May, the reaction in England was overwhelmingly hostile and Greig, as one of Packer's leading agents, attracted particular opprobrium. The Cricket Council, cricket's governing body in the UK, viewed his clandestine role in the recruitment of players as a breach of trust in his relationship with them and, consequently, on 13 May, they sacked him as captain. Later that day the *Daily Mirror* asked Brearley for his reaction to the news and he issued a statement regretting Greig's demise, especially given his inspirational captaincy in India. Discussing the candidates to take over against Australia that summer, Woodcock wrote:

> The favourite must be Michael Brearley of Middlesex, who was Greig's understudy in India. Like everyone else, he was rather dwarfed by Greig out there. But he is liked and respected by the players and he will almost certainly get into the England side on merit. [1]

Days later, Brearley received Greig's endorsement in *The Sun*. Complimenting him on his role in India, he commented,

> Mike was adept at man-management, aware of the players and, of course, totally reliable when I needed advice on and off the field. [2]

He was duly chosen to lead MCC against the Australians, scoring 4 and 47 in a match they lost by 79 runs. According to Robin Marlar in the *Sunday Times*,

> This was Brearley easing himself into the hot seat. With his keen mind to open up all the game's angles he is a leader to be respected but in 1914–18 terms he is a staff captain and not the type to lead over the top and somehow emerge unscathed. That was Greig, that was … Without the threat of the circus England under Brearley might well have had a better chance than England under Greig. The experience could have added an ever-finer edge to Brearley's steel. However, it is difficult

for an intelligent man to be a tough and successful cricket
captain for he will tend to see too much debate in the game.
Jardine, arguably unique, changed his personality: not that
Brearley has that fund of reserve at his disposal.'[3]

During the match he was appointed captain for the three
Prudential Trophy games the following week. In typical
English conditions, the home bowlers gave little away and
restricted Australia to 169/9 in their 55 overs. It was then that
most people saw for the first time the skull cap that Brearley
had first worn months earlier in Sri Lanka and that he was to
wear all that summer. According to Woodcock, it was 'shaped
like a mortarboard with the lid cut off'.[4] After enduring the
fastest bowling he'd ever encountered in the MCC-West Indians
match the previous year, he and Greig had visited Bill Swanick, a
manufacturer in Nottingham, who made protective headgear for
children who suffered from epilepsy. He gave them a polythene
shell which resembled a scrum cap to go under their cricket caps
with extra protection under the temples. (Greig never wore his.)
'My sole aim is to avoid death,' Brearley told the *Daily Mail*.
'There are fatalities in cricket and it's in the back of your mind.
You could be the victim of a 1,000-1 chance.'[5]

He gave his side a solid start but after his dismissal for 29 the
middle order panicked and they were indebted to some impish
batting by Knott to see them home by two wickets.

The ball continued to dominate in the second match at
Edgbaston. Electing to field first, the Australian bowlers used
the conditions to their own advantage, captain Greg Chappell
taking 5-20, aided by some undistinguished batting. England
were bowled out for 171 but it proved more than enough as
Australia were shot out for 70, a humiliating performance that
did wonders for English morale.

They began the final match at The Oval in style with Amiss and Brearley putting on 161 for the first wicket, the highest-ever partnership recorded in a Prudential match. Brearley played with greater freedom than hitherto, but after he was stumped off the leg-spinner Kerry O'Keefe for 78, Amiss played a lone hand for 108. Their total was less formidable than at one time seemed likely and with Chappell in sublime form his 125* took Australia to victory by two wickets amid driving rain. (Both captains wanted to finish the match that evening as the next day was Jubilee Day.) Brearley had looked the part in the three matches and the selectors named him captain for the first two Tests. 'Brearley may lack Greig's extrovert capacity for rousing crowds and motivating players,' wrote Arlott in *The Guardian*. 'He is, though, more tactful and more psychologically perceptive; genuinely conscious of the need for different approaches to different characters, he is likely to win loyalty by sympathy.'[6]

On the advice of the TCCB, the England selectors had picked their team on merit, which allowed for the inclusion of the three Packer players, Greig, Knott and Underwood, all of whom Brearley liked and respected. More important, he noted Greig's ability to get the best out of his men by involving them in team policy, a practice which Brearley continued. His reward was a loyal and united team in contrast to the faction-ridden Australians, 13 of whom had signed for Packer including the captain and vice-captain.

On a chilly morning at Lord's, Brearley was soon to have second thoughts about batting first on winning the toss as he and Amiss were quickly back in the pavilion. Although Woolmer, who made 79, and Randall batted with aplomb, the rest of the side made no impression against the Australian quicks and were out for 216 just before stumps. With most of the second day lost to bad weather, Australia looked to Chappell when play resumed on the third day. Although kept in check by the accuracy of the England bowlers, he established an effective bridgehead with his watchful 66, and with debutant Craig Serjeant prospering in a 100-run partnership with Doug Walters, the tourists were sitting pretty at 238/3. An aggressive spell by Willis, which gave him three important wickets, brought England back into the game and on the fourth morning he took the last three wickets to finish with 7-78, his best Test figures to date.

Australia led by 80 and, after Thomson bowled Amiss for nought, Brearley and Woolmer needed luck as well as skill in the cheerless conditions to keep their wickets intact. From 29/1 at lunch, Brearley was dropped at short leg shortly afterwards and twice edged Lenny Pascoe through the slips. Interspersed with much playing and missing, there were some crisp cover-drives and with Woolmer looking increasingly imperious they added 132 before Brearley fell on the stroke of tea caught in O'Keefe's leg-trap for 49. After tea, Woolmer went serenely on and, when bad light brought play to a premature end, he was still there 114* out of England's 186/2.

With Woolmer soon out on the final morning, England's resistance was based solely around Greig's 91 as Thomson and Pascoe made light work of his team-mates. His success under pressure won him enhanced respect from Brearley, who consulted him without in any way undermining his own authority; Greig didn't bowl a ball throughout the Test.

After England were all out for 305, Australia needed 226 to win in 165 minutes. Any hopes of a dramatic victory soon receded as both openers went early and with Willis, Old and Underwood keeping up the pressure they slumped to 71/5. It needed some firm defiance by David Hookes and Rodney Marsh to see them through the statutory 20 overs with the loss of only one further wicket.

For the second Test at Old Trafford, England brought in Miller for Barlow, giving them plenty of bowling options. In benign conditions Chappell won the toss and batted, only for his batsmen to fail to take full advantage. Half the side were out for 140 before a sixth-wicket stand of 98 between Walters, who made 88, and Marsh restored a sense of parity. With 35 minutes to go, Brearley, spurning the opportunity of taking the new ball, called up Miller for his second over of the day, and, in no time, he'd lured both batsmen to their doom. From 247/7 at the close, Australia took their score to 297 before disposing of both England openers cheaply, Brearley steering Thomson to slip. Woolmer once again came to the rescue, first in partnership with Randall, who made 79, and then with Greig, who made 76. By the time he was out for 137, England had progressed to 325/4, well on the way to a handsome first-innings lead of 140.

Despite a classic 112 by Chappell, one of his finest innings, Australia once again failed to pass muster, especially against Underwood. Persuaded by Brearley to experiment by bowling over the wicket and into the rough just outside the leg stump, the Kent spinner was happy to oblige and his 6-66 included the prize wicket of Chappell. Once he was out, Australia soon folded for 218, leaving England a mere 79 to win. With Thomson bowling at his most hostile, both openers endured some uncomfortable moments, but Brearley refused to be cowed, especially against the short ball, and played with real fluency. His 44 took his side to the cusp of a nine-wicket victory, England's first win at home for three years and only their second win against Australia in the previous 13 Tests. Not surprisingly, he was now appointed captain for the rest of the summer and, on his initiative, the selectors recalled Boycott, who'd recently ended his three years in self-imposed exile, for the Trent Bridge Test. He replaced Amiss, who'd looked tentative against the Australian quicks,

Mike Hendrick came in for Lever, who appeared jaded after his exertions during the winter, and a first cap was given to the young Somerset all-rounder Ian Botham.

Botham was soon to vindicate his selection with his memorable debut as the Australian batting flattered once again to deceive. On a plumb wicket they started steadily enough with Rick McCosker and Chappell steering their side to 94/1 at lunch. McCosker departed soon afterwards, neatly caught by Brearley at slip off Hendrick for 51, but the defining moment came immediately after the afternoon drinks interval. Keen to give Botham another shot after a loose first spell, Brearley recalled him at the Pavilion End and with his first ball, a rank long hop, he caused Chappell to play on for 19. He then followed up by claiming the wickets of Walters, Robinson, Walker and Thomson to finish with 5-74, success which he credited largely to Brearley for entrusting him with the ball at a critical juncture of the match and for his sensitive man-management. Having noted Botham's overuse of the bouncer when playing for MCC against the Australians earlier in the tour, Brearley advised him at the beginning of his second spell not to repeat the error, advice which Botham willingly accepted.

All out for 243, Australia fought back on the second day. Brearley was caught in the gully off Pascoe for 15, Randall was farcically run out by Boycott and England at 82/5 had surrendered their early advantage. Boycott, however, was still there and made Australia pay dearly for dropping him at slip shortly afterwards. Galvanised by the quirky brilliance of Knott, he grew in confidence and together they turned the tables with an unbroken partnership of 160. The next day, before another full house, both men completed their hundreds and, although the tail barely wagged, England still led by 121. They then dismissed Ian Davis and Chappell before stumps as Australia reduced their deficit to nine. On the Monday, the bowlers toiled hard on a placid wicket but Brearley gave nothing away by bowling them in short spells and handling his field adroitly. The dismissal of McCosker, fourth out for 107, provided an important fillip and after Underwood had disposed of Richie Robinson, prised out by Brearley's ingenious field placings, Willis returned to finish off the tail. Australia were all out for 309, giving England just over a day to score the 189 they needed for victory.

Having survived a testing examination by Thomson that evening, Boycott and Brearley began cautiously the following morning, but by dispatching the bad ball unerringly, they had advanced the score to 92/0 at lunch. With the weather closing in, both men accelerated afterwards with Brearley taking the lead before he played on to Walker for 81. He'd batted 261 minutes and hit 13 fours and his stand with Boycott had realised 154, the best opening partnership for England since Amiss and David Lloyd against India at Edgbaston three years earlier. Max Walker quickly sent back Knott and Greig, promoted in the pursuit of quick runs, but Boycott stood firm and, together with Randall, he guided their team to victory by seven wickets.

With scores of 135 and 80*, Boycott's return had been a triumphant one and after scoring his 99th century against Warwickshire the prospect of making his 100th hundred against Australia on his home ground entranced the nation. With expectations at fever pitch he barely slept before the beginning of the fourth Test but perfect batting conditions awaited him after England won the toss. Although Brearley was caught behind off Thomson for nought – he was admonished by Ian Chappell for not looking at the umpire – Boycott and Woolmer saw them through to lunch without further mishap. Woolmer departed soon afterwards, Randall flickered briefly but Boycott, eyes firmly on the great prize in front of him, prospered in partnership

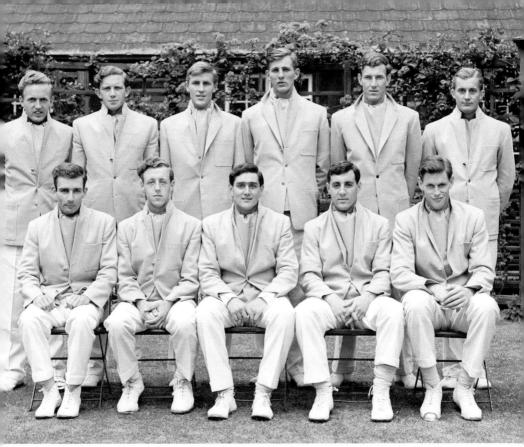

The Cambridge XI against Oxford, Lord's, 1962.

Brearley batting during his century against Oxford, Lord's, 1962.

Off to South Africa, October 1964: Brearley with his Middlesex team-mates, John Price, Peter Parfitt, Fred Titmus and John Murray.

Brearley's second Test: England against the West Indies, Lord's, 1976.

Brearley and Middlesex celebrate the winning of the county championship, 1976.

Hitting firmly to leg: Brearley batting against Australia in the Prudential Trophy, 1977.

Brearley on the day of his appointment as captain of England, May 1977.

England's slip cordon against Australia, Trent Bridge, 1977. From left to right: Willis, Miller, Hendrick, Greig and Brearley.

Celebrating the return of the Ashes, Headingley, 1977: Brearley with Willis, Greig and Knott.

Brearley opening the sports exhibition at Selfridges.

The England XI against Pakistan, Edgbaston, 1978.

Brearley introduces David Gower to the Queen, Lord's, 1978.

For services rendered: Brearley at Buckingham Palace, 1978.

with Greig, reaching his fifty in 175 minutes. Fortunate to survive a highly confident appeal for caught behind off left-arm spinner Ray Bright on 75, he sailed serenely on towards his destination. His moment came when, shortly before the close, he on-drove a Chappell half-volley to the boundary and raised his arms in triumph before being engulfed by half of Yorkshire.

After the Lord Mayor's Show there came the clear-up, as Boycott ground remorselessly on the next day. By the time he was last out for 191, England's total stood at 436. Their bowlers then pounded the brittle Australian defences, Mike Hendrick picking up Davis, then Chappell, caught at slip by Brearley for 4, Randall running out McCosker, and Botham dismissing Hookes and Walters. Having limped to 67/5 by stumps, they subsided to 103 all out in 31.3 overs the next day, Botham taking 5-21. With the overcast conditions ideal for seam bowling, Brearley enforced the follow-on and his early switch to Greig was rewarded with two quick wickets. By the time bad light brought play to a premature end, Australia were staring into the abyss at 120/4.

Heavy overnight rain on the Monday morning delayed the start till after lunch, but once play began the result was never in doubt, especially once Chappell was caught at slip off Willis. When Randall caught Marsh off Hendrick at 4.40pm, England had regained the Ashes on home turf for the first time since 1953. Having exchanged pleasantries with his demoralised opponents in their dressing room, and participated in a genial joint interview with Chappell for the BBC, Brearley joined his team-mates to savour their triumph. 'There was something strange about the occasion,' he wrote. 'It was like moments remembered from the past: players running for the stumps, people swarming on to the field, and great crowds beneath the pavilion balcony. The heroes of my childhood had won the Ashes and been exalted, and now we had done the same thing.'[7] Celebrating their achievement

– no England team had won three successive Tests against Australia at home since 1886 – an editorial in *The Times* singled out the captain for special mention. 'It is not disparaging to the virtually flawless captaincy of Brearley to say that he inherited a side already filled with the enthusiasm and motivation to perform splendid feats. He took over, nevertheless, at an unsettled time in less than happy circumstances, and, with great tactical perception, went on to lead England's team to comprehensive victories in three matches. That makes him a very good captain indeed.'[8]

The BBC's Christopher Martin-Jenkins reached a similar verdict about Brearley. 'He had a better side, too, but he missed hardly a trick in emphasising the point, manipulating his bowlers and fielders shrewdly and always keeping the pressure on his opponents. He is altogether a more complete captain than Greig … even better at getting the most out of his players and exploiting favourable conditions for his side.'[9]

Now that England had marked the Queen's Silver Jubilee by regaining the Ashes – their 1953 triumph had come in Coronation Year – the selectors were minded to omit the Packer players at The Oval. Their intentions found little favour with Brearley, typical of his conciliatory line towards WSC throughout. Not only did he continue to lean on Greig's advice on the field, he dined with him regularly off it. 'Brearley made it quite clear to the players that he was only captain because of the advent of WSC and he stressed that it was Greig who had built up such a good side,' wrote Knott. 'Throughout the series with Australia in the summer of 1977 the atmosphere was perfect in the England dressing room, and the credit for that goes to Brearley and Greig.'[10]

Brearley also understood the motives of the Packer players for greater financial security more readily than most, in line with his previous efforts to secure better terms for all professionals. When invited to become captain of England, he'd refused to give the authorities an assurance that he would repudiate an offer by Packer should he be approached, but he did agree that he would discuss it with the selectors. Contrary to the view of the TCCB, he opposed a ban on the Packer players from all first-class cricket, professing it would be neither fair nor sensible, since the standard of county cricket would decline, and he questioned their right to speak on behalf of the players without an extraordinary meeting of the Cricketers' Association. (When that meeting was held early in September, the players ignored Brearley's lead and voted for a ban.) During the Headingley Test he rejected a suggestion that a £9,000 cheque donated by several businessmen to the England team should exclude the three Packer players. He made it clear that they were a team and that every member should receive a share, which is precisely what happened.

That said, Brearley had his doubts about WSC, especially the control exerted by an individual outside the whole cricketing structure and the degree of commercialism involved. When he met with Packer, in company with Greig and Ian Chappell, the captain of the rebel Australian side, at England's hotel on the Sunday evening of the Headingley Test, he rejected his proposal to sign up the whole of the England team. (Not that he was in a position to accomplish this.) He stressed that he had no wish for confrontation between the TCCB and Packer and he supported a compromise masterminded by the businessman David Evans, namely that in return for Packer helping to finance Test matches in 1978 there would be a year's moratorium on the ban of his players, a compromise that the TCCB subsequently rejected.

England duly maintained their team for The Oval, aside from Lever replacing the injured Hendrick, but after the drama of Trent Bridge and Headingley the final Test was an anticlimax. The first day was lost to the weather and England batted poorly on the second day after Boycott and Brearley opened up with a stand of 86, each of them scoring 39. They were all out for 214 on the Saturday morning in what little play was possible. Australia struggled on Bank Holiday Monday before a late rally by Hookes and Marsh gave them a narrow lead by the close. The revival continued on the final day as Walker and Mick Malone flayed the bowling so successfully that they surged to 385 all out, a lead of 171. England had three hours to bat out time and although Brearley and Woolmer went cheaply they progressed to 57/2 before rain had the final say.

Away from England duty, Brearley led Middlesex to further triumphs: a shared championship with Kent, Gillette Cup winners for the first time and third place in the JPL. After narrowly beating Kent at Canterbury in the first round of the Gillette Cup, they saw off Warwickshire in the second round, Brearley's 82 winning the man of the match award, and made light work of Hampshire in the third round, thanks to a second-wicket stand of 223 between Smith and Radley. The semi-final against Somerset at Lord's was blighted by terrible weather. Six days were required to play the fixture and, because the weather forecast remained unreliable when conditions eventually permitted them to start, it was deemed necessary to limit the game to 15 overs each. Middlesex, without Brearley, who was playing for England at The Oval, won convincingly by six wickets and faced Glamorgan in the final.

Confronted with a damp wicket, Brearley, defying convention at that time, inserted Glamorgan and kept them on a tight leash throughout. Their 177/9 off 60 overs was hardly the most challenging of targets and while Brearley's dismissal to the first ball of the innings raised a few jitters, Radley, after an uncertain start, assumed control and his 85* was the lodestar which guided Middlesex to a comfortable five-wicket victory.

After their championship success the previous year, Middlesex maintained their winning ways, helped by the acquisition of West Indian fast bowler Wayne Daniel, whose pace and bounce brought him 71 wickets at 16.98. The early loss of Jones to injury was compensated by the emergence of Emburey, whose off spin provided balance to an already formidable attack, the best on the county circuit. The batting was more vulnerable and it leaned heavily on Brearley when he was present, his average of 68.33 far superior to the rest of his team-mates. Having begun with two fifties in his first three championship matches, he then struck prime form with 123* against Hampshire, 152 against Worcestershire, 82 and 17 against Nottinghamshire and 145 against Gloucestershire. In the second innings he was run out for 0 as Middlesex chased 75 to win in 12 overs against their opening pair Mike Procter and Brian Brain when it should have been 13 overs. Brearley sent a note out to the umpires pointing out their error but it was to no avail as his team had to settle for a draw.

By then Middlesex were beginning to lose some of their aura. Defeats to Leicestershire, Warwickshire and Northamptonshire in the first fortnight in August, all of them when Brearley was absent, underlined his value both as captain and opening batsman. The one match in which he was present during that time, against Surrey at Lord's, will linger long in the canons of great captaincy. During the first two days, only five overs had been possible in which time Surrey had made 20/1. On the third day they were bundled out on a damp pitch by Daniel, Selvey and Gatting for 49. As the wickets tumbled it gradually dawned on Middlesex that an outright win was still possible, especially if they could forfeit their first innings and compel Surrey to bat again in alien conditions. Because no one knew whether forfeiture was permitted by the Laws of Cricket, Brearley left the field to seek clarification with Donald Carr, the secretary of the TCCB, whose office was at Lord's. Carr told him that a side couldn't forfeit its first innings; only its second innings. Thus, Middlesex were obliged to bat for one ball before declaring, a stroke of inspiration, as once again their seamers rode roughshod over the hapless Surrey batsmen. Dismissing them for 87, Middlesex needed 139 to win in 88 minutes and with Arnold, Surrey's best bowler, unable to bowl, Smith and Brearley set about their task with gay abandon plundering 47 from the first seven overs. Thereafter the result was barely in doubt as they romped home by nine wickets with 11 balls to spare.

Following their defeat against Northamptonshire and a draw against Sussex, Middlesex enjoyed one piece of luck when their championship fixture against Somerset was rearranged to accommodate their weather-hit Gillette Cup semi-final. The match, played at Chelmsford so as not to interrupt preparations for the Gillette Cup Final, enabled Middlesex to win seven crucial points, seven more than they would have done on the original rain-soaked dates. Bad weather had also decimated the championship hopes of Kent, who'd led the table for most of August, so that when the final round of matches began on 7 September, it was Gloucestershire, four points ahead of both Kent and Middlesex and with a home match against Hampshire, who appeared the favourites. Middlesex travelled to Blackpool and, sent in by Lancashire on a turning wicket, they lost Brearley for 0. Only Mike Gatting with 50 looked comfortable as they were bowled out for 148, two runs short of a bonus point.

The pitch continued to pose problems for batting and with Phil Edmonds in fine fettle Lancashire were shot out for 108. Building on their lead of 40, Brearley batted doggedly for 41 before Radley and Gatting, with 61 and 60 respectively, carried on the good work. Middlesex declared early on the third morning, setting Lancashire 278 to win, and with Edmonds and Emburey exploiting the wicket to the full, they dismissed them for 186. Victors by 91 runs, they waited to see whether they were champions. Gloucestershire played beneath themselves and lost by six wickets, but Kent won a fluctuating game against Warwickshire by 27 runs, giving them a share of the championship with Middlesex.

Middlesex's success capped a memorable season for Brearley, especially since he equalled Peter May's unparalleled feat of 1957 of leading England successfully through a Test series (West Indies) and his county (Surrey) to the championship in the same year. His exploits won him the BMW-Lord's Taverners' Cricketer of the Year and an appearance on BBC Radio's *Desert Island Discs* – a rather stilted affair since the presenter Roy Plomley clearly knew little about cricket – and, later, an OBE in the 1978 New Year's Honours List.

Now that Woolmer and Amiss had joined Greig, Knott, Underwood and Snow by signing for Packer, Brearley, with Barrington once again the manager, was tasked with leading an inexperienced side to Pakistan-New Zealand that winter. While they could boast a powerful attack, albeit one unsuited to Pakistan's dead wickets, a middle order of Brian Rose, Derek Randall, Graham Roope and Mike Gatting looked suspect. Much would depend, as ever, on Boycott, whose intriguing appointment as vice-captain, a decision much favoured by Brearley, had taken him one step closer to his ultimate ambition of captaining England.

Chapter 9

Misfortune in Pakistan

NEVER had an England tour departed in such uncertain circumstances as Brearley's tour to Pakistan-New Zealand, with the ruling in the High Court regarding the International Cricket Conference (ICC)/TCCB ban on all WSC players from Test and county cricket imminent. *The Guardian*'s Frank Keating, there to see them off, was struck by the chemistry between Brearley and Barrington. 'Manager and captain make a fascinating duo. The old Sergeant Major and the knowing Sandhurst-type swot, Barrington is amiably approachable, Brearley has a slightly patronising edge. They became firm friends in India last winter. Brearley knows Barrington has been "over the top" in sport more times than Dwight Stones. There seems a huge and mutual respect between the son of the Reading private soldier who started working in a garage at 14 for 17s 6d a week and the Cambridge double first who also came joint top of the Civil Service examination.'[1]

No sooner had England arrived in Pakistan than word reached them that Kerry Packer had won a crushing victory safeguarding his players from the ICC/TCCB ban. The news clearly caught them off guard. Prejudice had overtaken foresight.

'All the talk is about Packer,' Barrington wrote to his wife Ann. 'It was a shock judgement. It's going to be a real problem unless they all get together.'[2]

After starting the tour with the worst of a rain-affected draw against the Pakistan Board Patron's XI at Rawalpindi, England (no longer MCC) journeyed to Faisalabad for their second fixture. Getting there proved something of a nightmare since their lack of landing lights meant that the team were compelled to make a three-hour journey on a filthy corporation bus on a road full of holes. On a pitch conducive to batting, Brearley missed out a second time against United Bank as Boycott and Rose scored centuries in England's first innings of 284/1 declared. With bat dominating over ball, the match ended in stalemate.

Against the North West Frontier Governor's XI at Peshawar, Brearley enjoyed better fortune. Returning to the ground where he scored 312 in 1967, he and Boycott put on 105 for the first wicket, the latter compiling another century, before England's pace attack ran through their opponents, giving them victory by 212 runs. After visiting the Khyber Pass, they travelled to Lahore, venue for the first Test, in fine fettle. Opposing them was a young Pakistan side, under Wasim Bari, which hoped to compensate for the loss of their Packer players with a number of promising young batsmen such as Haroon Rashid and Javed Miandad and a top-flight leg-spinner in Abdul Qadir, the best that Brearley ever faced.

The Test was marred by crowd disturbances. The first stoppage on the second afternoon featured the crowd attacking the police after they hit a boy who'd run on to the field to celebrate opener Mudassar Nazar's century. Warned by the British High Commission that demonstrations were possible, Brearley had told his side that if there was any trouble they should congregate in the middle and stick together rather than run off. When trouble duly occurred, Willis recalled the scene. 'Coughing and spluttering, ten of us gathered in the centre of the pitch as per our instructions only to see the back of our gallant captain in the direction of the dressing room.'[3] They followed him off but once they realised they weren't the object of the unrest they relaxed. The martial police quickly restored order, and after an early tea the game continued.

The second stoppage the next day was altogether more ominous. The trouble stemmed from the recent overthrow and imprisonment of the Pakistan prime minister Zulfikar Ali Bhutto by the head of the military, General Zia-ul-Haq, and the imposition of martial law. Bhutto's fate provoked waves of resistance in Lahore, his principal stronghold, and because public meetings were forbidden a Test match offered an alternative means of rallying the faithful. When Mrs Nusrat Bhutto and her daughter Benazir, neither of whom were cricket fans, appeared at the ground, they immediately became a target for their rivals, the Pakistan National Alliance, who set fire to the stand where they were sitting. So enraged were the crowd that the two teams barricaded themselves in the pavilion until the military police restored control. When play resumed after the rest day the police and army outnumbered the crowd and security thereafter remained tight, even in the provinces. At Bahawalpur the guard outside Barrington's room snored all night keeping him awake.

The Lahore disturbances overshadowed the tedium of the cricket. Mudassar Nazar's first-innings century took 557 minutes, the slowest ever in Test cricket, and Pakistan batted into the third day before declaring. Despite the alien conditions, the England bowlers toiled hard, not least their debutant off-spinner Cope, the protégé of Johnny Wardle, who advised him to always deploy his best four fielders in the four most prominent positions. He relayed this advice to Brearley who, recalling his year in the

Cambridgeshire team, smiled at him and said, 'Your adviser didn't happen to be a certain well-known left-arm bowler?'

Cope recalls how, for his first bowl in Test cricket, Brearley opted for a gully rather than a silly point, his own preference, for a batsman inclined to play with an open-faced bat. 'First ball I got a bat-pad, and it went to silly point. Gully dived, and he was inches away from it.

'And Brears walked up to me. He said, "I'll never interfere again. All I will say to you is, can we attack? And can we defend?" And he left me to it. There's a lot in a captain who gives you that.

'I thought he was a good captain, certainly a thinking captain. He did ask questions, and he tried to understand you. But he tended to look round at some of the players who were with him who were better players than he was. He was finding that part of it demanding.'[4]

Having claimed Wasim Raja as his first Test victim, Cope then appeared to take a hat-trick on his debut by dismissing Abdul Qadir and Sarfraz Nawaz with successive deliveries before having Iqbal Qasim caught at slip inches above the ground by Brearley. As a delighted Cope was congratulated on his achievement by the umpire and his team-mates, Brearley thought he might have taken the ball on the half-volley. Cope assured him that it was a clean catch and that the umpire was happy with it, but Brearley remained unconvinced and said that in the interest of the series he felt honour-bound to recall Qasim. 'A complex character, Mike,' recounted wicketkeeper Bob Taylor. 'I've seen him stand his ground in a Test and refuse to walk, even though everyone knew he had snicked the ball and yet his honesty robbed Geoff Cope of a hat-trick in Cope's first Test.'[5]

Replying to Pakistan's 407/9 declared, Boycott and Brearley began steadily with a half-century partnership before the latter was sent back by the former and was unluckily run out for 23.

Despite 63 from Boycott, England were floundering at 162/6 till a painstaking 98 from Miller carried them to safety.

Victory in the first two one-day internationals at Sahiwal and Sialkot either side of Christmas proved some compensation for the shoddy travel and accommodation and the boredom associated with long dark evenings. En route to Hyderabad, venue for the second Test, the bus broke down twice and the England team, in blazers, had to get out and push. Once there, their hotel, according to Barrington, was on the point of falling down. 'To give you an idea I have the best room but the lights are poor and the carpet; well I wouldn't put it down in my garage … No hot water, mosquitoes by the thousands and on top of this nowhere to go, and dust everywhere.'[6]

On a dead wicket, England's satisfaction at dismissing Pakistan for 275 soon diminished by their failure to cope with Abdul Qadir's leg-spin, bowling round the wicket into Willis's footmarks. After Boycott was run out for 79, they collapsed to 191 all out, losing their last seven wickets for 54, Qadir finishing with 6-44. Although Pakistan built a handsome lead, Wasim Bari took caution to excess by delaying his declaration till just before the close of the fourth day. With Boycott surviving two appeals in the second over, the mood in the England camp was tense that evening. Early the next morning Barrington answered a phone call from Brearley asking that he bowl to him in the nets in a manner similar to Qadir. He was at the nets before 8am and bowled according to instruction, helping Brearley get his feet in the right place. The session proved invaluable for, despite surviving a number of lbw appeals, both he and Boycott defied everything that Qadir and company could throw at them. They put on 185 for the first wicket and assured themselves a draw. The one issue still at stake was whether both batsmen could reach their hundreds. Boycott, by playing a few shots and claiming the extra half hour, did, but Brearley started blocking and was out for 74 just before the close. 'I became obsessed,' Brearley admitted to *The Observer*'s Scyld Berry afterwards. 'I became obsessed with the concept of purity in the not-out.'[7]

After drawing with a Punjab XI at Bahawalpur and losing the final ODI at Lahore, attended by Jim Callaghan the British prime minister, the team travelled to Karachi for the final Test, where they became embroiled in a major rumpus. The origins of this rumpus were bound up with the struggles which governed Pakistan cricket. Factional infighting throughout the 1970s had weakened its board of control and discredited it in the eyes of the players, so that when stalwarts such as Mushtaq Mohammad, Zaheer Abbas and Imran Khan defected to Packer it was the board who were deemed culpable. It was thus to restore their credibility and that of the national team that elements of the board, egged on by Omar Kureishi, the manager of Pakistan's tour to England in 1974, sought to recall the WSC players for the final Test. With Packer's blessing the trio returned home, much to England's indignation. Led by the senior players such as Boycott, Willis and Old, they expressed their opposition to all WSC-contracted players being able to play in official Tests, and on arrival at Karachi, they drafted a statement to this effect.

In the middle of this crisis an inconsequential one-day game against Sind XI at the lovely Gymkhana Club ground in Lahore had unforeseen consequences. In the fifth over of the day, a delivery from opening bowler Sikander Bakht reared off a dusty surface and broke Brearley's forearm as he instinctively protected his face. In obvious pain, he hurled his bat away, staggered a few paces and sank to his knees. It was several minutes before he was able to leave, escorted by Bernard Thomas, looking dazed and shattered. 'We knew something had broken because we heard a loud crack,' recalled Gatting. 'Brears was philosophical

– he always is – but you could see he was downcast.'[8] An X-ray at a local hospital confirmed a clean break and Brearley decided to return home to have an operation to ensure that he gained the full rotating movement of his arm. Before he left that evening, in a joint press conference with Barrington in the team room, he read the players' statement opposing the selection of WSC players for official Test matches. He stressed that their opposition wasn't simply about the Karachi Test, but was as much concerned with the forthcoming West Indies-Australia series, since the West Indies Board of Control had indicated their intention to play their WSC players. Strike action wasn't something he willingly countenanced but, faced with the growing militancy of his team following his departure, his hand might well have been forced.

Arriving home, Brearley was met by the chairman of selectors Alec Bedser and he was immediately whisked off to see a doctor. He was then booked into Birmingham General Hospital, where a small stainless 4½in steel plate was fixed over the bone fracture by consultant orthopaedic surgeon Roy Pearson, who'd treated a number of top sportsmen. During his four-day stay there in a £40-a-night private room, paid for by Cornhill Insurance, he was inundated with phone calls and press visits asking for his comments about the escalating crisis in Pakistan. According to Tony Greig, writing in the *Sydney Sun*, the threatened strike was the work of Boycott and his cronies. Anyone who knew Brearley knew that he wouldn't resort to such brinkmanship. He always stood for compromise not division. Accusing Boycott of double standards, Greig declared that he should be the last person to determine who should play. His ability to avoid fast bowling had long been a talking point among cricketers. By some stroke of fortune, he'd steered well clear of the game's best fast bowlers for the past five years.

Greig's paean of praise to Brearley failed to move him. Declaring that he was wrong about England's motives, he called his words 'ill-timed' and urged him to apologise to Boycott, whose brinkmanship, and that of his team, had brought a climbdown from the Pakistan Board. The Test went ahead without the Packer players and fizzled out in a dull draw.

Brearley's loss was much regretted by the team, who'd grown accustomed to his collegiate style of leadership. 'Brearley was a consultative captain,' recalled Brian Rose, the captain-elect of Somerset. 'He liked to talk to his players, his bowlers particularly, and explain to them what he was thinking. What I learned most from Brearley was the importance of thinking ahead. He would always be thinking about where he wanted to be in five or ten overs' time, and he would quite often talk to his bowlers about that as well, so that they knew exactly what he wanted from them.'[9]

There were a couple of dissenters, however. Brearley and Boycott hadn't always seen eye to eye, chiefly because of the latter's insatiable demand for practice, which had meant less opportunity for the others. Brearley had also fallen out with Edmonds, having omitted him from the first Test for a personal misdemeanour. 'I hadn't been getting on too well with Brears,' recounted Edmonds. 'I felt ambivalent about his departure. Everyone was saying what a terrible captain Boyks was. All I know is that when Brearley was in Pakistan I didn't do much, and when Boycott took over, I got 7 for 66 at Karachi in the third Test.'[10]

The other dissenter was Botham who'd disappointed with his attitude. During the first net of the tour at Rawalpindi, his attempt to slog the spinners to all parts had created such a poor impression with the senior players that Brearley began to wonder why they had chosen him for the tour. 'Brearley thought I was an oaf for a long time,' Botham later declared. 'I don't think he was prepared for a hulking lad from Yeovil who wanted to conquer the world. He is a fellow for symphonies, for slow and thoughtful music. He likes meditating and working people out. In me he saw only a wild youth who wouldn't do as he was told. He thought I was undisciplined, vulgar and crude. For several months he treated me with something approaching contempt.'[11]

Omitted from the first Test after sustaining dysentery, Botham's return was marred by a heated altercation with Brearley in an ODI. 'I was at midwicket and the ball went to deep cover. I didn't know which end to back up. I chose one and the throw came in. I found Brearley standing behind me. He wanted to know why the hell I wasn't at the other end. I told him that I didn't have eyes in the back of my head. He said that I always had an answer. And I said: "Well perhaps I was bloody well right for once." That was the end of it, and the game carried on. I wasn't upset because it was all in the heat of the moment but Brearley was.'[12]

Ignored and frustrated, Botham unburdened himself to Barrington on the golf course and Barrington advised him to have a heart-to-heart with Brearley. He did so only for Brearley to tell him that, attitude aside, he considered him a lesser all-rounder than either Old or Miller. Botham replied that he would prove him wrong, something he was able to do in New Zealand when Brearley saw him in a different light. 'We spent some evenings together drinking and chatting,' recounted Botham. 'After I scored 150 and taken 8 wickets in a Test he said, "Well maybe you have got Chris Old covered." We laughed about it and had a few dinners together.'[13]

'I was hostile at first,' Brearley admitted, 'and in Pakistan we wondered why we'd brought him. He was brash, played like a cheerful, wild hitter from club cricket.

'He played terrifically well in New Zealand under Boycott. He showed a lot of guts in his battles with Hadlee and he bowled his heart out.'[14]

Brearley was in New Zealand, courtesy of a free flight from British Airways, to comment on the second and third Tests for the *Daily Express*. He arrived the day before the second Test at Christchurch and joined the team for the traditional pre-Test dinner. Aware of the delicacy of the situation, he saw Barrington and Boycott as soon as he arrived and agreed he wouldn't spend much time in the dressing room or attend the pre-match discussion. He was thus annoyed to read, in a Christchurch popular daily, a quote from a London paper that he'd been banned from the England dressing room. As it was, Boycott had asked his opinion on what he'd do if he won the toss. Brearley advised him to field first, advice Boycott rejected since he decided to bat. England ended up winning that Test and drawing the series but New Zealand hadn't been the happiest of trips and Brearley, fitness providing, would soon be back at the helm.

Chapter 10

Good Enough?

ON Sunday 16 April Brearley returned to the cricket field against a Guernsey Invitation XI and pronounced himself fully recovered from his fractured forearm, although he carried a plate screwed to the bone for the next year or so. A half-century for Middlesex against MCC was an encouraging start but it proved to be something of a false dawn. It said much for his character that despite his dearth of runs all season he continued to give everything to his captaincy. 'One of the reasons Brearley was so respected by the England team,' wrote Leo McKinstry, Boycott's most recent biographer, 'was that he never let his regular crises of personal form interfere with his leadership.'[1] The same couldn't be said of Boycott. Having always hankered after the England captaincy, he proved unable to rise to the challenge when deputising for Brearley in Pakistan and New Zealand. Diplomatic gaffes aside, his sense of insecurity, his constant moodiness and obsession with his own game failed to motivate his team-mates. During the second Test, his failure to accelerate, as England chased quick second-innings runs, so frustrated the side that Botham deliberately ran him out; then his failure to declare on the final morning caused

146

more consternation before Willis took the decision for him. With Barrington, the manager, expressing reservations about his leadership on his return, his fate was finally sealed. 'Mike's reappointment will meet with the approval of every England player,' Willis wrote in his diary when Brearley was chosen as captain for the ODIs against Pakistan.[2] As luck would have it, a chipped finger sustained against Derbyshire's Alan Ward prevented him from playing and it was Boycott who led England to a convincing victory in the first match; and Willis in the second one following Boycott's withdrawal because of a sore thumb. It was an injury that ruled Boycott out of the Test series against Pakistan, but his absence was barely noticed, since the tourists, unable to adapt to English conditions, offered little opposition.

In the first Test at Edgbaston, Pakistan fell easy prey to Old, who took 7-50 in their first innings of 165. England began circumspectly and Brearley, after surviving several lbw appeals, ran himself out for 38 when going for a risky second run. With centuries from Radley and Botham and an attractive 58 from David Gower, on debut, England amassed 452/8 before declaring at tea on Saturday, 287 ahead.

The Pakistan openers Mudassar Nazar and Sadiq Mohammad batted fluently that evening, putting on 94 for the first wicket, till the former was out just before the close. On the fourth morning, Sadiq and the nightwatchman Iqbal Qasim held out for 45 minutes, much to the growing frustration of the England quicks. Willis, who'd already bowled two bouncers to Qasim, then went around the wicket to him and with his first ball he bowled another bouncer which struck him in the face. 'That was wrong, in my opinion,' wrote the England wicketkeeper, Bob Taylor. 'Iqbal Qasim was only an obdurate tail-ender. Bob was far too good a bowler to need recourse to such tactics.'[3]

As Qasim was led bleeding from the field not to return, Willis refused to show any outward regret, concerned that inquiring after him would break his concentration.

Qasim's injury cast a pall over proceedings. Sadiq was out in the next over and Pakistan collapsed from 123/1 to 231 all out, but England's comprehensive victory was overshadowed by the furore caused by the injury. The Pakistan manager Mahmood Hussain denounced Willis's tactics, calling them unfair and in breach of the 1976 ICC agreement that instructed captains to ensure that no fast short-pitched balls should be directed at non-recognised batsmen. His comments drew little sympathy from Brearley who issued a self-righteous statement justifying his team's tactics. 'Although Qasim was a nightwatchman, he batted showing a good defence. We had tried everything and what do you expect?' He remained defiantly unapologetic at the feisty post-match press conference, making clear that he had no complaints about the way that Willis had bowled. His words failed to convince the critics. Woodcock wrote that Qasim's injury 'showed the two umpires at their weakest, Brearley, the captain, at his most indifferent, and Willis, his bowler, at his most callous'. That kind of bowling had been condoned for too long. 'Something has got to be done to save cricket from those vandals who want to make a blood sport of it.'[4] The *Daily Telegraph*'s cricket correspondent, Michael Melford, took issue with Brearley's contention that Qasim's role as a nightwatchman made him fair game for the quick bowlers. He was clearly not equipped to defend himself against that sort of ball which, in fact, would have taxed most batsmen. 'The umpires have a duty to intervene, especially in a decade when the bumper has been bowled excessively. But as one who believes that the principal responsibility lies with the captain, I am afraid that on this occasion, the scholar-captain, like Homer, nodded.'[5]

As the press continued to lambast Brearley, the TCCB issued a statement 'bitterly regretting' the incident and reminding him of his responsibilities of enforcing existing legislation. He did reluctantly agree to their suggestion that he and Wasim Bari should exchange lists of non-recognised batsmen exempted from bouncers, and advised Willis, in private, to show more sympathy to any future batsman he hit. (In 2005 he chided the England team for failing to check on several Australians hit on the head or the body by short balls.) More important, he called for the general introduction of helmets, an innovation whose time had all but come. The ferocity of WSC cricket and the number of head injuries during its first year had prompted a burgeoning use of helmets, with Amiss leading the way with a fibreglass motorbike helmet with a metal grille, and, early in 1978, the Australian Graham Yallop, playing against the West Indies, became the first batsman to wear one in Test cricket. A series of head injuries, including Qasim's, during the early part of the English season continued the trend and by the time England toured Australia that winter most of their batsmen had taken to wearing the lighter, more comfortable helmets now available. 'It makes so much sense to me to protect one's head that I am astonished at the outcry against helmets,' wrote Brearley at the time. 'They can be helpful not only against the quickest bowlers or on fast or uneven pitches, but also against medium-fast bowlers in order to give the batsmen more confidence in playing the hook or the pull. If protecting the head encourages stroke play and prevents serious injury, surely everyone should approve.'[6]

With safety the overriding issue, the case for helmets became ever greater and, looking back on his career, Brearley thought their introduction had not only improved the game, they had rejuvenated his batting, giving him greater confidence against the

short-pitched ball. Back in 1978, they were considered something
of an eyesore, not least when Brearley opened the batting in the
Lord's Test in a white crash helmet with protective bars across
the face of it. Up against a gentle Pakistan attack on a placid
wicket, his appearance provoked general derision, and after being
hit three times on the pads he was lbw to left-arm seamer Liaqat
Ali for 2. His partner Gooch, arrayed in a white sunhat, marked
his return to Test cricket with a stylish 54 and Gower confirmed
the good impressions of his debut with another fifty, but, once
again, it was Botham who stole the show. His spectacular 108
dominated England's 364, which proved more than adequate
against the hapless tourists. All out for 105 in their first innings,
they initially showed greater resolution when following on before
they were blown away on the fourth morning by Botham. Using
the humid conditions to maximum effect, he took 8-34 to give
England victory by an innings and 120 runs.

The third Test was decimated by the weather but not before
Brearley had given his Yorkshire critics further ammunition
with another failure, caught behind off Sarfraz for nought. The
hostile reception which greeted him opening the innings was
even more jarring on his return as shouts of 'Boycott, Boycott'
rang out. The selectors kept faith with him by appointing him
for the New Zealand series. Playing against them for Middlesex
at Lord's, he received a painful blow on the glove from opening
bowler Richard Hadlee and his damaged finger was bad enough
to prevent him batting in the second innings.

He was back for the first Prudential Trophy match at
Scarborough, where, once again, he was stalked by Boycott's
ghost as the Yorkshire crowd gave him the bird. England won
the match by 19 runs and the second one by 126 runs, placing
them in good heart for the Tests. On winning the toss at The
Oval, New Zealand had the better of the opening session,

prompting Brearley to berate his team at the lunch interval for their lethargy. His words had a galvanising effect because their opponents collapsed from 131/1 to 224/7 at the close. All out for 234, New Zealand fought back the following morning with debutant fast bowler Brendan Bracewell sending back Gooch for 0 and Brearley for 2. According to Willis, this was the England captain's darkest hour to date. 'Generally, Mike can be philosophical about dismissal, and after the few minutes of silent meditation that every batsman needs after being out, he is fairly cheerfully back amongst us. Today, things were different. He sat in the corner of the dressing room for about 15 minutes, first staring at the floor and then studying a book. It was some time before Mike rejoined us.'[7]

A maiden century from Gower gave England a narrow lead of 45 before Botham and Edmonds exposed the fragility of the New Zealand batting. After a blank fourth day their hopes for survival rested on a defiant innings from former captain Bevan Congdon. With Edmonds beginning to drift, Taylor suggested to Brearley that he convey his concern to him and, when Brearley acted on his advice, his homily so irritated Edmonds that he bowled Congdon with an absolute beauty. That ended the tourists' resistance. Needing 138 to win, England made it by seven wickets thanks to a hard-hitting 91* by Gooch, but another failure by Brearley kept the celebrations muted. According to Alex Bannister, the selectors could carry him for the moment but could they afford to have him captain in Australia when he was short of Test class? 'But such is Brearley's present form, or lack of it,' wrote Woodcock, 'that if he were not the captain he would be out of the side, and the days are past when that is an accepted practice. Because England are at ease under Brearley and play the better for being so, it is much to be hoped that he will, as it were, pull through.'[8]

As the runs dried up, Brearley's unorthodox stance came under critical scrutiny. Brian Close, Len Hutton and Richie Benaud were among the luminaries who offered him advice, the latter pointing out that whenever he played the ball it nearly always went off square to the wicket. According to Robin Marlar, who dissected his technique in the *Sunday Times*, both his feet were on the ground, which indicated that the bat was ahead of the delivery during the bowler's approach, and there was a gap between his hands. This meant his bat was used for protection – of person and wicket – rather than for assault. Only if it was held with both hands together at the top of the handle could there be a full swing. Marlar suggested to Brearley that he have a net with Ted Dexter and, in a session before the Oval Test, Dexter advised him to stand still, pick the bat up straight and avoid the early pick-up, advice he accepted, albeit marginally, mainly because the high back-lift he'd pioneered in 1974 had served him well, especially against the rising ball. 'When, four years later, I found myself in a bad patch ... many critics who had little knowledge or memory of the contribution this upright stance with high back-lift had made to my improvement as a batsman now pinned the responsibility for my decline on it. And I, equally obstinate in being wedded to a method that had perhaps become rigid, was unable to notice that at times my head went up and down like an oil-well pumphead as the bowler bowled. I was nodding like a mechanical donkey.'[9]

As a sop to the critics and to accommodate the return of Boycott at the top of the order, Brearley agreed to demote himself to number five. His *Via Dolorosa* continued at Old Trafford where he made only 9 in Middlesex's defeat by Lancashire in the quarter-final of the Gillette Cup. Once again, he was singled out for derision by sections of the 20,000 crowd whenever he misfielded. 'I was surprised by the animosity to Brearley,' wrote

Alan Gibson. 'Some of it was good-natured ribbing but there were some unpleasant undertones. What harm has he ever done them?'[10]

'We were in the field,' recalled Edmonds, 'and Brears was having a nightmare, with the ball following him around, and he fumbling it at every opportunity, much to the delight of the Lancashire crowd. Brears took some frightful abuse. But he made a point of placing himself in the most important fielding position of the moment, at short midwicket to a leg-side player. Lesser men would have found somewhere to hide.'[11]

At Trent Bridge, Brearley, on winning the toss, elected to bat and Boycott once again celebrated his return to Test duty with a century. He and Gooch put on 111 for the first wicket and by the time Brearley entered to a lacklustre reception, the score stood at a healthy 301/3. With Richard Hadlee in full spate he endured a torrid examination of his technique and mere survival seemed the limit of his ambition. In time, he unveiled a number of crisp cover-drives and after three hours he reached a painstaking fifty, only his third that season. On his dismissal shortly afterwards, his mood was one of relief rather than elation as he received the congratulations of his team-mates. 'At first, he was scratchy, clearly tense, and to be frank, he didn't bat particularly well at any stage of his innings,' confided Willis to his diary. 'He needed some luck, but after what he has been through recently, he was due for a large share. As he reached fifty, most of the team gathered on the balcony to applaud. It was a genuine gesture of real pleasure for the man who has bound the side together.'[12]

All out for 429, the luck continued to favour England, since New Zealand were compelled to bat on a pitch that was exposed to the elements. Adhering to Brearley's instructions to bowl short of a length because of the lift that would accrue, Botham proved their nemesis by taking 6-34 and, when they

followed on 309 behind, he and Edmonds consigned them to
an innings defeat.

Botham was again rampant in the third Test at Lord's with
match figures of 11-140. New Zealand led by 50 on first innings
but as England went out to field again Brearley paused at the
dressing room door and said, 'Look if we get stuck in, we are
capable of bowling this lot out for less than a hundred.' Acting
on Illingworth's advice, he gave Botham the new ball and he,
together with Willis, caused mayhem in New Zealand's ranks.
Reduced to 37/7 at the close, they were all out for 67 on the fourth
morning and England survived some early shocks to win by seven
wickets, giving them a clean sweep in the rubber. Whatever his
limitations as a batsman, Brearley was the overwhelming choice
of the players to lead them in Australia, and his appointment at
the end of the Lord's Test was little more than a formality. He'd
given some thought to the team he wanted and was successful
on all counts. In particular, he secured the choice of Tolchard
as deputy wicketkeeper to Taylor in preference to the more
gifted David Bairstow of Yorkshire, prompting the resignation
of John Murray from the selection panel. Equally contentious
was Boycott's loss of the vice-captaincy to Willis. Dismayed by
his demotion, Boycott sought a meeting with the chairman of
selectors Alec Bedser and the tour manager Doug Insole on 11
September. They told him that they'd heard reservations about
his captaincy in New Zealand the previous winter and, more
important, Brearley had expressed a reluctance to have him as
his deputy. Armed with these revelations, Boycott arranged to
see Brearley the next day. He later wrote:

> It was an odd meeting and I cannot to this day work out
> precisely what it proved. Brearley was very ill at ease, which
> surprised me. He was, after all, rightly celebrated as a man

with a talent for dealing with people. Yet he had the gravest difficulty explaining just why he did not want me as his vice-captain.[13]

When Brearley mentioned that he'd found Boycott's advice to be brusque and patronising, Boycott attributed this to Brearley's inferiority complex as a player in comparison to him.

> I think my presence on tour as vice-captain made him unsure and nervous to the point where he took the easy way out and very rarely discussed things with me as captain to vice-captain. Certainly, we had not related much on the tour of Pakistan – at least we agreed on that. I represented a threat and Willis did not.[14]

'Geoff has never understood his own unpopularity,' commented Botham. 'He couldn't see why we liked Brearley. He just thought Mike was a man born with a silver spoon who could not bat much and who had made it because of his background.'[15]

One other disappointment of the season for Brearley was Middlesex's failure to retain the championship primarily because of a lean spell in June when they lost twice, to Kent, the eventual champions, and Warwickshire. He wasn't the only batsman to fall some way short of his best, but with the bowlers, led by Daniel and Mike Selvey, doing sterling work, the team recovered to finish third, winning eight of their last ten matches, culminating with a ten-wicket defeat of Surrey in which Brearley scored 65* and 25*. A season of fluctuating fortune had ended on a high. 'Rarely has an England captain been under such severe stress and strain as was Mike Brearley in 1978,' wrote the editor of *Wisden*. 'His critics were legion, particularly the Yorkshire contingent who favoured Geoff Boycott.'[16] Yet, according to Alex Bannister,

Brearley emerged with the utmost credit. 'Throughout the difficult season not one word of complaint came from him. At Press Conferences he met challenging and sensitive questions fearlessly and without resentment.'[17] Such qualities would be needed in abundance throughout the forthcoming tour to Australia when, once again, he would have to account for his run famine.

Chapter 11

The Ashes Retained

AFTER the tribulations of a disappointing season with the bat and the organisation of his benefit, Brearley finished the 1978 season exhausted. Reclusive by nature, England's new cricket captain could easily have passed for the philosophy lecturer he'd once been, undertaking research in some university backwater. The cricket journalist Ivo Tennant recalls that his aunt was seated next to Brearley at a luncheon when he was captain. 'By the time she asked him what he did for a living, she had formed the distinct impression that he was an academic. He disillusioned her by saying that he played cricket. "What, all the time?" she replied. Rather than taking offence at not being recognised, he appeared rather pleased.'[1]

Invariably accompanied by a pile of novels, he read Paul Scott's *The Raj Quartet* in one of the treatment rooms during the long break for rain in the Headingley Test against Pakistan. A man of few close friends, his material needs weren't great. A casual dresser, he didn't smoke, drank sparingly and drove a modest Volkswagen. Shunning the celebrity world of sponsors' drinks parties, charity dinners and television chat shows, his milieu was the theatre, the concert hall or a quiet meal out.

As captain he would carry out his duties conscientiously but would often seek refuge thereafter in his own company or with non-cricketing friends. (He has always chosen his friends carefully and dislikes people claiming a closer association with him than is actually the case.) Uneasy when accosted by strangers and resentful about press intrusion into his private life, his natural reticence was tested in 1978 when granted a benefit by Middlesex, since success depends to some extent on the beneficiary's willingness to hobnob with all and sundry. Despite being overwhelmed by a bulging diary, Brearley did his share of selling pontoon tickets in the pub, autographing bats and hosting glittering dinners with guests such as John Cleese, Tim Rice and Fred Trueman, all of which helped him raise the tidy sum of £31,000.

After completing his benefit programme, he managed a week's break in mid-Wales before returning for an extensive two-week practice in the Lord's Indoor School with MCC coach Don Wilson, in which he made some adjustments to his technique. The exaggerated bat-lift which he'd used for the previous few years was abandoned in preference for a more orthodox stance. Prior to the team's departure from Heathrow on 24 October, there were the usual team talks and press briefings. Brearley emphasised the need for good communication, to avoid cliques and to play positive cricket, especially important given the rival attraction of WSC. Besides having a talented squad, Brearley was fortunate to have an accomplished managerial team comprising of Doug Insole, Ken Barrington and Bernard Thomas. Although Barrington had been a popular manager on the two previous tours, it was thought essential in light of WSC to have an experienced administrator and with Insole, the recent chairman of the TCCB, they picked the ideal man. Brearley later described him as the best manager he'd encountered: 'He was efficient;

he gave excellent advice, sparingly; he was a friend, confessor, disciplinarian and solace to the players. He also created an easy and relaxed atmosphere in the team room that was normally attached to his own bedroom.'[2]

Another bonus was the harmonious relationship with the travelling media. Brearley arranged to hold press conferences the day before the Test, on the rest day and immediately on the Test's conclusion, an arrangement that worked pretty well.

On arrival in Adelaide, they were met by Don Bradman and decamped to a high-rise motel complete with rooftop swimming pool to shake off their jet lag. They then began five days of intense practice before their first match, a gentle warm-up against South Australia Country XI at Renmark on the banks of the River Murray. Then it was down to serious business against South Australia, one of only four first-class matches prior to the first Test at Brisbane. It was here that they had their first sight of Rodney Hogg, a fair-haired fast bowler with a devastating turn of speed, whom Brearley compared to Brian Statham. Not only did he take 4-43 in England's first innings, he hit Radley on the forehead, undermining his confidence for the rest of the tour.

Eighty-one behind on first innings, the bowlers, led by Edmonds, hit back in South Australia's second innings, dismissing them for 149, but scoring 229 for victory proved too daunting an assignment. Hogg had the better of Boycott for the second time in the match as they were bowled out for 196, their first defeat against South Australia since 1925. It was, as *Wisden* recorded, a chastening start for Brearley, but he didn't overreact. He accepted that the team had played badly and they would need to guard against further complacency. He was as good as his word as he led from the front with an undefeated century in a rain-affected draw against Victoria. On a sluggish pitch and in cheerless conditions, it wasn't pretty to watch – he managed only three boundaries in his 116* – but his first century for well over a year did wonders for his confidence.

He stood down for the match against New South Wales, which they won by ten wickets, but he was back to score 59 against Queensland Country XI and 75* and 38* in the six-wicket win against Queensland. While consecutive wins were a welcome boost, the free-scoring approach of the batsmen gave cause for concern. Brearley admonished Randall for giving away his wicket against New South Wales after completing a century and told the out-of-form Gower to keep his ambitions in check until he'd sized up the pace of the wicket. With the cream of Australia playing WSC and the Test team under Graham Yallop something of an unknown quantity, England started firm favourites, but the tension was evident at the eve-of-Test meeting in their Brisbane hotel. The niggling among the players moved Brearley to anger and he felt depressed enough at the end of it to take a nocturnal walk along empty streets with Insole.

In keeping with the new emphasis on cricketing razzamatazz, a vintage car procession and the descent of sky divers formed the backdrop to the opening day of the Test to celebrate Brisbane's 50 years of Test cricket. In humid conditions ideal for swing bowling, Brearley was happy to lose the toss, especially since Willis, Old and Botham soon reduced Australia to 26/6 and they barely recovered to 116 all out. Although Brearley, batting at number five, was one of several failures in the England upper order, 75 from Randall, 44 from Gower and 49 from Botham enabled them to make 286, giving them a lead of 170. Fine centuries from Yallop and Kim Hughes, Australia's two best batsmen, brought them back into the game, but with the tail contributing little, England's target was only 170. While Boycott, Gooch and Brearley all failed for the second time, an undefeated

74 from Randall and 48* from Gower ensured a seven-wicket victory by mid-afternoon on the final day.

From Brisbane to Perth and the first major controversy of the tour. Boycott, still deeply affected by the death of his mother and his recent loss of the Yorkshire captaincy, was also struggling for runs, which helped explain his tetchy mood. Upset by his cheap dismissal in England's first innings against Western Australia, he let out his frustration in the pavilion over Brearley's decision to bat first on a sporting wicket in earshot of several television cameras. He then blotted his copybook further by swearing at umpire Don Weser and calling him a cheat for turning down a confident lbw appeal against Kim Hughes in Western Australia's second innings. Weser reported Boycott to the Umpires' Association, but no further action was taken once Boycott, on Brearley's insistence, apologised to the umpire. Sensitive to Boycott's plight, Brearley didn't overreact to his occasional barbs and made every effort to spend time with him in his hour of need. He advised him to keep playing, listened more frequently to his technical observations and defended him vigorously in the media, not least his seven-hour 77 in the second Test, which he deemed central to England's success. 'We haven't come all this way to Australia to understand Geoffrey Boycott,' he remarked at one press conference following intense media coverage of the Yorkshireman's character.

On a well-grassed wicket at the WACA, the Sheffield Shield champions, Western Australia, were no match for England's pace attack – dismissed for 52 and 78. Particularly telling was the performance of Hendrick whose eight wickets in the match had cost a mere 34 runs. John Inverarity, the opposing captain, told Brearley that he considered him the pick of the bowlers so far on the tour, comments that helped win him selection for the second Test instead of Edmonds.

On an overcast morning, Yallop's decision to field first appeared vindicated as England struggled to 41/3, Brearley among the men out, caught behind off left-arm seamer Geoff Dymock for 17. It took a fourth-wicket stand of 158 between the obdurate Boycott and the exquisite Gower to rescue them and take them to 309 all out.

Instead of opening with Willis, Brearley gave the new ball to Lever and his hunch paid off with Lever trapping Graeme Wood lbw for 5. Australia could only manage 190, although a belligerent 81 from Peter Toohey, in which he won a battle of wills with Botham, caused unrest in the England camp. 'We had one more over to the new ball and I was bowling to Toohey,' recalled Botham. 'I thought to myself, well, he'll be expecting an accurate over to slow him down before we attack with a harder ball, so I tried a double-bluff. I bowled bouncers. The first one dropped just where I wanted a man. I was furious and he hit the next three to the boundary. Brearley wasn't too pleased. We had a right row, one of our best.'[3]

Brearley also became engaged in a frosty exchange with umpire Tom Brooks over the bowling of bouncers to Dymock, a lower-order batsman, following a pre-match pact by the two captains whereby the lower order were exempt from bouncers unless they proved hard to dislodge. The pact had worked to Hogg's advantage in the previous Test, since he'd batted without a helmet and top-scored in the first innings at Brisbane, much to Botham's frustration, and this time the beneficiary was Dymock. His survival for over an hour prompted Brearley to inform umpire Robin Bailhache that he now warranted a bouncer or two with the new ball. Bailhache agreed but his colleague Brooks objected, insisting that it was the umpire's responsibility to protect the tail. Brearley disagreed, believing that anyone who walked to the wicket accepted a risk. As it was, the matter never came to a head since Hendrick bowled Dymock with his second ball.

It was during this partnership that Brearley became embroiled in one of the most acrimonious confrontations of his career involving Edmonds, his most trenchant critic. As discussed in a later chapter, their relationship had deteriorated over time and Edmonds had infuriated Brearley in the previous Test by bowling two bouncers out of the blue. Disillusioned to have been dropped and made 12th man at Perth, he'd prepared the third-day drinks and lunch just prior to the interval when he fell into conversation with some spectators. The conversation continued as England left the field until an irate Brearley ordered Edmonds back into the pavilion and tore a strip off him for failing to look after the team adequately. Being told that he should participate more, whatever his disappointment, merely fuelled his long-standing sense of grievance towards Brearley. Squaring up to him, he said, 'Get off my back, Brearley, or I'll – fix you.' Such was the hostility between the pair that only the timely intervention of Lever prevented a real fracas. Although both protagonists later confessed to overreacting, Brearley shouldered the bulk of the responsibility.

'It was, I think, more my fault than I have acknowledged. Phil had done all the things he should have done, I was hot, and I was tired, and I flew off the handle. He was sitting with his feet up, and I felt that there should have been more response from him. He would have said that to show more respect would have been crawling, no doubt. It was as if he really resented being 12th man. But it is difficult in these circumstances to say if that was right, or how my response was conditioned by my experience of him.

'He flew off the handle in response to the fact that I unreasonably flew off the handle. It was a real face-to-face. But

I don't think I would have hit him. I have not hit anyone since I was a child.'[4]

Leading by 119, England made heavy weather of their second innings, not least Brearley who was out for nought, caught behind off Hogg, one of his ten wickets in the match. Set 328 to win, Australia were never in the hunt once Wood departed for 64, the victim of a dubious caught-behind decision by umpire Brooks, one of several errors he made in the match. Although Brearley wouldn't comment on the umpiring, others weren't quite so restrained and, disenchanted by the growing flak he attracted, Brooks announced his immediate retirement from Test match umpiring, an unfortunate end to a distinguished career.

After an exciting draw in the return match against South Australia, in which Brearley demoted Boycott to number eleven in England's second innings as they chased 239 for victory, they repaired to Melbourne for Christmas. Always a lonely time away from their families, the team found some consolation in their entertaining traditional Christmas lunch and fancy-dress party.

The following day, Brearley received a nasty blow to the eyebrow from fast bowler Jonathan Agnew, one of England's top young cricketers in Melbourne on a Whitbread sponsorship scheme, when batting against him in the nets. Although the injury required six stiches, Brearley declared himself fit for the third Test and elected to open with Boycott to enable the out-of-form Gooch to bat at number four. On a pitch of unpredictable bounce, Australia batted first and were indebted to a century from Wood. A trifle fortunate to finish the first day at 243/4, they lost their last six wickets for 15 once debutant Allan Border was out for 29. Brearley commended his team for their effort and urged them to bat properly, but it wasn't to be. Egged on by the partisan crowd, Hogg was soon among the wickets, dismissing Boycott and Brearley in his second over. He ended with 5-30 as England were shot out for 143. Although Brearley upset his hosts by blaming the pitch for their demise, his batsmen had erred tactically by their tendency to play back. Led by Botham and Emburey, the bowlers gave it their all, but a winning target of 283 proved some undertaking for a side short of runs. They endured the worst of all starts with Brearley out for nought, driving loosely at a delivery from Dymock he should have left alone. Although Boycott, Gooch and Gower provided some resistance, nobody could master Hogg, who took another five wickets to finish with a match aggregate of 10-66. Brearley, in contrast, was left ruing a record of 37 runs in six innings, in addition to two dropped catches at Melbourne.

After suffering his first defeat as England captain in 16 Tests, the debate about his place in the team resurfaced. 'Can a man who is neither holding his catches nor scoring runs justify his place in the side?' wrote *The Guardian*'s Paul Fitzpatrick. [5] Comparisons with former England captain Mike Denness, who dropped himself after scoring 65 runs in the first three Tests on the previous tour of Australia, were made, and Brearley did consider his position. He accepted that his lack of runs reduced his value to the side, but reckoned it had little effect on his captaincy, and bolstered by the support of Insole, Barrington and Willis he vowed to keep going. 'Others enjoyed keeping the thought alive,' wrote Brearley. 'Tony Greig, for example, who came to have tea in my hotel room in Sydney the day before the fourth Test, remarked on the irony of my having the same room that Denness had had four years before. It was not until a year later I learned that Denness's team had stayed in another hotel.' [6]

To help him prepare for the Test, Brearley leaned on the professional expertise of Dr Arthur Jackson, the medical hypnotherapist he'd first met two years earlier through Willis, and now in two sessions Jackson managed to get him to relax with his quiet voice.

With England looking somewhat rusty since Perth, and Australia back in contention, the fourth Test now assumed a critical significance. In blistering heat, the tourists threw away the advantage of winning the toss, their only success in six Tests, with an abject batting display. Boycott went early and Brearley's start was so tentative that a wag shouted out, 'Brearley, you make Denness look like Bradman!' He was eventually bowled by Hogg for 17 and only Botham with 59 did himself justice. All out for 152, they looked no better in the field as Australia finished the day at 56/1. At the instigation of Hendrick, Brearley called the team together for a meeting in the manager's room back in the hotel. He quietly berated them for their slipshod performance and demanded a wholehearted effort on the morrow. His homily was vigorously endorsed by Hendrick and Taylor, who wrote in his tour diary that evening: 'It was good captaincy in my opinion – another skipper might have let it ride, but I think he judged our mood just right. We wanted to be told we were rubbish and I can't wait to get at them tomorrow.'[7]

The next day England duly found their resolve with a plucky display in the field, despite the absence of Willis, who was nursing a stomach ailment. With Brearley's deft field placings and clever manipulation of the attack, Australia, 126/1 at lunch, were restricted to 248/7 by the close. The following morning Brearley again came into conflict with the umpires over the question of bowling bouncers at Dymock. Dismissed for 294, the home side's lead of 142 looked all the more formidable once Hogg had Boycott lbw to the first ball of the innings. It could have been worse had Randall not survived a highly confident lbw appeal off Dymock when on 3 and Brearley enjoyed his fair share of fortune. Urging each other to keep concentrating through a tense afternoon, they survived to tea at 74/1, by which time the heat and Randall's constant jabbering was beginning to unsettle the Australians.

Following a shower and a change of clothing, the England batsmen returned to the fray and played with greater authority. They brought up the century partnership and Brearley reached his fifty, only then to be bowled by a turning delivery from occasional left-arm spinner Border. Although his 217-minute vigil had contained only two fours, the value of his innings couldn't be underestimated. 'Everyone was genuinely delighted for Brears and considering the heat and the state of the game it was a great effort,' wrote Gower.[8]

With England 133/2 at stumps, nine in arrears, they approached the rest day in better heart. Brearley told the press that he believed his side could win provided they could establish a lead of over 200. On resumption, Randall continued his stonewall tactics. With Gower and Botham feeling unwell, the emphasis was overwhelmingly on defence, and when Randall eventually reached his century in 411 minutes it was the slowest century in Ashes history. By the time he was lbw to Hogg for 150, he'd batted England back into contention. Not surprisingly his effort won him little appreciation from the crowd or the Australian media, which slated his team for their slow scoring. Yallop also weighed in confessing himself mystified by Brearley's tactics. Brearley, in turn, kept his own counsel, opting for an evening at the Sydney Opera House with his parents, out in Australia to watch him, and Taylor to see Benjamin Britten's *Albert Herring*.

England began the final day 162 ahead with four wickets in hand and were bowled out for 346, leaving Australia to score 205 for victory. They began brightly enough but two wickets for Hendrick and the run out of Wood brought them back to earth.

With the ball now turning appreciably, Brearley switched to his off-spinners, Miller and Emburey, and preyed on the nerves of the Australians by crowding the batsmen. Unable to withstand the pressure, they subsided to 111 all out, leaving England victors by 93 runs. As the home media turned their guns on their shell-shocked side, Brearley, drinking champagne, called his side's win the most satisfying under his leadership. His aggressive captaincy was lauded by former Australian leg-spinner turned critic, Bill O'Reilly, and the English press corps paid their dues to the only England captain, aside from Hutton, to regain the Ashes and then retain them. According to Scyld Berry, his leadership was the difference between victory and defeat, while Paul Fitzpatrick described it as one of the most dazzlingly brilliant campaigns of his career. 'For the major part of four days England were in a seemingly hopeless position, but that incisive attack on the final day won a battle that appeared lost.'[9]

After beating Northern New South Wales by nine wickets, the team headed for Tasmania without Brearley, who took the opportunity to attend a WSC game at the Sydney Cricket Ground (SCG) with 45,000 other people. While harbouring a number of reservations about WSC, he was impressed by the spectacle of night cricket, which accentuated his belief that some form of compromise with Packer would become necessary. Shortly afterwards he received an offer for $50,000 winner-takes-all by Packer for a match between the WSC Australian players and England. The letter was published in a Sydney paper before Brearley even received it, suggesting it was primarily a publicity stunt, and having contacted both Insole and the TCCB, he rejected it as impractical given their congested itinerary.

England's success in retaining the Ashes couldn't conceal the frailties in their batting, which were once again manifest in the fifth Test at Adelaide. Inserted on a lively pitch, Hogg and his new-ball partner Alan Hurst caused mayhem with the upper order as they slumped to 27/5 and only a brilliant 74 from Botham saved them from total embarrassment. Once again, their bowlers rescued them, giving England a first-innings lead of five.

With Hogg and Hurst causing further trouble in the second innings, they were indebted this time to Taylor with 97 and Miller with 64 to steer them into calmer waters. Requiring 366 to win, Australia briefly sparkled before they fell away, losing their last eight wickets for 45.

Brearley's delight at another victory did little to curb his growing irascibility as the strain of the three-and-a-half-month tour began to exact its toll. Normally philosophical on dismissal, he reacted with fury when given out caught off his shoulder in the first innings at Adelaide. He then lashed out at Botham for not bowling to his field in the third ODI – the first one had been abandoned – the only occasion, according to Gower, when Brearley came close to losing control on the field all tour. England's loss by four wickets, making the series one each, meant that a deciding match was necessary, something the weary tourists could have done without. Inserted on a damp wicket at Melbourne, Brearley batted resolutely for 46 during which he ran out Bairstow attempting a sixth run on Melbourne's vast expanses, but his team were dispatched for 94 and they were well beaten by six wickets. Subjected to heckling by some drunken home supporters before going to the presentation ceremony, Brearley was in no mood for diplomacy when somebody said they couldn't hear him. 'If you lot shut up, you might learn something,' he retorted before giving up in mid-sentence and abruptly departing the scene.

He'd previously clashed with victorious supporters at the end of the Melbourne Test and during the Sydney Test he criticised the crowd for throwing fruit at Boycott. 'Australian crowds are not, these days, notable for their subtlety or wit, their stock insult (concealing, dare I surmise, their own underlying fear?) alleging that "all Pommies are poofs".'[10] His own aloof, cerebral manner in turn struck few chords with his audience. The cricket historian David Frith wrote:

> The softly-spoken, greying, dark-featured man with the little-boy manner in the field and the air of a philosopher off it never ceased to puzzle or infuriate Australians, and will not be forgotten, even if few of his deeds outside those of controller-in-chief will be remembered. History will show.[11]

Brearley's mood barely improved by the time England arrived in Sydney for the final Test. Irked by the chaotic practice facilities, a feature all too familiar of the tour, his exasperation at losing yet another toss was such that he stalked off leaving Yallop to converse with the television commentator alone.

Having called for one final effort from his exhausted team, Brearley could have no complaints as his bowlers, led by Botham, dismissed Australia for 198. Only Yallop with a superb 121 offered any resistance, the next top score being 15.

Eighteen not out overnight, Brearley took 54 minutes to add to his score on the second morning as Boycott and Randall went cheaply, but then he began to find his touch in his most fluent innings of the series. He added 69 for the third wicket with Gooch and seemed destined for a big score until, on 46, he lofted the leg-spinner Jim Higgs to cover. With Gooch scoring 74 and Gower 65, England gained a lead of 110. Demoralised by their repeated failures, the Australian batting without Border, unaccountably omitted, once again caved in all too easily to Emburey and Miller, who took nine wickets between them.

Although England needed a mere 34 to win, the interval between innings gave rise to one of the greatest controversies of the whole series. The trouble began when the umpires Don Weser and Tony Crafter informed Brearley as he was padding up that Yallop wished to use the old ball. Despite Brearley's objections – it would be to Australia's advantage to start with a ball that their spinners could grip – the umpires overruled him, assuring him that there was nothing in the laws to prevent Yallop from doing so. Brearley insisted there was but he couldn't quote chapter and verse and it was only when England had reached 12/0 that Insole found the relevant passage in Law 5 which states that either captain may demand a new ball.

Despite the furore, Brearley survived to make 20* and guide his side to a nine-wicket victory. Amid the celebrations of a 5-1 win – no England captain, or for that matter any captain, had won five Tests in one series in Australia – he paid tribute to the professionalism of his side, particularly to Miller whom he considered the find of the tour.

Although the tour party broke up even before the majority departed for home they came together for an evening of presentations and speeches at the London Press Club dinner. Best of all was Brearley's self-deprecating contribution. 'I don't want to boast,' he declared, 'but I must say that I was very gratified to be the person to score the winning run in the final Test.' He paused and smiled. 'Indeed, I was gratified to score any run.' His Test batting average of 16.72 had indeed given him some sleepless nights, but his captaincy remained of the highest order. Alex Bannister remarked in *Wisden* that Yallop 'was no match for Brearley's tactical shrewdness, thoughtful planning, and general know how of how to run a Test side. Around Brearley's quiet determination and honesty was forged a team spirit which speedily overcame the one serious crisis of the winter.'[12] Boycott thought Brearley did a magnificent job on and off the field, Taylor rated it the happiest tour he went on and Gower commended Brearley for combining authority with sociability. 'He did not like Australia – I can't think of anyone further removed from the brash Aussie image,' declared Willis, 'but his captaincy on his first tour out there was a model for anyone wishing to learn the game.'[13]

From an Australian perspective, the esteemed cricket journalist Peter McFarline wrote that, batting aside, Brearley had enjoyed a magnificent tour, hiding his disappointment under the contentment of England's achievement. 'Brearley's standing within the team was amazing ... Few captains in the game's long history can lay claim to arousing that kind of devotion in other men.'[14] It was an accolade that has stood the test of time.

Chapter 12

A Missed Opportunity

AFTER a year short of runs, Brearley hoped for better things from the 1979 season. One of the wettest Mays on record afforded him few opportunities but 73* against Essex and 148* against Gloucestershire provided valuable preparation for the World Cup – to be held in England in June.

The second World Cup, officially called the Prudential Cup, lacked some of the drama and glamour of the inaugural one, especially since Australia chose to send a second-string side. While the West Indies once again started as clear favourites, England also fancied their chances and they began in confident fashion against Australia before a full house at Lord's. Winning the toss on a cool, overcast morning, Brearley employed his secret weapon just before lunch when he brought Boycott into the attack. He responded by removing opener Andrew Hilditch and captain Kim Hughes in the space of six tidy overs and, once Border was out for 34, the rest of the batting offered little, leaving England 160 to win. They lost Boycott and Randall early on but Brearley hunkered down while Gooch played his shots and their third-wicket stand of 108 propelled them towards a comfortable victory.

After an easy win against Canada, England faced a stern test against Pakistan, much strengthened by the return of their Packer players. In autumnal conditions at Headingley, their batting failed dismally, with Brearley out for his second consecutive nought, and only a ninth-wicket stand of 43 between Taylor and Willis gave them a veneer of respectability. Requiring 166 to win, Pakistan were undone by excellent bowling by Hendrick and at 34/6 they appeared beaten. A defiant 51 by Asif Iqbal kept their hopes alive and after he was caught by Brearley off Willis, Imran Khan, batting at number nine, took up the cudgels. Once again Brearley resorted to Boycott and once again he delivered by dismissing the last two men, to give England victory by 14 runs.

By finishing top of their group, England faced New Zealand in the semi-final. In sunny conditions at Old Trafford, they were sent in to bat and received their customary bad start. Brearley, however, played sensibly for 53, Gooch made a spectacular 71 and a late flourish from Randall took them to 221/8 off their allotted overs. Opener John Wright provided the grit in the New Zealand innings and after he was run out for 69, the lower order took up the baton so that the result came down to the final over, sent down by Botham. With 14 needed, it proved a tad too much for New Zealand and England won a fluctuating match by 7 runs. Afterwards, Edmonds recalls driving back to London with Brearley. 'It was a bit of a tense trip. He kept saying: "How can we possibly beat the West Indians?" I felt then that he was not expecting to win, and that he was going to be satisfied with a good personal performance. I thought that then. It was rather cynical of me to think that.'[1]

Up against the might of the West Indies in the final, England chose not to risk Willis's fitness and erred by playing only four front-line bowlers. Fielding first, they took the early honours, and when Old deftly caught and bowled Clive Lloyd for 13 they were placed uneasily on 99/4. Richards was still there, however, and the entry of the hard-hitting Collis King turned the match irrevocably in the West Indies' favour. Taking aim at England's hapless part-time bowlers, Boycott, Gooch and Wayne Larkins, they added 139 in 21 overs and, after King was out for 86, Richards continued to dominate with his imperious 138*.

Scoring 287 to win against the powerful West Indian attack would tax any team, but Boycott and Brearley withstood the early assault and proceeded carefully to tea. With a score of 79/0 off 25 overs, Brearley now sensed the need to accelerate but was persuaded by his delighted team-mates to keep going in a similar vein. 'I'll never forget the scene in the dressing room at tea,' Edmonds declared. 'All the guys round the trolley were congratulating them, and Derek Randall was saying things like, "Magic, skip. If one of you is there at the end, we've won it." And I was at the other end of the dressing room, saying what is going on? We have to go and slog the weak links!' [2]

The failure to go after the occasional off spin of Richards proved a costly error as England only scored 50 runs in the next 13 overs. By the time Brearley was out for 64, 158 was needed in 22 overs and with Garner in typically miserly mood, England's plight became ever more desperate. They lost their last eight wickets for 11 runs and the match by 92 runs, a much greater margin than at one time appeared likely.

After the World Cup, England played host to India in a four-Test series which was marred by bad weather. The tourists could boast several fine batsmen in Gavaskar, Viswanath and Dilip Vengsarkar, but their bowling lacked the aura of old now that their illustrious spinners were fading. Their limits were all too evident during the first Test at Edgbaston. England batted first on a plumb wicket and made hay with Gower scoring 200*,

Boycott 155 and Gooch 83 in their total of 633/5 declared. Their bowlers then took over, dismissing India for 297 and 253 to win by an innings.

England continued to dominate in the second Test at Lord's in a match ruined by bad weather. Having bowled out India on the opening day for 96, Botham taking 5-35, they built up a lead of 323 before Brearley declared on the fourth afternoon. He then took a stunning catch to dismiss Gavaskar for 59 to give Botham his 100th Test wicket, but centuries by Vengsarkar and Viswanath, and further stoppages for bad weather, gave India a hard-earned draw.

A swashbuckling hundred by Botham was the highlight of the rain-ruined third Test at Headingley. After three failures opening, Brearley dropped himself down the order to number seven for the final Test at The Oval, but scores of 34 and 11 hardly brought an upturn in fortune. Building on their first-innings lead of 103, a century by Boycott set up an England declaration on the fourth afternoon. Requiring 438 to win, India began the final day at 76/0 and in perfect conditions for batting, Gavaskar, supported by Chetan Chauhan and Vengsarkar, played to the manner born. Before the match, he'd been invited to dinner by Brearley at his home, along with a number of his team-mates and their wives. As the wives talked about shopping at Selfridges Brearley asked Gavaskar if he intended to acquire anything prior to his return home, and he replied, 'Yes, and I hope to get it at The Oval.' Playing flawlessly, he batted with increasing freedom and when tea was taken at 304/1, his side seemed on course for a historic win. India continued to flourish afterwards but England then slowed down the over rate and with 49 needed off eight overs, Brearley recalled Botham. He responded with the vital wicket of Gavaskar for 221, followed by those of Yashpal Sharma and Yajurvindra Singh, as India faltered in the home straight. At close of play they were nine runs short of victory with two wickets left.

After three seasons of success, Middlesex fell away badly, dropping from 3rd to 14th in the championship, recording only three wins, their worst performance under Brearley's captaincy. The appalling weather didn't help nor did the absence of their Test players, but inferior performances, especially the new-ball attack, were also apparent. They promised something better in the limited-over campaigns, but were badly beaten by Yorkshire in the quarter-final of the Benson and Hedges Cup and by Somerset in the semi-final of the Gillette Cup. In the JPL, they performed more to standard, coming fourth, and, keeping a promise Brearley had made to Botham, they outplayed the favourites, Kent, in their final match at Canterbury, enabling Somerset to celebrate their second title in two days. It was small consolation for a season that had promised something better.

Chapter 13
'Physician Heal Thyself'

IN his 2015 introduction to *The Art of Captaincy*, Brearley wrote: 'One thing I do understand better: that it may be harder to lead oneself than others ... I sometimes feel that being a slow learner I might now be better able to encourage the modest batsman-me to do moderately well in Test cricket rather than poorly.'[1] He is more willing to admit to failings in cricket than in other walks of his life and he still at times replays moments of bad thinking which led to unnecessary Test dismissals, citing examples of an injudicious stroke, or an ill-judged run. Was he berating himself too much? After all, all batsmen from the Test arena to the village green look back with a certain regret to moments of impetuosity that caused their dismissals.

Brearley's assessment about his unfulfilled potential is supported by plenty of ex-team-mates and critics who contend that he was a better player than his Test record suggests. They point to a career aggregate of over 25,000 runs with 45 centuries, mainly on uncovered wickets, and that between 1974 and 1982 he was invariably one of the top Englishmen in the national batting averages. Often compared to Mike Denness, another captain who struggled to make runs in Australia, it is worth noting that his predecessor, despite having an inferior career average, averaged 39.69 in Tests and scored four centuries at this level. The fact that most of these centuries were against lesser attacks only underlines Brearley's failure to avail himself of similar opportunities when up against the Pakistan-New Zealand attack of 1978 and the Indians in 1979.

Although Brearley's failure to live up to potential is accepted fact, we shouldn't push this assessment too far. John Woodcock, in a typically prescient piece, wrote, in 1964, that he was an outstandingly competent player rather than an outstandingly natural one and Brearley himself, when discussing his batting in *The Cricketer* that year, admitted that he would never take control. The same couldn't be said about Denness.

Invariably described as correct, composed and methodical, Brearley possessed the ideal temperament for an opener. His proficiency against the quicks inspired confidence in his partners and attacking fields didn't bother him, since it gave him the opportunity to score in the open spaces. Before each delivery he would check his stance and pick-up and ease the tension by humming various melodies, his favourite being Beethoven's *Razumovsky Quartets*. (Playing against Haseeb Ahsan of the Pakistan Eaglets in 1963, he asked the umpire to stop the bowler from whistling as he bowled.) Always a stickler for middle stump guard, he would move towards the off stump to help him decide what to play and what to leave. Unflinching against the short ball, he would get into line, riding the bounce well and successfully neutralise movement with soft hands. When his team-mate Simon Hughes saw him hit a century against Bob Willis on a damp pitch at Lord's in 1980, his admiration for his batting soared.

Aided by the invention of the helmet, Brearley felt more confident about hooking the short ball to supplement his trademark deflections and glances and his rasping square cut. Primarily a front-foot player, the result of his upbringing and Fenner's easy-paced wickets, he used the pace of the ball well and hit through the line, the off-drive and the cover-drive being the most potent weapons in his armoury. So flawless was his timing that he only used two Gray-Nicolls bats a season, compared to some hitters who used eight or nine.

A highly accomplished player of spin, he was hard to dismiss, although a canny bowler such as Somerset's Vic Marks would make him earn his runs by setting a one-saving field and force him to play some big shots, something he was loath to do. As a batsman he lacked power and struggled to lift the ball over the infield, especially on sluggish wickets, in comparison to Gatting, whose lofted drives he so greatly admired. Content to play within his limitations, Brearley's mental toughness helped him get through the tricky periods and he tended to score runs for Middlesex when they were most needed, his consummate century against Underwood on a dust bowl at Canterbury in 1980 a case in point. Circumspection and accumulation were less appreciated, however, if acceleration was the priority, and later-order batsmen resented their captain's instructions to hit out when he'd taken 70 overs to score as many runs.

At Test level, against true pace and with fewer loose balls, these limitations, especially his restricted range of shots off the back foot, proved more of a liability. According to Derek Randall, when Brearley walked out to bat with those three lions on his jersey, his pride was self-evident, yet for all his customary grit he was constantly under siege, liable to get out to a good ball defending. As an opening batsman he was invariably more vulnerable to pace rather than spin with Lillee his chief nemesis, dismissing him on seven occasions and Hogg on five, invariably caught behind or at slip, caused by his tendency to move across the crease when playing defensively and his failure keep side on. Tony Lewis later wrote:

> I knew him from Fenner's as an excellent player but saw at the higher level one technical flaw that denied him many big innings – he did not naturally maintain a wholly sideways posture through a stroke. His right shoulder came around strongly and opened him up to the bowlers.[2]

Rather than highlighting any technical flaws, Brearley attributed his lack of success at international level to defects of character, especially his failure to overcome the feeling of inadequacy that stalked him throughout. 'When I walked onto the big stage of Test cricket, I was often too tense, made mistakes that I would not have made when facing similar bowling in county cricket,' he later wrote.[3] Even during his salad days at Cambridge, he confessed that his ideal of relaxed concentration when batting eluded him and so, not surprisingly, the harsh glare of Test cricket only increased the pressure. Having made 0 and 17 against the West Indies on his debut, he had one more chance to prove himself. Three days before the second Test at Lord's, in the grounds of Shenley Mental Hospital, where he was due to attend a course, he was struck down with a stomach ache so bad that he was forced to lie down, curled up, under a hedge. That tension never deserted him as he continued to underperform at the highest level.

John Arlott thought he was always over-anxious to prove himself as an England batsman and, consequently, was never able to live up to his full ability.

> In Test matches his batting becomes introverted. He seems to worry rather than to play naturally (which is easier to

recommend than to do). He is constantly out edging balls outside the off stump: so are others, but not quite so frequently as Brearley. Some expert advisers feel his footwork is sometimes inhibited by anxiety.

Whatever the explanation, he often plays himself in and then gets out. He has reason to feel stressed, for he has had little sympathy from crowds.' [4]

'Arlott was right,' Brearley later wrote. 'I had to struggle in Test cricket with an inner voice which told me that I had no right to be there. I would then become more tense, try harder than ever, and play further below par. This inner saboteur even undermined success. If I scored 50, I would find it pointed out to me that one of their best bowlers was missing, or that they were tired, or that conditions favoured the batsman. In this mood, I would undervalue the shots I played well and overvalue those that I rarely played. I would remember the streaky shots.' [5]

According to Gooch, Brearley was bothered about his failure to score a Test century, especially since Boycott wasn't slow to point out who was the better batsman, something he has continued to do ever since. 'I saw it get to him in the dressing room and that inner tension may explain his occasional explosions of temper which quickly faded away.' [6] 'Mike would always give praise to others but got very little praise himself and probably he was a person who needed support,' noted Emburey. [7]

On later reflection, Brearley regretted his failure to make the effort to find a mentor who not only could talk to him about his approach to batting but who could also understand his shortcomings. 'I, however, would ask for advice only during periods of bad form, and would then move from one well-meaning colleague to another, often bewildered by the conflicting pieces of advice gained from people who, however generous, were not committed to an ongoing process with me, and nor I to them.'[8]

What does seem surprising is his failure to consult his opening partner, Boycott, the supreme technician and a perceptive coach, who later expressed his disappointment. 'A man who could take so much intelligent interest in other people found it hard to talk about his major professional weakness. That was an oddity and a pity. I might have been able to help him but I certainly did not want to embarrass him.'[9]

It has been suggested that the cares of captaincy might have reduced his effectiveness, but while the additional scrutiny didn't help, it ignores the fact that his average of 24.80 in his first eight Tests before he became captain was little better than his overall one of 22.89. Brearley has written that his five years away from the game may have impeded him, since he didn't have a technique he could rely on until he was well over 30; yet even when in vintage form in county cricket, not least in 1981, he couldn't reproduce that same form at Test level. Willis thought that his decision to demote himself down the order – he batted in every position for England between number one and seven – was flawed because it signified a lack of confidence in his batting. Yet while it is true that, arguably, his three best innings for England – 91, against India at Bombay, 81 against Australia at Trent Bridge and 74 against Pakistan at Hyderabad – were all as an opener, his average in that position – 23.03 – was remarkably similar to his overall Test average; at the same time, his best series, against Australia in 1979/80, saw him bat down the order.

Only twice in ten series did he average over 30 – in Pakistan 1977/78 and in Australia 1979/80 – and in five others he averaged less than 20. He never scored a Test century and the majority of his nine fifties lacked sparkle. According to Steven Lynch, the deputy editor of the *Wisden* Group, he has the second slowest scoring rate among batsmen who have scored more than 1,000 runs in Tests, with 29.80 runs per 100 balls. (We don't have reliable figures for many of the early Test matches.)

His figures also suggest a remarkable consistency throughout his Test career. There was no particular stage when they differ markedly from the general norm nor was there any one country against whom he particularly succeeded. Against Australia, for instance, his 37 innings realised 798 runs at an average of 22.80, which was almost identical to his overall Test average. 'Our jobs are laid bare by the statisticians,' Brearley wrote in *The Art of Captaincy*. 'One consolation is that it makes it hard, in the long run, for a cricketer to kid himself,' and his statistics point to a fundamental truth articulated by Boycott: that for all his dogged resolution, he lacked that essential class to succeed at the highest level. [10]

Chapter 14

In Jardine's Shadow

ON 30 May 1979 the great schism which had ruptured the cricket world for the two previous years was finally healed. Deeply in debt, the ACB felt compelled to come to terms with WSC and, although they nominally regained the right to run cricket in Australia, they found themselves in thrall to the Packer organisation. His Channel Nine network was granted exclusive rights to broadcast and promote cricket in Australia for ten years.

To help the ACB restore its ailing finances, England reluctantly agreed to tour there for a second consecutive winter to participate in a triangular one-day competition with Australia and the West Indies and in a three-Test series against Australia. Given Brearley's desire to begin his psychotherapy training, it was by no means certain that he would tour again, but after receiving the full endorsement of his team-mates he declared himself available. Well aware of the challenge that awaited him from a full-strength Australian side bent on revenge, Jim Laker, the former England off-spinner turned broadcaster, wondered whether Brearley had committed his first serious blunder by going. 'Will the Brearley myth be blown sky-high during the toughest assignment he has yet undertaken? I have a horrible feeling this may be the case ...'[1]

The runes were bad from the start. Articulate and logical in presenting his case at selection meetings, Brearley invariably succeeded in getting the side he wanted, but Australia 1979/80 proved an exception to that rule. Keen to have the strongest possible side now that the WSC players were once again eligible for Test cricket, Brearley wanted to pick Alan Knott, who, by agreement with Kent, had given way mid-season to their promising young wicketkeeper Paul Downton, once he'd finished at university. Knott recalls Brearley contacting him to sound him out about touring again, something he'd previously repudiated. He told him he wouldn't be available, but on the night of the selectors' meeting, Brearley, with the backing of two other selectors, rang again in a final effort to persuade him to go. Knott said he would discuss it with his wife and when Brearley rang back he declared himself available, provided his wife and family could accompany him for several weeks during the latter part of the tour. This reasonable request seemed too much for selectors such as Peter May, who cautioned that they couldn't have players dictating to them, and, consequently, the chairman Alec Bedser contacted Knott the following morning to say that he hadn't been selected after all. His Packer team-mate Underwood, however, was chosen ahead of Edmonds in a side that otherwise contained few changes from the one to Australia the previous winter.

While the TCCB accepted the gruelling itinerary, which was geared towards the interests of television rather than the players, they did object to the one-day playing conditions used in WSC and many a detail remained unresolved at the time of the team's departure. Relations between the two boards had already been strained by England's refusal to play for the Ashes in an abbreviated Test series, and the additional tour guarantee that the TCCB had forced out of the ACB as Brearley pushed for better financial terms for his players.

Able to earn more as a university lecturer than a cricketer, Brearley had consistently felt aggrieved by the financial insecurity confronting most professionals. Even Test match players struggled to make a living – reflected in the meagre sum of £3,000 per player for the four-month tour of India and Australia in 1976/77, a tour which attracted two million spectators. When Middlesex won the championship in 1976, he ensured that photographers and interviewers paid for the privilege, a policy he subsequently pursued with England, and with Packer bringing more money into cricket, he was persuaded to use his new-found status to cash in. In *The Return of the Ashes*, Brearley admitted that making money for the sake of it pricked his Puritan conscience, but, according to Willis, he drove a hard bargain in commercial matters to help establish his psychotherapy business. On the 1978/79 tour of Australia he refused David Frith's request to join the editorial board of his new *Wisden Cricket Monthly*, citing too many commitments, unless he was handsomely remunerated.

His reputation for money-making – one newspaper erroneously described him as the first £1,000-a-week cricketer – was such that several years later the letters column in *The Times* included the following contribution:

> As for the dreaded and discredited word 'professional', was it not that exceptionally shrewd cricketer Mike Brearley who quite recently defined a professional [sportsman] as someone who would do almost anything for money?[2]

Days later there came a brief reply:

Mr David Gravell wrote: 'Was it not … Mike Brearley who recently defined a professional [sportsman] as someone who would do almost anything for money.'

It was not.

Yours faithfully,

Mike Brearley [3]

Even before they'd left for Australia, Brearley denounced the hate campaign in their media directed against his team and when they arrived to unflattering headlines, he faced renewed pressure to accept conditions already rejected by his board. The main points in contention were the uniform, as England considered the coloured stripes on the shirts and trousers were too gimmicky, the use of a white ball in day matches, which they found difficult to pick up, and the restrictive field placings, which disadvantaged them compared to the other two teams who'd played under these conditions in WSC. Although they settled for a solid sky-blue uniform for one-day matches, they stood firm over the ball and fielding restrictions, much to Australian resentment. England's hypocrisy in the matter of the tour conditions was odious, fulminated *The Age*, and Ray Steele, the ACB treasurer, under pressure from the promoters, publicly berated the team for refusing to move with the times. Boycott wrote, 'You can imagine how it seemed to the Aussie public: the Poms were whingeing again. It should have been sorted out before we got there and Mike would have been spared the responsibility of spelling out truths which could only make him unpopular – although as it happened the whole team was behind him in our discussions at the team meetings.' [4]

After draws against Queensland and Combined Universities and two one-day wins against Northern New South Wales, where they played with a white ball, England were thrown into the cauldron with a day-night ODI against the West Indies. Recalling their slow start in the World Cup Final, they figured that there wasn't room in the same side for both Brearley and Boycott and thus chose to omit the latter, a decision that was to have profound repercussions. Batting first on a slow pitch at Brisbane, Brearley, now sporting a black bushy beard to look more abrasive, and Randall put on 79 for the first wicket before Brearley was brilliantly caught by Gordon Greenidge for 27. With Peter Willey making a hard-hitting 58* and Gower a useful 44, England finished their 50 overs on 211-4. Rain reduced the West Indies' target to 199 in 47 overs and with Dilley and Botham bowling well to defensive fields, they were kept in check. Eventually they needed three to win off the last ball, at which point Brearley irked the 6,000 crowd by dispatching every fielder to all corners of the ground, including the wicketkeeper Bairstow who crouched in front of the sightscreen with one glove off in case he had to throw in quickly. After Botham bowled Croft to give England victory by two runs, their opponents and the Channel Nine commentators questioned their tactics, claiming it wasn't in the spirit of the game, but Brearley was unrepentant. Delighted by England's first win over the West Indies since 1974, he led the prolonged celebrations in their hotel afterwards.

Boycott's omission from the one-day team stirred him into action. After making a century against Tasmania, he repeated the feat against South Australia, putting on 174 for the first wicket with Brearley, who made 81. In a match brimming with incident, Brearley soon clashed with opposing captain Ian Chappell, who was returning from a three-week suspension for abusing an umpire. What irked Chappell was Brearley's indication to the umpire, on appeal for a catch, that he'd played the ball into the ground. 'We can do without the ball-to-ball commentary,

Mike,' he muttered to him at the end of the over. 'You do the batting, we'll do the appealing and leave the umpiring to the umpire.' Later Chappell parodied Brearley's opposition to the Australian restriction of leg-side fielders by bowling to him with every fielder on that side; then, when batting, he argued with the umpire after a leg bye was signalled a dead ball, an act which landed him in further trouble.

Boycott's two centuries didn't win him selection for England's first ODI against Australia till Miller's late withdrawal gave him a chance to show his true worth. Needing 208 to win, he led the run chase against Lillee and Thomson with 68 off 85 balls, making a mockery of the assumption that he couldn't play one-day cricket, and when his team-mates faltered in mid-innings, a valuable 27 by Brearley saw them home. Boycott then went one better in the next match with a superb 105 that set up another win against Australia, this time by 72 runs. The win raised England's morale but it did little to mitigate Boycott's resentment at his omission from the first ODI. 'Mike Brearley had to be found a place in the side because he is captain, that is common sense,' he wrote. 'But I would back myself against him as an opener in any competition known to cricket, so it didn't help my frame of mind to see him walking out in my position while the newspapers announced that I had been left out because I couldn't play the game.'[5]

His alienation was further accentuated by his omission from the tour selection committee and his conviction that England's preparations for the first Test lacked professionalism. After a frivolous fielding practice and unsatisfactory nets at the WACA, he took his frustration out on Brearley when Brearley requested his assessment on the state of the Test match wicket. He told him in colourful language that he'd given his advice before and it had been ignored so what was the point? 'It was a thing said on the spur of the moment and born of intense annoyance,' recalled Boycott. He accepted Brearley's contention that the poor practice facilities were hardly his fault, 'But I felt that as captain he was responsible for the way a practice was run and that he should have curbed some of the skylarking.'[6]

Handicapped by a shoulder injury to Hendrick which forced him out of the tour, England gave a first cap to Dilley, controversially omitted Gooch and played three spinners in a lopsided batting order that had Randall opening with Boycott and Miller batting at number five. Australia, in turn, included only four non-Packer players and looked all the stronger for the return of their stars such as Lillee, Marsh and captain Greg Chappell. On winning the toss, Brearley elected to field first and outstanding swing bowling by Botham made early inroads into the home side's batting. It needed a polished 99 from Kim Hughes to lift them out of the mire and take them to 232/8 at the close. The next morning was dominated by an unseemly wrangle involving Lillee and his aluminium bat, the brainchild of his good friend and business partner Graham Monaghan. There was no law against using such a bat and alive to the potential of a pre-Christmas marketing ploy Lillee seized his opportunity. After a couple of shots which produced a discordant sound, Brearley complained to the umpires about the damage the bat was doing to the ball, still only eight overs old. 'I told Lillee that if I came out with sandpaper wrapped around my bat, he might not be too amused and the umpires could tell me to take it off,' he informed the *Daily Mail*.[7] While Lillee protested that there was nothing illegal about his bat, he failed to convince Brearley, who said that one couldn't cover every contingency in the laws. After ten minutes of animated discussion with the umpires and both captains, Lillee finally deferred to higher authority and reluctantly accepted a wooden bat from Greg Chappell, but in one final act of defiance he threw his aluminium bat away in disgust towards the pavilion. According to Barrington, Lillee's antics was the worst flouting of the umpire's authority that he'd witnessed, but in an era of inflated player power he escaped with a mild reprimand.

All out for 244, Australia soon fought back, Lillee dismissing both Boycott and Randall for ducks. The middle order contributed little with some reckless shots and only Brearley, batting at number six, stood firm, playing Lillee and Thomson as well as anyone. Finally, at 123/7, he found a reliable partner in Dilley and together they negotiated the final session unscathed.

Fifty-six overnight, Brearley only added another eight runs before being caught behind off Lillee, but his 64 and Dilley's 38* took them to within 16 of Australia's first innings. An opening stand of 91 between Bruce Laird and Julien Wiener and 115 from Border consolidated their position, and although Botham struck back with 5-98, giving him 11 wickets in the match, 356 to win was a tall order, especially after the early loss of Randall. Brearley hoped that England could bat through the final day but Boycott's 99* aside, they once again lacked application and were all out for 215. In retrospect he thought that some of the batsmen were secretly unnerved by an image of Australian toughness. 'We lost contact with our own combative powers, and surrendered to the legend of Lillee and the Perth pitch.'[8]

After a heavy defeat by the West Indies in front of an anti-English crowd at Brisbane on Christmas Eve, Brearley's men returned to winning ways in the ODI against Australia at Sydney on Boxing Day. The home side recalled Ian Chappell and he responded with a brilliant 60*, but when batting with Lillee in the closing overs, he pretended to send Bairstow to the boundary, while Lillee taunted Brearley for failing to run him out. As the crowd laughed, Brearley stood bewildered for a moment and then turned his back with a shrug of the shoulders. 'Lillee and Chappell may have thought they were being funny when they ridiculed Brearley and may have seen their gestures as gamesmanship to goad the crowd into a greater anti-Pom and in particular anti-Brearley mood,' wrote Underwood. 'But their behaviour was not becoming from two of Australia's most talented cricketers.'[9]

Thanks to Boycott's unbeaten 86, England won by four wickets but their win was marred once again by boorish crowd behaviour, a sign of changing times and the gladiatorial atmosphere generated by WSC. Boycott had written the previous year that the Hill at Sydney used to be amusing, sharp and cutting but not unfriendly, now it was simply foul-mouthed and crude. In the first England-West Indies ODI at Brisbane, Bairstow was hit by a refilled beer can; in the previous Australia-England ODI at Sydney, Underwood had been struck on the neck by a large block of ice and now, back at the SCG, a piece of metal was thrown at him. According to Brearley, fielders placed on the boundary were at risk, and in a radio interview prior to the second Test at Sydney he warned on local radio that 'someday, somebody is going to be killed in front of an Australian crowd. You can't go within 15 yards of the boundary, yet people on the radio say the field placings are silly – that you should have somebody out deep.' He added that he was happier playing in front of Pakistan crowds where they were protected by a barrier and the hostility wasn't directed at his team. His comments were applauded by Bob Radford, secretary of the New South Wales Cricket Association, but he was in a minority. Greg Chappell said Brearley must have been playing on different grounds to him – Australian crowds compared favourably with English football fans – and Ian Johnson, secretary of the Melbourne Cricket Club, expressed amazement at Brearley's claims.

Unseasonably bad weather in Sydney, a saturated wicket left uncovered during a storm on New Year's Eve while the ground staff partied and an injury to Boycott all called for some hard choices before the match began. A ricked neck and damaged finger sustained while playing golf had jeopardised Boycott's chances of playing, although his injuries elicited little sympathy from his team-mates. They thought he was opting out because of the state of the wicket and that he owed it to the team to play. On the morning of the match Brearley ordered Boycott to take a fitness test in front of the physiotherapist Bernard Thomas. Thomas reckoned he was fit to play and when Boycott continued to insist that he wasn't, Brearley blew his top. 'When I say that,' wrote Boycott, 'I mean he went crazy, raging round the dressing room shouting at the top of his voice. It would have been quite a performance from anybody. From him it was amazing. Bernard Thomas quietened him down and we ended our argument on a slightly more composed plane.'[10]

With the wicket still recovering from its recent drenching, play couldn't begin on time. Conditions were still far from perfect when the umpires called the captains together after lunch on the first day to ascertain their views. One down in a three-Test series, Brearley was keener to play than Chappell, knowing that he had Underwood, the great exponent of drying wickets, at his disposal, but as luck would have it, Chappell won the toss and inserted England. From the moment that Boycott was bowled by Dymock for 8, England struggled and finished an abbreviated day on 90/7. The next morning, they were all out for 123 but fought back valiantly, dismissing Australia for 145, 42 of which came from Ian Chappell, playing his first Test for four years.

Having pulled themselves back into contention, England then let it slip again, losing three wickets that evening, including Boycott caught off an unplayable ball from Lenny Pascoe for 18.

With some solid defence a priority, Brearley promoted himself to number four and, together with nightwatchman Underwood, played with great composure the next day. 'I enjoyed the experience of batting with Mike, especially in Sydney,' recalled Underwood. 'He is unselfish and the sort of cricketer who will always come down the wicket, saying encouraging things, and offer assistance when we are in difficulty ... I remember going through some torrid spells and looking down the wicket at Mike's wry smile concealed by the helmet and thinking to myself, "There must be easier ways to earn a living."'[11] With a series of pushes and nudges, the pair added 48 before Brearley was out just before lunch caught behind off Pascoe as he tried to glide him down to third man. He made only 19 but in the circumstances his innings was worth many more. Underwood continued to battle away for 43 and Gower, after an uncertain start, played majestically for 98* in England's total of 237. With the wicket now playing much easier, they needed an early breakthrough if they were to stop Australia getting the 219 required for victory. Despite some marginal decisions going against them, Underwood gave them hope by taking the first three wickets. Had Greg Chappell been given out caught behind off Dilley at 100/3, England might still have won, but the Australian captain rode his luck to the full and his 98* saw his side home by six wickets. Afterwards Brearley came as close as he ever did to criticising the umpires over the Chappell decision, though, in truth, their batting had once again been their undoing.

They continued to get the better of Australia in the ODIs, a two-wicket win at Sydney guaranteeing their place in the WSC final, but Boycott's disenchantment remained clear in an interview he gave to Tony Francis of ITV. Complaining that no one ever listened to him, he said that he was disillusioned with the whole set-up on the tour. When the story appeared in the

London *Sunday Telegraph*, Boycott admitted to manager Alec Bedser and Brearley that he'd made the remarks but claimed they were off the record.

For the first of the best-of-three-match final, England bowled well and, thanks to Brearley's shrewd field placements, they limited the West Indies to 215-8 in their 50 overs. A good start gave way to a loss of momentum in mid-innings, leaving Brearley and Bairstow with much to do. Needing 15 to win off the final over bowled by Holding, they whittled it down to four off the last ball but Brearley could only find Lloyd at long-on and they lost by two runs.

The second final at Sydney was an altogether one-sided affair. In ideal conditions for batting, England could only make 208-8 (Boycott 63), and with Greenidge and Richards in regal form West Indies cantered home by nine wickets.

England's insipid batting was once again on display in the third Test at Melbourne. After Boycott and Gooch gave them their best start for some time with an opening partnership of 116, the latter going on to make 99, the middle order proved no match for Lillee and Pascoe, losing five wickets for 22. Brearley and Taylor took the score to 231/6 at the close. The next morning the England captain continued his resistance, finding a stalwart ally in Lever, his efforts unappreciated by the large Melbourne crowd. (The police insisted that all the offensive banners about him, the most humorous comparing him and his bushy beard to Ayatollah Khomeini, the Iranian revolutionary leader, were removed.) His fifty, reached with a sumptuous off-drive off Lillee was greeted with boos and catcalls, as was his dropped catch off Laird later in the day. The hostility generated by his opposition to WSC innovations and his comments about the unruly Sydney crowd accentuated the antipathy felt by many Australians towards him on previous trips. Brearley wrote:

During the tour of Australia in 1979/80, I was seen by the man in the Sydney street as the embodiment of all that's bad in the British. I talked too much, too glibly, and with the wrong accent. And when they had a go at me on the field I ignored them, like the stuck-up Pom that they knew I was. That beard, too, which led to the nickname 'Ayatollah', and that I had grown to express my capacity to be rough and abrasive, struck them as archaic and foreign. I also bore the brunt of the hostility directed, in the aftermath of World Series Cricket, against English cricket for the refusal to go along with some aspects of the new playing conditions.[12]

A Sunday newspaper devoted its front page the next day to a condemnation of the crowd who jeered him, and John Edwards, the Australian team manager, said that such behaviour made him ashamed to be an Australian. 'Brearley may not be one of the greats, but he is a fine captain and a highly respected fellow who goes out of his way to make this tour successful. He is always the first bloke to come into the Australian dressing room, with a cold bottle of beer, after our boys have had a hard day in the field.' The call went unheeded. Woodcock wrote that in 30 years of touring with England sides, he'd never met such a consistent and humourlessly aggressive campaign as the one directed against Brearley. According to Bedser, the ill will passed all limits and entered the unsavoury realm of persecution. 'One came to the conclusion that part of the public and media had been brainwashed by events, and my respect for Brearley grew. A lesser man might have cracked. Brearley emerged stronger and more dignified than could have been expected, and was a great credit to his country.'[13]

For the most part Brearley remained unruffled by the crowd's belligerence – indeed it energised his batting – but his indifference towards them served only to widen the breach. Near the end of the tour, Bob Hawke, the president of the Australian Council of Trade Unions and later the country's prime minister, told him he thought he could have mollified the hostility if only he'd communicated in some way with them like Greig would have done, an opinion that Brearley accepted.

Brearley's 60*, one of his finest innings for England, helped them reach 306, but their total posed few problems for the Australian batsmen. With Greg Chappell scoring a century and brother Ian 75, they amassed 477, before Lillee struck again with another flawless exhibition of swing bowling, the best that Brearley ever witnessed. He quickly accounted for Boycott, Gower and Willey and when Brearley fell to Pascoe for 10, they were reeling at 92/6. A typically defiant century from Botham offered some hope of saving face till Lillee returned to mop up the tail, giving him match figures of 11-138, and Australia, needing a mere 103, cruised to victory by eight wickets.

In the post-mortems afterwards, Brearley summed up the tour as 'pretty bad'. It had shown them up more than he'd thought. He said that they had greatly missed Hendrick and speculated whether he'd been too relaxed with certain players. Certainly, that was the view of Boycott and Willis who both criticised his attitude to coaching. Nets were organised in a lackadaisical fashion, Barrington didn't exert the same influence as before and a general lack of discipline pervaded throughout the tour. *Wisden* was inclined to agree. 'With problems in all departments, Brearley was not as positive as he might have been in countering them. He is not a captain for laying down the law. The England sides under his command have been happy sides and he seemed reluctant to risk spoiling that harmony by remonstrating with his batsmen even when they continued to display a lack of discipline and sense of responsibility.'[14]

Brearley, for his part, admitted that, on his fourth successive winter away, the incessant travel and cricket had taken its toll. 'I felt very tired during the tour, and needed even more than before to get away from the cricketing environment whenever I could … In 1979/80 I did not spend enough time with the team off the field. I did not know fully enough what their problems and feelings were.'[15]

After the exertions in Australia, England had one final commitment to fulfil. To celebrate the 50th anniversary of the formation of the Board of Control for Cricket in India (BCCI) they had agreed to play a one-off Test against India at Bombay. Expecting a slow turner similar to the one they had played on three years earlier, they could barely believe the grassy pitch that awaited them, the work of a new groundsman who feared the damage the England spinners could inflict on the Indian batsmen. As it was, the pitch and the overcast conditions rebounded to England's advantage as Botham, at the height of his powers, proved close to unplayable. Having removed Gavaskar for 49 on the opening day, he then caused mayhem with his team-mates, five of his six victims being caught by Taylor, who took ten catches in the match, a world record.

Replying to India's 242, England looked equally at sea against the moving ball and at 58/5, including Brearley lbw Kapil Dev for 5, they appeared to be heading for the rocks. Botham and Taylor were just beginning to steady the ship when Taylor was given out caught behind by umpire Rao. As he stood there flabbergasted, Viswanath, the Indian captain, asked the umpire to rescind his decision, a magnanimous gesture which, for all its nobility, Brearley disapproved of because it undermined the umpire's authority. The umpire obliged and Taylor celebrated his reprieve by adding 171 with Botham, whose 114 was primarily responsible for England's lead of 54. He wasn't finished yet because, in an astonishing display of skill and stamina, he bowled unchanged through India's second innings, destroying them with figures of 7-48, becoming the first man to take ten wickets and score a century in a Test. England won by ten wickets and Brearley was lavish in his praise of his all-rounder, placing him on a pedestal alongside Sobers. Yet great all-rounders don't always make great captains – certainly this was the case with Sobers – and Brearley in his high estimation of Botham was about to commit one of the greatest errors of his cricketing career.

Chapter 15

Demob Happy

ON Brearley's return from Australia he stated his intention not to tour again. His decision wasn't a surprise. Aged nearly 38, he'd tired of touring and was keen to begin his training as a psychoanalyst, but invigorated by his batting in Australia he declared himself available for the forthcoming home series against the West Indies, believing that he could help blood his successor. The selectors, however, thought otherwise. Conscious that England's tour to the Caribbean the following winter presented a daunting challenge, they wanted the new captain to be appointed as soon as possible. With few of the current squad deemed officer material, and reluctant to choose an outsider not worth his place in the team, they opted for Brearley's preference, Botham. Appointed to the tour committee in Australia, Botham had impressed Brearley with his natural feel for the game, his technical expertise and the sensitive manner in which he'd handled the prickly Boycott. There were those selectors such as Close, Botham's former captain at Somerset, who thought that giving him the captaincy, in addition to his many other roles, was placing too much weight on young shoulders, but he was outvoted by Bedser and Barrington, both of whom had been in Australia. The news was made official when Middlesex happened to be playing Somerset at Taunton at the end of May, and Brearley greeted Botham with a namaste – the Indian greeting with hands together – when he came out to bat. 'As it turned out, it was, I admit, a mistake,' Brearley later wrote about his choice of Botham. 'He was too touchy about criticism. He found it hard to captain himself, to find that blend of restraint and freedom that I think he needed ... Worst of all, the pressure had got to him, and England had lost the superb qualities of their best player.'[1] In retrospect, Botham wished Brearley had been asked to stay on during 1980 to help him adapt to his new role. 'It was callous of them to throw him at the West Indies for his first two series,' recalled Brearley. 'They could have kept me on for part of that first series, or even all of it, helping Ian to absorb what was needed for the job. Then he could have taken the side away in the winter with the media pressures less intense on him.'[2]

While Botham grappled with the demands of the England captaincy, Brearley was fully absorbed with Middlesex's flying start to the season, which saw them unbeaten in all competitions during the first two months.

On returning from Australia, he'd been asked by his county how he planned to rectify the disappointments of the previous season. He replied that he would become more proactive running the pre-season nets himself, intervene more on technical matters and insist on punctuality. Fielding and warm-up sessions became obligatory before each day's play in the opening weeks and discussions about the opposition were held before each match. One welcome addition to the Middlesex staff was the arrival of Vintcent van der Bijl, the giant Natal seamer and one of the best bowlers never to have played Test cricket. When the Middlesex chairman, George Mann, informed Brearley that the county had signed van der Bijl for the year, on the mistaken assumption that Daniel would be touring England with the West Indies, his response was decidedly lukewarm. Resentment aside that he hadn't been consulted, he harboured doubts about signing a white South African. Yet, whatever his reservations, Brearley made every effort to make van der Bijl feel part of the team and he soon changed his mind when he realised that they'd unearthed a gem. Intelligent, articulate and personable, van der Bijl proved to be a unifying figure by seeing the best in others. 'Vintcent was a breath of fresh air,' recalled Brearley 'not only as a terrific cricketer and a useful batsman but he was also an excellent influence on the dressing room.'[3] Brearley especially admired his capacity to take responsibility for things he didn't do right, shunning the tendency to find fault elsewhere. Van der Bijl in turn thought Brearley the best captain he'd ever encountered, particularly the way he understood players and tried to help them attain their own aspirations within the body of the team. Yet alongside Brearley's sensitivity, van der Bijl also discerned his toughness, his relentless search for excellence and his refusal to counter the easy option. When Gehan Mendis, Sussex's opening batsman, hit him for four during the Benson and Hedges quarter-final, van der Bijl turned to apologise to Brearley, who threw his hat to the ground and kicked it in annoyance. 'Mike, that was totally unnecessary,' he told him and Brearley, unreservedly accepted the reproach, admitting that he'd been childish.

Against Sussex in the championship, van der Bijl, bowling one of his best spells, beat the bat repeatedly and Brearley came up beaming, commending him for a fantastic over. The next over when he dismissed Imran Khan with a full toss which he hit to mid-wicket, Brearley merely said, 'A bit lucky weren't you?'

Against Yorkshire, van der Bijl was appalled to see Brearley moving to silly point to greet the incoming batsman Bill Athey, thinking it a waste of a fielder. On second thoughts, he accepted that Brearley must have his reasons for crowding the bat and he bowled a wide half-volley in the hope that Athey, feeling hemmed in, would drive too early. He was caught behind much to Brearley's delight, not only at the fall of a vital wicket, but also because van der Bijl had understood his plan and executed it without a word passing between them.

It wasn't only Brearley's captaincy that was flourishing, he was scoring runs in all forms of the game with a broader range of strokes than hitherto. Beginning with 134* against Lancashire in Middlesex's second championship game, he followed this up with a century against Surrey in the Benson and Hedges Cup zonal match. Surviving a blow to the head off Sylvester Clarke, the fearsome West Indian fast bowler, he battled through to win the Gold Award. 'Brearley's innings was refreshing in its mastery,' reported Alan Lee in the *Sunday Telegraph*. 'Gone was the hustled, hurried figure of recent summers. Here was a man playing with the confidence of his early career – decisive, punishing and with a notable freedom.'[4] It was the same with the JPL. After beginning with a duck, he shed his inhibitions thereafter with consecutive scores of 65, 43, 109*, his first ever century in the 40-over game, 63, 40* and 53 as Middlesex won their first six matches in this competition.

He also made useful runs in Middlesex's total of 195 in the Benson and Hedges Cup quarter-final against Sussex at Lord's, but with their opponents closing in at 146/2 it needed all his ingenuity to stem the flow of runs and bowl them out for 166. It was during the tense final overs that he became embroiled in an unseemly altercation with Imran Khan, Sussex's main hope for victory. As captain of England, Brearley had felt honour-bound to abide by the constraints of that office, but now free of those constraints he began to express his emotions more openly, something which his psychoanalytical training had encouraged him to do. Consequently, according to Emburey, he became more volatile during the later stages of his captaincy and less tolerant of mistakes. The spark which lit this particular fuse occurred when the non-striker Imran complained to umpire Jack van Geloven about the number of bouncers Daniel was bowling at his team-mate Tony Pigott, at which point Brearley, fielding at mid-on, chose to intervene. He told Imran that he couldn't expect to bowl bouncers at Middlesex and then object when Middlesex returned the compliment. He should shut up and leave such matters to the umpire. The altercation became increasingly heated and when Imran marched towards him and raised his bat Gatting stepped in to act as mediator. He recalled how 'Brears got very annoyed with me as well. But I persisted because they were eyeball to eyeball and looked to be on the point of a punch-up. "Look," I said, "don't be silly. Leave it. Come on." Anyway the drama gradually subsided, Wayne went on bowling, and thank goodness we got them out.' [5]

Unlike Brearley who played down the spat afterwards, van Geloven, no stranger to robust exchanges, described it as the worst language he'd ever heard in his life, and the TCCB asked both counties to conduct inquiries into the incident. While Sussex reprimanded Imran, Middlesex cleared Brearley of swearing and, after both counties had submitted reports, the TCCB considered the matter closed.

Brearley's volatility was again on show during the Middlesex-Surrey championship match at The Oval. On an uneven pitch there, he'd toiled manfully against Sylvester Clarke to score 91, his most satisfying innings of the season, but his efforts were unappreciated by some barrackers on the East Terrace. Irritated by their response to him taking evasive action against a venomous delivery from Clarke, Brearley walked towards them and offered them his bat. 'I had this shouting on Saturday and get it every day from these ignorant fools. I'm not going to take it and be stiff upper lip any longer,' he told the *Daily Mail*.[6] When an overweight Sussex supporter soon afterwards shouted some abuse at him while he inspected the damp outfield at Hove, the legacy of his spat with Imran, Brearley turned to him and said, 'You're not only very rude, you're very ugly as well.'

On 26 June Middlesex were brought back down to earth, losing to Northamptonshire in the Benson and Hedges Cup semi-final. It was their first defeat of the season and others followed, especially in the JPL where their form fell away. Against Derbyshire at Lord's with the weather fast closing in, Brearley bowled Emburey who went for 11 in the over, instead of Daniel, enabling Derbyshire to win on a faster run rate. In van der Bijl's estimation, it was the only tactical error he made all season.

After this defeat Brearley organised a team practice the next day and called in the players one by one to the committee room. There, he and Mike Sturt, the chairman of selectors, sought their explanation of the team's faltering performance and asked them what should be done. According to van der Bijl, it was the first time he'd heard of players being counselled individually; later, at a players' meeting, it was Butcher who noted that they were all too intent on the outcome of the match rather than approaching each session as a unique challenge. From that meeting, Brearley introduced team discussions before every session of play so that each player would know what was expected of them.

They remained leading championship contenders with draws against Northamptonshire and Kent and wins against Hampshire, Yorkshire and Essex. Against Kent, Middlesex

fielded two new caps who were to play a significant part in the
county's success over the next decade. Following the decline
of Mike Smith, and the failure of Butcher and Wilf Slack to
make the opening slot their own, Brearley astounded his team
by opening with Paul Downton, previously Knott's deputy at
Kent, since Downton normally batted in the lower order. They
put on 160 for the first wicket and for the rest of the season
they formed a reliable opening partnership. The other debutant
was Simon Hughes, a 19-year-old seamer from Ealing, then a
student at Durham University. He recalled Brearley helping him
enormously by giving him a bowl early in the Kent innings and
encouraging him to go all out for wickets.

In early August Middlesex suffered consecutive defeats
by Leicestershire, their first in the championship, and by
Gloucestershire on a declaration. Reflecting on the match, the
Gloucestershire opening bowler Brian Brain wrote:

> Brearley seems more relaxed now that he doesn't have the
> cares of the England captaincy on his shoulders. He's still
> very much in control out on the field but he'll have a laugh
> and a joke as well during the game. And although he's never
> been a man for the card schools, he doesn't lock himself away
> any more. Instead he'll stay on the fringe of the card schools,
> catching up on his mail but happy to join in the banter. It's
> ironic that he's having his best batting season for years after
> all the traumas he went through about his form in Tests. [7]

After these losses, Middlesex bounced back with handsome
victories against Nottinghamshire and Derbyshire. On a mild
pitch at Uxbridge, Middlesex lost the toss and saw Derbyshire's
leading batsman, Peter Kirsten, in fine touch. In time Brearley
noticed that he was becoming restless so he placed men on the

boundary, cutting off his favourite square cut and forcing him to take singles at the beginning of the over, tactics which helped to further frustrate him. After an hour or so of unorthodox fields, he reverted to more conventional ones and almost immediately Kirsten, attempting an extravagant drive, was bowled by van der Bijl. Later that evening Kirsten confided to his fellow South African, 'Mike's a great captain, isn't he? I felt pressure from him throughout my innings. He always seemed to be one jump ahead.' Despite losing their last eight wickets for 35, Derbyshire led by 56 on first innings but splendid bowling by van der Bijl restricted them to 142 in their second innings, and a first-wicket stand of 138 between Brearley and Downton set up a nine-wicket victory.

Against Sussex at Hove, Middlesex were the beneficiaries of a rank misjudgement by the opposing captain, John Barclay, who, on winning the toss, gave them first use of a benign wicket. They responded positively, Brearley leading with a century, much to Barclay's dismay, and he was in low spirits when he met his opposite number for a drink at close of play. As they reviewed the day's events, Brearley agreed that Barclay had erred by fielding first but, in line with his theory that a captain's importance is often exaggerated, he stressed that once the decision had been made the outcome was largely out of his control. 'He had no reason to throw me a crumb of comfort but, as I drove home that night, I felt more at peace with the world than at any time during the day,' Barclay wrote.[8]

A draw against Sussex meant Middlesex required ten points from their penultimate match against Glamorgan at Cardiff. A total of 163 in their first innings was hardly the stuff of champions but four wickets for both van der Bijl and Hughes gave them a narrow lead of 23. In the remaining overs on the second day, Middlesex made 48/0 and then, on the third morning, Brearley excelled with a superb 125*, one of his finest innings, which enabled him to challenge Glamorgan to score 235 in 67 overs. Once again, their attack proved too powerful for their opponents, dismissing them for 162 with eight overs to spare to give them the championship for the third time in five years. As the team celebrated, van der Bijl embraced Brearley, who paid tribute to him and his 85 first-class wickets at 14.72, and to Hughes, whom he rated as one of the best bowling prospects in the country.

After consecutive championship hundreds, Brearley made it three in a row with 104 against Kent in their final match, his innings notable for its skill against Underwood on a drying wicket at Canterbury. It helped him to a first-class average of 47.45 for the season.

Middlesex also triumphed in the Gillette Cup, repeating their double of 1977. After easy wins against Ireland and Nottinghamshire in the early rounds, Worcestershire away presented a greater challenge in the third round, but after a sound start, they folded all too easily. Requiring 125 to win, Brearley and Radley had to battle against former England spinner Norman Gifford on a difficult wicket. They made it through to tea after 25 overs, Brearley 17*, only for one of his players to look up from his game of cards and ask him, 'Is that all you've got?' In easier conditions afterwards, they went on to win by ten wickets, and their reward for a comfortable victory over Sussex in the semi-final was a showdown with their local rivals, Surrey, in the final. The day before the match van der Bijl recalls visiting the betting tent and being astonished to see that Middlesex were quoted at 5/2, while Surrey were 6/1. He told the person behind the counter that the odds didn't seem right and the bookmaker replied that was the difference between the two captains, Brearley being a cut above Roger Knight of Surrey. The next day Brearley proved his worth by inserting Surrey and keeping them hemmed in by his masterful field placings and shrewd bowling changes. The arrival of van der Bijl and Hughes that season had led to the demotion of Selvey, who only played in the final because of an injury to Edmonds. With Brearley acceding to his request that he bowl before Hughes, Selvey responded positively by bowling his 12 overs unchanged for a mere 17 runs in addition to taking two vital wickets. Middlesex started tentatively in pursuit of their target of 202, losing Downton and Radley early. Gatting helped Brearley take the score to 121 before he upset his captain by swinging wildly at Robin Jackman and losing his off stump. Fortunately, Butcher seized the initiative with a spectacular cameo and, with Brearley steadily accumulating, Middlesex won with over six overs to spare, thus becoming the first county to win both the championship and the Gillette Cup in the same year. For his leadership and his unbeaten 96, Brearley deservedly won the man of the match award from Ian Botham.

He continued his run spree the next day, his 50 helping his team to a five-wicket victory over Hampshire to give them third place in the JPL. 'That season was the most mature the team ever got,' Selvey later recalled. 'As an all-round attack it was one of the best that county cricket has seen. You weren't going to struggle too hard in those circumstances.'[9] At the same time Brearley's own contribution shouldn't be underestimated. 'It is no coincidence that Middlesex's outright Championship titles have come either side of his spell as England captain,' commented *Wisden*. 'Both as captain and batsman he is vital to the side.'[10] It was a highly satisfying observation of someone nearing his 40th birthday, but his best was yet to come.

Chapter 16

The Art of Captaincy

'EVERY good captain leads his side in his own way as suits his personality,' declared Brearley in *The Art of Captaincy*. 'He must be willing to follow his hunches.'[1] He certainly practised what he preached. Neither a remote captain like Len Hutton who rarely consulted, nor a charismatic one like Tony Greig, who led by example, nor a consensual one like Colin Cowdrey who disliked imposing himself, Brearley was very much his own man, both autocratic and egalitarian, cerebral and passionate by turn.

Few claimed to know him well. His first-class mind, his highbrow interests and singular personality saw to that. For a man conditioned by success and who hated failure, life was a serious business. The captaincy of England and a career in psychoanalysis hardly lightened matters but those who penetrated the Brearley reserve discerned the alter ego: witty, genial and at ease with those he trusted. Appreciating in particular the camaraderie of the county circuit, he loved the dressing room banter, and had an infectious laugh, as well as a mischievous sense of humour. Van der Bijl recounted having a soda siphon fight with him in a bar at Scarborough during which they accidentally sprayed an old lady dressed up to the nines, who graciously brushed aside their profuse apologies.

Resenting being typecast as an intellectual, Brearley, unlike most of his predecessors, had that priceless ability to relate to all types – Fletcher had never realised till recently that he'd been to public school – reserving a special admiration for self-made craftsmen.

The years spent researching psychoanalysis had given him a profound understanding of other people and he enjoyed the challenge of bringing the best out of his players by engaging with them both individually and collectively. He later wrote:

> I wanted a team of 11 people who were all potentially captains and thinking like captains, thinking about the game, others' and their own. That make life a bit more difficult. You get arguments and debates. But to get a team together that is vital. [2]

If the Middlesex side Brearley inherited was riven by cliques, the championship ones he nurtured comprised many strong characters with a cutting edge to their humour. John Barclay recalls that if things didn't go their way in the field, they would start bickering with each other, but, for the most part, the personal slights took second place to the cause of winning. By standing up to powerful characters – he was willing to drop a senior player if form or conditions dictated – fighting for the interests of his team and helping those in trouble, Brearley fostered the right spirit. 'We had a good bunch of individuals,' recalled Radley, 'but Brearley made us a much sharper team.' [3] 'Not only highly intelligent, but extremely sensitive, he seemed to quickly understand people,' wrote Simon Hughes. 'He would make a statement and gauge a reaction or ask a question and listen carefully to an answer ...He was brilliant at making people feel important.'[4]

Drawing on his winter work in a therapeutic community where junior members had a say in the way the clinic was run, making them more productive, he would involve his younger players in team policy. Gatting recalls how, in one of his first matches for Middlesex, Brearley came up to him in the field and sought his opinion, an astute ploy which, increased confidence aside, encouraged him to concentrate more intently. In 1980 it was one of the younger players, Butcher, who brought to Brearley's attention the team's lack of focus after their successful start to the season, an observation that Butcher repeated at a players' meeting. Jolted out of their complacency, Middlesex returned to winning ways and Brearley credited Butcher for their improvement. In the opinion of van der Bijl, it was this public recognition that transformed Butcher's season, while Butcher himself acknowledged the debt he owed his captain. 'The marvellous thing about Brearley was that he made you believe in your own ability and I was looking for someone in charge who was strong ... Brearley was a hard man but he commanded a lot of respect. With Brearley there was no favouritism; if he had something to say everyone heard it.'[5]

Brearley's efforts to get the younger players to assert themselves more and have the confidence to try things won the allegiance of two newcomers, Downton and Hughes. The former recalls complaining at a dressing room talk that he couldn't get team-mates to give him catching practice before play and Brearley immediately rectified this oversight, while the latter wrote:

When I was about 19, Brears came up to me in the middle of a session and said, 'What do you think?' I said, 'What do you mean?' He said, 'What do you think we should do, who should we bowl next?' He obviously felt I was drifting a bit and wanted me to concentrate more on the game. But more than that, asking me at the age of 19 what did I think we should do, all of a sudden, he's got me as a bloke. After that I'll walk through walls for him. And it made me think about the game in case he asked me again, so it was clever on two counts. The way he worked with people was phenomenal![6]

Hughes, though, does recall one occasion when Brearley's relationship with the younger players found him out. During pre-season training at Lord's in 1981, he was engaged in a conversation with him when Kevan James, the young Middlesex all-rounder, approached them. They exchanged pleasantries and after James moved on, Brearley turned to Hughes and said, 'Who's that?'

For all the cosy chats, the genuine interest in people's welfare and the softly spoken advice, Brearley was a hard taskmaster. 'Perfectionism can of course emerge as obsession with safety, simple avoidance of risk,' he wrote in *The Return of the Ashes*. 'But without perfectionism where is the drive to improve? Like Boycott, I too am kept going by the lure of the ideal.'[7] Wistful not to have been born in Yorkshire since he greatly admired the uncompromising manner in which they played their cricket, he placed two of their kith and kin, Brian Close and Ray Illingworth, in the pantheon of great captains. (After his appointment as England captain, he took the latter out to dinner to pick his brain.) Gower, who played under both Illingworth and Brearley, noted that, while the latter's style was more persuasive, he was equally tough and combative. 'On the surface he was a gentle person, with his slow friendly smile,' wrote Brian Johnston, 'but underneath he was tough and strong willed, and expected to get his own way.'[8]

Demanding total effort all the time, Brearley wouldn't allow heads to drop during a long stand and those who dozed off in the field or opted out of going for catches would receive a verbal lashing. 'Brearley was a ruthless captain,' wrote Peter Roebuck at the end of his final season. 'On the field he could be brusque [at Weston he told Simon Hughes to "go where I damn well put you"] and I expect he needed to be to retain charge of a team so strong in character.'[9] 'Sometimes he was intimidating,' concurred Hughes, recalling those reprimands he received for his apparent casualness. 'He wouldn't tolerate negligence or people holding something in reserve through fear of failure.'[10] On one occasion during his first season, as Middlesex battled to bowl out Essex to win the match, Hughes's failure to follow instructions exasperated his captain till a vital wicket restored harmony. 'I know a lot of things I wasn't very good at, in terms of the leadership attitude,' Brearley later admitted. 'Irritability, anger as well though you might call that passion ... Sometimes at Middlesex I would be very angry with somebody or other ... and I would take it out on a very nice bloke like Mike Smith or Mike Gatting. I'm blushing telling you the story.'[11]

Off the field he could be equally irate. Once he was so enraged after Butcher had run out two team-mates in one session that he stormed out of the dressing room at Lord's and let forth some choice expletives over the balcony.

At Middlesbrough in 1974, he railed at the team for giving a higher priority to the Scotland-Yugoslavia World Cup football match than their match against Yorkshire; and at Cheltenham in 1980 he lost his cool with his players' obsession with a popular card game while they batted. (Brearley was always sensitive to the fact that few of his team-mates watched him bat.) Launching into a ten-minute harangue, he concluded by imposing a ban on card games during the hours of play for the foreseeable future, a sanction that produced a stunned silence before Emburey piped up, 'Right, whose deal is it?'

He also met his match from an unlikely source. Concerned that the Lord's lunches, regarded as the best on the circuit, were having a detrimental effect on his team's fitness, Brearley went to see Nancy Doyle, the fiery Irish lady who ran the catering, to ask her to cut back on the largesse. 'Tell you what, Michael,' she spat at him. 'I won't tell you how to bat if you don't tell me how to cook.'

Despite his great erudition, Brearley had the capacity for making complex things appear quite simple, easily understood by his players, which, according to Barclay, was his greatest strength as a captain. From the moment he took to the field, Brearley liked to stamp his authority on all parts of the game. Standing normally at first slip, collar invariably up, he kept in touch with the rest of the team through constant eye contact and by chivvying, encouraging and applauding them. Sometimes he would jog up to the bowler in mid-over to consult him; otherwise he would be taking soundings from his neighbours in the slip cordon, especially his good friend Radley, and bring in Smith from fine leg, while plotting his next move.

An astute reader of pitches, Brearley would choose his combination of bowlers and from which end they bowled depending on the conditions and the opposition. A believer in a balanced attack, he was always looking to seize the initiative by shuffling his bowlers around and encouraged them to bowl different lengths to different batsmen. He would sometimes open with his spinners if the ball was turning and once, when Yorkshire were batting out time at Lord's in 1980, he placed a fielding helmet at short mid-wicket for Edmonds to try to induce the batsman to hit against the spin, since striking the helmet while the ball was in play would then have gained the batting side five penalty runs.

That same year he experimented with another unorthodox ploy by bowling a few overs of lobs which landed over the batsman's head on top of the stumps in the manner of Charles Palmer, Leicestershire's captain in the 1950s, when they were desperate for a breakthrough, a ploy which, a lack of wickets aside, met with scant approval from team-mates and opponents alike.

Fortunate to have such a powerful attack, he would coax additional overs out of strike bowler Wayne Daniel by promising to introduce him to an attractive brunette in the Tavern, and if Emburey was bowling badly he would keep niggling him simply to provoke a positive response. He gave a high priority to spinners and set an orthodox field for them except for stationing a silly mid-off to combat the growing fashion for pad play.

Setting his fields precisely – he'd move the slip cordon forwards and backwards depending on the firmness of a batsman's grip – and placing his best fielders in the most prominent positions, Brearley kept making adjustments, especially when the bowler required them. Knowing that Kent's Bob Woolmer liked the cover-drive, he had Selvey bowling at him wide of the off stump with two slips and two gullies. In 45 minutes, he scored 6 before he chased another wide one from Selvey and was caught at second slip. On another occasion, in a JPL match at Leicester in 1978, Gower was in sight of a hundred when he noted Brearley dispense with his long-on for Edmonds, inviting him to hit over the top. Rising to the bait, Gower went for glory, only to miscue Gatting to long-off.

In a critical situation masterminding the defence of a small total, Brearley was at his most imperious. Simon Hughes wrote:

> Teams seemed to visibly wilt as soon as they lost a couple
> of wickets and a new batsman succumbed to the feisty

bowling and a cacophony of sound round the bat which he orchestrated. The opposition disliked the urbane cockiness of this bunch of southern show ponies and bolted for the warmth and security of the dressing room.[12]

Having a great memory for the strengths and weaknesses of opposing batsmen, Brearley possessed that special knack of doing precisely what the opposition least wanted him to do. Amiss used to object to the amount of short-pitched bowling he received against Middlesex, an objection that received scant sympathy from Brearley. It was his fault, he retorted, because of his tendency to take his eye off the bouncer. Another deemed suspect to the short ball was Somerset's Vic Marks, who recalled Brearley getting very animated at first slip and berating Daniel for bowling too full at him. Sometimes he directed the field in the batsman's face. After Marks had hit Gatting for four, Brearley shouted down the pitch, 'Oh Gatt, you know he's only got one shot.'

Conversely, the bouncer was often used as a ploy to snare those who were compulsive hookers. Barclay remembers Imran batting against Middlesex at Lord's in 1982 and was well set when Brearley recalled Daniel for one over before tea and put his best two fielders out in the deep. After three full-length balls, Daniel dropped one short and Imran, unable to resist the challenge, hit it down square leg's throat. He returned to a silent dressing room, inconsolable, to get a wigging from his team-mate and good friend the South African Garth Le Roux.

Brearley's tactical wiles sealed the fate of Derek Randall, a notoriously bad starter, at Trent Bridge the previous year. Having been dismissed second ball in the first innings, mishooking Simon Hughes to deep square leg, Randall had Brearley to stay the night before his second innings. As they drove to the ground, they discussed the likely tactics that Middlesex would employ against Randall, with Brearley suggesting that his second ball would be a bouncer. Sure enough, when Randall came to the wicket, Brearley told Hughes to give him a bouncer second ball in the near certainty that Randall would be unable to resist the challenge. The bait was duly offered and Randall fell for it completely, holing out once again to deep square leg to complete an inglorious pair.

Yet for all his reputation for motivating his players, Brearley failed categorically in his relationship with Edmonds, a top-class spinner, a more than useful batsman and a superb fielder. Born of an English father and a Belgian mother and raised in Zambia (then Northern Rhodesia) during the last years of Empire, his family was ostracised by the white settlers because of their support for African nationalism. It was this unconventional background which shaped his feisty personality, his dislike of authority and forthright opinions, evident when joining Middlesex in July 1971 while still at Cambridge.

With their Cambridge pedigree, their low boredom threshold and their manifold interests outside cricket, Edmonds and Brearley appeared to have much in common. 'I liked him, I liked the fact that he was such a talented cricketer,' Brearley said. 'I enjoyed his company, and we had dinner together often. We talked a lot, and argued a lot. His company was always very stimulating. He was refreshing, and I liked his views on cricket even when I didn't agree with them.'[13]

United by their commitment to positive cricket, often by resorting to the unorthodox, Edmonds was a stalwart ally of Brearley during his formative years as captain. He recalled the help he gave him when he was struggling to assert his authority over the old pros, especially John Murray, whose wicketkeeping was now more prone to error than in his prime. 'And I used to be fielding at, say, cover, with Brears at mid-off, and I'd be making remarks like "Well catch the bloody ball then!" Brears would hear, and he was very much on the same side. I was his boy, he was feeling exactly the same kind of impatience.'[14]

But after they were both capped for England in the mid-1970s, their relationship began to unravel as their mutual regard gave way to mutual contempt. 'He[Brearley] had this need to dominate the dressing room intellectually,' declared Edmonds, who later regretted his propensity to challenge him on every score. This was certainly the view of his wife, Frances, who later wrote of Brearley: 'He has become the guru, the fundi, the eminence tres grise of English cricket ... And how dumb, mon cher Philippe-Henri, to be on the wrong side of a legend.'[15]

His constant barbs to Brearley's suggestions did him no favours, Brearley declaring that he was the most difficult person he ever captained. According to Titmus, 'if Mike became heated, he (Edmonds) would look down on him from his great height and pat him on the head and say, "Keep your cool, Michael. Don't lose your rag." Brearley would fume, "Don't pat me on the head," as we all stood around trying not to laugh at his humiliation.'[16]

'For some reason, Phil could always wind Mike up,' commented Bob Taylor, who played with both of them for England. 'Phil seemed to think that Mike wasn't the only man in the squad with a Cambridge degree and he would be rather assertive about that. Mike would sometimes fly off the handle at Phil, even though a man of his intellect and psychological depth should surely have realised that Edmonds was just trying to rile him. I suppose every man has his blind spots and Edmonds was certainly one with Mike.'[17]

Hughes, a debutant for Middlesex in 1980, noted the rift between the two men when bowling to Edmonds in pre-season practice. 'The pitches are much harder and drier than the club ones I'm used to, and one or two of my deliveries bounced shoulder high,' he wrote in his diary. 'One, unfortunately, ended up as a vicious bumper which shaved Edmonds's nose. He came marching down the wicket and swore at me, but Brearley said, "Well bowled." There are plenty of rumours that they don't get on.'[18]

As Edmonds's fortunes continued to plummet, most notably after 1978 when he lost his England place and was demoted to Middlesex's fifth choice bowler, he began to feel increasingly slighted by Brearley, which in turn diminished the quality of his bowling. When called on to bowl, there would be quarrels about field placings. While Edmonds liked to have one or two men back for the big hit, Brearley opted for a more orthodox mid-off to stem the flow of runs. 'I used to get especially annoyed with Brears when I would anticipate a batsman hitting over the top, and tell him I wanted a man out,' Edmonds recalls. 'Brears would refuse, and tell me to keep the man saving the one. Lo and behold, four runs over my head, and I'd be furious.'[19]

On one occasion, Nottinghamshire's Clive Rice clouted a short ball from Edmonds through mid-wicket and when Edmonds asked for a fielder to be placed there, Brearley resisted, saying that he wouldn't set a field for bad bowling. An argument then ensued which Rice found as embarrassing as anything he'd witnessed on a cricket field.

On another occasion, when Brearley denied him the field he wanted, Edmonds deliberately tossed the next six balls down the leg side. 'I think we both felt that the other failed to appreciate our point of view,' wrote Brearley. 'What I interpreted as contempt for my idea he experienced as uncertainty about his ability to put it into effect.'[20]

Edmonds also thought that Brearley inhibited less experienced bowlers. He wrote:

> Brearley was a batsman-captain, and he gave the impression that he believed no bowler should ever bowl a bad ball. If you bowled a bad ball, he would kick the earth in frustration, as if his entire master-plan had gone awry. He put a lot of pressure on his bowlers in that way – Dermott Monteith, Simon Hughes, Embers in his early days, Mike Selvey ... It would upset some bowlers. It would annoy me, and I'd get distracted from bowling sometimes. [21]

Another source of dissension was Edmonds's batting. Having seen Brearley score a pawky 60 or 70 in as many overs, he resented his instruction to go in and hit for the team. He often would respond with a 'mindless combination of blocking and slogging' which in turn would exasperate his captain. 'You would be playing for a draw,' Brearley said, 'and they would have a defensive field, with one man in the deep. And Edmonds would invariably manage to put the ball down long leg's throat.' [22]

He felt that Edmonds didn't make the best of his ability either as a batsman or bowler. 'He hasn't learnt enough. He often bowls worse to ordinary players. John Emburey is different: better on green wickets, a good nibbler of the ball. He is not as capable of bowling the really good ball that gets top players out on good wickets, and on a real spinners' wicket he is unlikely to get the results Phil would. But Phil is always trying to attack – and often you want a bowler to be defensive.' [23]

While Brearley readily admitted that he could have handled Edmonds better and that other captains such as Boycott and Gower gained more out of him, it should be said that his Middlesex team-mates thought that Edmonds's provocative character was primarily responsible for the rift. According to Downton, he didn't give Brearley the respect he expected and Emburey wrote: 'The pity of the deteriorating Brearley-Edmonds relationship was that whereas Brearley respected Phil's ability, Philippe did not have the same respect for Brears's capabilities.' [24]

Several years after his retirement in 1982, Brearley met up with *The Times* sports writer Simon Barnes, who was writing a biography of Edmonds. Barnes recalls it as one of the most intimidating interviews he ever conducted. 'I was impressed by his coldness, his sense of certainty, his intellectual contempt for some of Edmonds's problems with him. I was also impressed by the way he willingly confessed that his dealings with Edmonds represented personal failure. If Edmonds had failed so had he.' [25]

Shortly after the publication of *Phil Edmonds: A Singular Man* in 1986, author and subject were in a railway carriage on the way to a Test match up north when Brearley walked in. 'It was a meeting both men would have avoided,' recalled Barnes. 'But now, it was impossible, without gross discourtesy, to avoid a conversation lasting two and a half hours. So we all sat together and the two of them had that conversation, with very little rancour, and a tacit admission was made that each represented the other's greatest failure in the sporting life.' [26] It was the beginning of some form of reconciliation.

Brearley's attempt to forge a healthy team spirit equally applied to his captaincy of England, especially on tour when homesickness could be a particular curse. To help ease such pangs, he encouraged the company of wives and girlfriends and he tried to ensure that those out of form or favour didn't feel neglected. Never a great drinker himself, he would rarely linger at the bar or join the younger players in hearty camaraderie up town, but when he did venture out, he was invariably good company, taking an interest in one and all.

On succeeding Greig in May 1977, he kept the Packer divisions in check during that summer's series against Australia, in stark contrast to their opponents. This set the tone for his 31 Tests in charge in which harmony overwhelmingly prevailed. Drawing on his powers of human insight, he made sure every member of the team was valued through constant consultation and encouragement. 'The first thing to say about Mike Brearley is that he is simply a very nice man,' wrote Gooch. 'Part of his brilliance as a captain was the fact that he could relate to all people … That to me, was the secret of his success: his man-management and handling of people.'[27]

It was a common refrain. Bob Taylor declared that Brearley never flaunted his phenomenal intelligence. He recalled accompanying him to a dinner party at the home of John Inverarity, the Western Australia captain, on the 1978/79 tour and struggling to hold his own as the conversation became increasingly highbrow. 'Mike saved the situation for me; noticing that I was quiet at the dinner table, he kept bringing me into the conversation in which I could make a contribution; and whenever somebody started another dialogue, Mike would steer the conversation back to more mundane matters … Of course I was Mike's representative because he had invited me to the dinner, but it was typically thoughtful of him to take care of me.'[28]

Graham Dilley's anxiety on his first England tour eased when, during a game of handball, Brearley came over to him, put a hand on his shoulder and said, 'Picca[his nickname] you'll be all right.' 'It may not have meant a lot to him or anyone else who overheard the remark,' Dilley wrote, 'but to me that was the moment of my acceptance in the party.'[29]

When Paul Allott first played for England – against Australia at Old Trafford in 1981 – he was amazed at the relaxed atmosphere

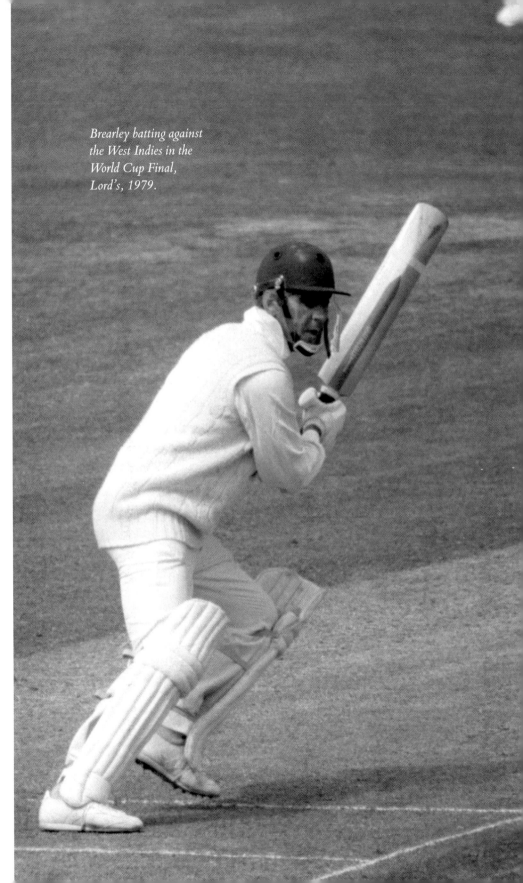

*Brearley batting against
the West Indies in the
World Cup Final,
Lord's, 1979.*

An accomplished slip fielder, Brearley catches Bishan Bedi, The Oval, 1979.

Leading Middlesex to victory against Surrey in the Gillette Cup, Lord's, 1980. Brearley was also man of the match.

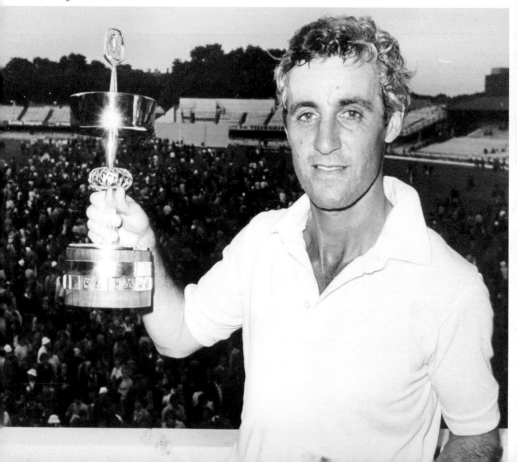

Back from Australia sporting a beard, the object of some comment there: Brearley with Graham Dilley, Heathrow, February 1980.

Brearley caught at slip off Lillee, Headingley, 1981.

Lillee celebrates another Brearley dismissal, Edgbaston, 1981, but the England captain was to have the last word in an incredible match.

Retaining the Ashes, Old Trafford, 1981. Brearley with England's hero, Ian Botham.

Brearley receiving congratulations from Australia's wicketkeeper Rodney Marsh, Old Trafford, 1981.

Leading his county to a fourth championship in his final season: Brearley and Middlesex, 1982.

Brearley with Tim Rice and Prince William at a charity dinner at the Guildhall, 2008.

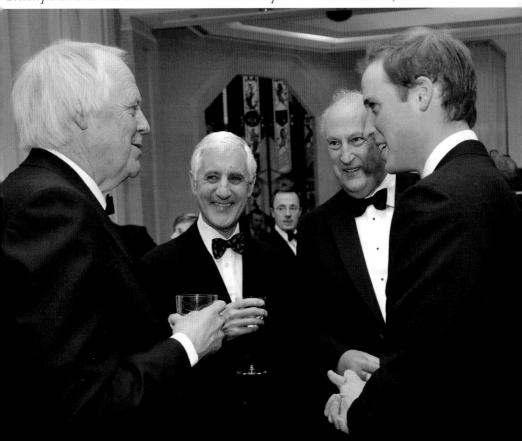

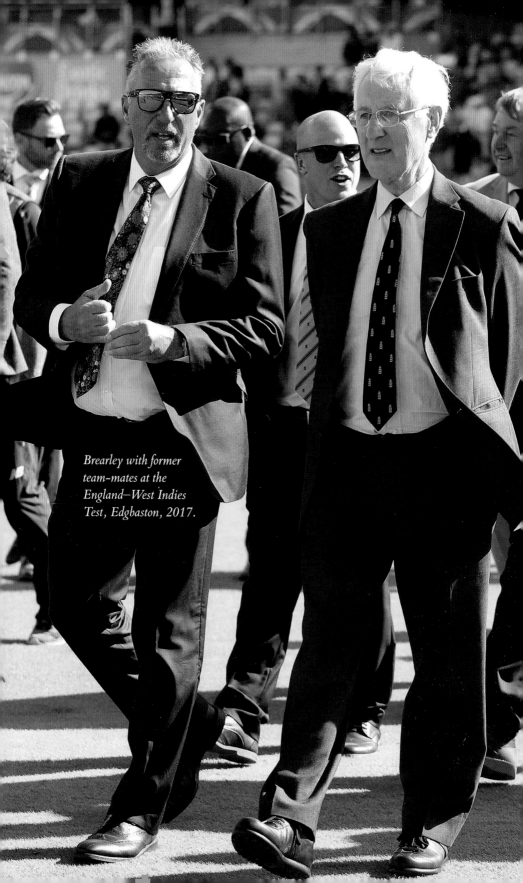

Brearley with former team-mates at the England–West Indies Test, Edgbaston, 2017.

in the dressing room. 'But Brears never minded the high jinks or the drinking as long as they performed out on the field.'[30]

For all his competitiveness, Brearley's concern for his players meant they would go the extra mile for him. He liked to talk to them before the start of play and consult a bowler about field placings, something that Dilley had never seen before. Lever recalled Willis having an inferiority complex about his bowling and Brearley, knowing this, would be superbly reassuring, convincing him that he was better than the batsman. 'Brears shared with Fletch (Keith Fletcher) that priceless ability to get people to play for him,' declared Lever. 'You bowled those extra overs for him, even though you were in trouble.'[31] When Hendrick was asked to name the best captain he'd played under, he replied Brearley without a doubt 'because he had that amazing ability to make you feel that you were the only person in the country who was capable of running in and doing the job he wanted you to do at that specific time'.[32]

Gooch's mortification at being dropped for the first Test against Australia in 1979/80 was mitigated to some extent by Brearley's explanation for the decision and the confidence he still had in him. On that same tour, Gower also recalled Brearley's encouragement when he was experiencing a lean spell with the bat, even taking him to a party with friends of his. The next day he scored 98. He later wrote:

> As to his own players, he had the amazing capacity to empathise with you and intuitively sense whether it was an occasion for the carrot or the stick. He could have a quiet chat with you or simply engage in a general conversation about nothing in particular, the subtext to which was simple: 'I'm watching, I'm on your side.'[33]

According to Taylor, Brearley was the only man who could handle Boycott and Botham properly, 'the former by quiet cajolery and Botham through a mixture of leg-pulling and firm leadership'.[34]

A fellow opener and grafter, Brearley respected Boycott's single-minded approach to batting, and made due allowances for his mercurial personality. Before the Headingley Test in 1977, as expectations of Boycott's 100th hundred reached fever pitch, Brearley, appreciating the strain he was under, excused him from the pre-Test team meeting to help him relax; and during the 1978/79 tour to Australia when Boycott was beset by personal problems and loss of form, he proved a sympathetic shoulder to lean on. He later wrote that someone such as Boycott needed encouragement and reassurance. More than one might imagine, especially if he wasn't doing so well. He'd want to know, for example, that the ball that had just got him out would have accounted for W. G. Grace, Don Bradman and got all the rest of them out too and that he hadn't done anything wrong.

After Boycott's double failure in the match against Western Australia, a match in which he was forced to apologise to the umpire for swearing at him, his confidence was at such a low ebb that he felt inclined to miss the second Test. Brearley, along with manager Doug Insole, persuaded him to think again, and he subsequently complimented him on his painstaking 77, writing that he was 'overcome by a wave of admiration for my partner, wiry, slight, dedicated, a lonely man doing a lonely job all these years'.[35]

Even when Boycott spoke out against Brearley or boasted about his superior batting, Brearley didn't overreact to his jibes. He treated him fairly, sought out his views and was sensitive to the fact that he'd never felt appreciated. When Boycott sparked fury on the tour of India in January 1982 by playing golf in the middle of the Calcutta Test when supposedly ill and unable to field, an act which ended his England career, Brearley, by then a *Sunday Times* columnist, was more sympathetic than most. Boycott wrote in his autobiography, 'His attitude was balanced and honest and I don't think you can ask for more; certainly, I never did. I suppose at the end of the day I felt that Mike understood me. He did not always agree with me but he did not try to change me. If I wanted extra nets, he would be the first to make the arrangements; when I appeared undemonstrative on the field he never mistook it for lack of interest.' [36] Acknowledging his natural approach which made cooperation logical, Boycott reckoned he would have been an even better player had Brearley captained him more frequently.

In the case of Brearley and Botham, it was a case of polar opposites aligning harmoniously in the same orbit. According to Brearley, 'Part of his appeal to me, as to others, consisted, I think, in his being so different in character from me. He is physically strong and outgoing. I am weak and comparatively introverted. He has charisma as a player, I do not. He is blunt, optimistic and young, I am more sensitive, perhaps more pessimistic – and ageing!' [37]

The suggestion that Brearley, 13 years Botham's senior, was fortunate to captain him at the beginning of his Test career when he was at his most eager and productive contains some truth. According to Lever, 'Brearley realised at a very early stage in Botham's career that for all his massive talent and boundless self-confidence, the youngster desperately needed someone to believe in him. And Brearley showed Botham that he did by giving him his head and never trying to restrain his natural attacking instincts.' [38]

It is true that Brearley had rather neglected Botham in Pakistan in 1977/78, but the latter's stellar performances in New

Zealand weeks later convinced him that he was somebody special who could turn a game. 'We need a bit of magic now, Both,' was a constant refrain over the years and Botham invariably responded. Leaning on his greatest asset, his ability to understand every player and what motivated them, Brearley possessed the priceless knack of getting the best out of Botham. Not only did he consult him and act on his advice – Botham told him he was gripping the bat with his bottom hand too hard – he was happy to give him responsibility, appreciating that he needed to be in the thick of the action. He did, however, use him predominantly as an attacking weapon, mainly resisting the temptation to over-bowl him.

In his debut Test against Australia at Trent Bridge, his first spell was profligate but Brearley trusted him with a second spell at a critical stage and advised him to use the bouncer sparingly. 'When I helped bowl out the Aussies that day,' Botham wrote in his autobiography, 'I hardly sent down a bumper at all. Yet, if Brears had not pushed the right buttons, the combination of my nervousness, my desire to do well and my sheer bloody-mindedness might have had an altogether different result.'[39]

At Headingley, during Botham's whirlwind century against India in 1979, Brearley signalled to him from the pavilion that he should block, knowing full well that he would do the opposite; at the tea interval on the same ground during his 149* against Australia, Brearley playfully asked him why he was batting so slowly in comparison to Dilley. In the field, Brearley often tapped into his competitive instincts by alluding to some rivalry, real or imagined. If he began to flag, he would goad him by comparing his lack of pace or hostility to some bowler Botham didn't rate. In Australia's first innings at Headingley in 1981, he ridiculed his new sidestep action and told him to concentrate on running in hard, instructions Botham carried out to good effect with 6-95.

Later that series, on the final day of the Old Trafford Test as England pressed for victory, Brearley told him to bowl quicker, which, sarcastic response aside, – 'It must be hard standing at slip all day at your age' – had its desired effect.

In their constant exchange of ideas when fielding together in the slips, Botham impressed with his tactical acumen and on the tour to Australia in 1979/80 he was co-opted on to the tour committee. The way he handled his seniors such as Boycott convinced Brearley he was the heir apparent and on renouncing the England captaincy he lobbied hard for Botham to succeed him. A year later the boot was on the other foot when, following his removal from the England captaincy, Botham was relieved to see Brearley back in control. His former captain went out of his way to restore his confidence by reminding him of his inordinate ability and predicting great things for him in the forthcoming Test. 'There are those who credit Ian Botham with the lion's share of making that memorable series turn out the way it did,' wrote Emburey. 'In my view, it is both uncharitable and inaccurate to deny Brearley an equal share of credit. The quiet man ... had a huge influence in coaxing the best out of Botham, and indeed the rest of us, at a time when it would have been only too easy to feel dejected.'[40]

Off the field, Brearley liked Botham's friendliness, boyish humour and zest for life and admired his commitment to the team, not least his personal support when he was short of runs. Even their contrasting lifestyles presented no problem, since Brearley was relaxed about his players' private lives provided they performed on the field. 'I don't ever remember having to speak about his behaviour after hours,' he later recalled, 'although it's true I might not have known what was going on.'[41] In the opinion of Edmonds, Brearley and Botham were close because they didn't pose a threat to each other. 'Beefy needed to dominate a dressing room physically whereas Brears wanted to shine intellectually. Brears relied heavily on Both's animal strength and they respected each other enormously.'[42] Downton, briefly Brearley's opening partner at Middlesex, thought his insecurity as a batsman enhanced his admiration for Botham's willingness to take on all comers.

As long as he was getting the best out of Botham, Brearley felt able to cut him some slack, not least at net practice, a ritual Botham always disliked, especially once the Tests had started.

Yet for all the banter and high jinks, Brearley would pull rank when necessary. There were explosive spats on the field when he refused to give Botham the third slip he craved, or when Botham failed to bowl to the field that he'd given him. At Sydney, during the 1979/80 Test series, it was Botham's impulsiveness with the bat that landed him in trouble. An irresponsible swipe against Greg Chappell in the second Test, after a plucky 43 by the nightwatchman Underwood had played England back into the game, earned him a stinging rebuke from Brearley.

Off the field, Brearley admonished Botham and Hendrick in Tasmania on the 1978/79 tour for constantly saying there were only two Tests to go before they returned home. He acknowledged that their comments were made in all innocence but pointed out that there were lesser players on the tour who were homesick and hearing these comments merely exacerbated such feelings. On tour to Australia the following year, he vetoed Botham's sailing trip with the New South Wales leg-spinner Kerry O'Keefe, telling him that he must have treatment for his fibrositis from Bernard Thomas instead. Gooch noted that in the verbal battle between the two of them there would only ever be one winner. At the lunch interval on the final day of the England-Australia Test at Edgbaston in 1981, Taylor recalled Botham's reluctance to bowl again. As they were about to go out and field, Brearley saw him putting on his Nike tennis shoes and told him to get his bowling boots on. When Botham once again expressed reluctance, Brearley's voice changed and he repeated his order which Botham complied with. 'A lesser captain would have ducked down to him and Beefy would have got away with it,' Taylor commented.[43] 'I don't know what it is, but I took stuff from him that I'd clip other guys round the ear for,' Botham later admitted. 'There is something about Brears. He knows how I feel and what I am thinking. He makes better communication with players than any other captain I've known.'[44]

Without his influence and man-management of him, Botham acknowledged that things might not have gone so smoothly for him in his early years. He also admitted that Brearley's retirement did him no favours because, thereafter, there was no one to stand up to him and keep him on the straight and narrow. 'To captains like myself, Bob Willis and Mike Gatting, who had grown up with Beefy it was sometimes a problem that we were of a similar age,' commented Gower. 'It was different with Brears, he was so much older and therefore found it easier to assert authority.'[45] Yet age aside, this was a relationship based on genuine respect and affection, so that even now there are very few people to whom Sir Ian defers to more than Brearley.

Chapter 17

Annus Mirabilis

WHILE England were undergoing a traumatic tour of the West Indies, Brearley spent his winter teaching and training to be a psychoanalyst. After leading Middlesex on a short tour to Zimbabwe in the autumn, he briefly took time out over New Year to lead an International XI against the Indian Board President's XI to mark the golden jubilee of the Bengal Cricket Association. The Lancashire all-rounder Jack Simmons, who went primarily to gain first-hand experience of playing under him, wrote: 'He was impressive, did everything I expected, was jovial or strict at the right time, would go out with the lads sometimes, stay away on other occasions.'[1] Accommodated in a luxury hotel in Calcutta and well feted throughout, the International XI's lack of practice showed as they were soundly defeated by their hosts.

In January 1981 Brearley began a ten-year stint as a school counsellor at Westminster, one of the most academic schools in the country, then under its charismatic headmaster John Rae. 'Michael Brearley, the England cricket captain, comes to lunch with the scholars,' Rae wrote in his diary on 29 June 1979. 'We discussed the possibility of his teaching a few periods a week at Westminster. He says he wants to teach not classics but something in the overlap between psychoanalysis and literature. In the long run, he will be a psychoanalyst, in the short run, he will help to strengthen and stimulate our non-specialist studies. The one thing he doesn't want to do is to coach cricket.'[2]

His appointment came about through his friendship with Jim Cogan, the Undermaster at Westminster and Master of the Queen's Scholars, who was an outstanding teacher of English and a talented cricketer. He, Brearley, Richard Stokes and Tristram Jones-Parry, two other pillars of the Westminster common room, made up a hilarious but keenly contested foursome on the fives court. (The others were surprised at how competitive Brearley was.) Every year they used to play the Harrow masters, and their captain Dale Vargas recalls Brearley as a very useful addition to the Westminster team (John Rae also played on occasions) in what was always a very spirited contest followed by supper and much genial conversation.

Brearley appeared confident and relaxed in the Westminster universe. In addition to providing individual counselling, he taught psychodrama – free dramatic expression – to small classes. Trusted, popular and well regarded by his charges, he was successful at getting them to talk, and his impact was such that, come his second year, he increased his commitments from one day a week to two.

Delighted to have landed such a prize catch, Rae appreciated his discussions with Brearley on the nature of leadership. 'On one occasion, he took me to task for seeing the headmaster's role so much in terms of confrontation, of battles to be won and enemies to be defeated,' he wrote in his memoirs.[3] When Rae confessed to an ongoing tension with certain critics in the common room, normally the old guard, Brearley assured him that the same thing happened in all groups, not least in the England cricket team. If an awkward customer was dropped or retired, another member soon took over. Several years later, when Rae wrote his *Letters from School,* in which he uses imaginary names and situations to discuss his own relationship with the parents, Brearley called it a stimulating book that would challenge educational conservatives and liberals alike.

As the 1981 season beckoned, Middlesex were everyone's favourites to repeat their success of the previous year. While their failure to entice van der Bijl back for another season was a big loss, they managed to sign Jeff Thomson on a one-year contract, although a hernia operation soon ended his contribution. Consequently, in the opening matches, they fielded an all-Test side: Brearley, Downton, Radley, Gatting, Butcher, Barlow, Emburey, Edmonds, Selvey, Thomson and Daniel – a unique feat in the championship.

An unusually wet start to the season hampered their progress, causing Brearley some frustration. After dispensing with the experiment of opening with Downton, he was soon to forge a new opening partnership with the West Indian-born Wilf Slack. A relative newcomer trying to establish himself in the first team, Slack felt inhibited batting with Brearley because of his tendency to express disapproval whenever he played a loose shot. When confronted with this unwelcome truth, Brearley relaxed and his improved relationship with Slack enabled the latter to play with greater freedom.

Although lacking the enthusiasm of the previous year, Brearley's run harvest continued. In June he scored four centuries, including 132* against the Australians, becoming the third Middlesex player after Patsy Hendren and Peter Parfitt to score two centuries against them, with the best batting of his career. Describing his century against Hampshire at Basingstoke, Alan Gibson wrote in *The Times*:

Brearley has never been exactly an elegant batsman but has become a polished one; if you take the distortion; rather like a Victorian mahogany table, of no intrinsic beauty but shining from many years of assiduous toil. [4]

His success stood in direct contrast with his team, since Middlesex had only gained one championship victory by the middle of June. When Butcher asked him what his motivation was that year, he replied somewhat frivolously, 'To score so many runs that they're forced to pick me against Australia solely as a batsman alone!' That was fine, said Butcher, but what about his ambitions for the team. Acknowledging some truth in his implied criticism, Brearley called a team meeting and Butcher repeated his remarks. They were endorsed by Barlow, who added that Brearley hadn't been as firm and determined as the previous year. Downton broadened the discussion by observing a reluctance of the players to help each other at morning practice and out of that meeting came a new resolve to re-establish old bonds.

Brearley's problems at Middlesex were nothing compared to Botham's with England. It was his misfortune that all of the 12 matches when he was in charge happened to be against the West Indies and Australia; but without one victory to his name, the reservations about his leadership were beginning to mount. 'Right to the very end,' wrote Gooch, 'Ian never quite learned the art, which Mike Brearley perfects, of making individuals feel good about themselves and also part of a motivated unit who expect to win.'[5] Besides Botham's limitations in man-management and his undue sensitivity to criticism, his travails were compounded by his own dramatic loss of form. After England lost the first Test to Australia at Trent Bridge, Brearley had been informally approached through a third party to see whether he would be prepared to return to the captaincy. He indicated his willingness to do so, but the selectors chose to stick by Botham for the second Test at Lord's. Although his team managed a respectable draw, the match was a humiliation for him personally as he was dismissed for a pair. Intent on resigning the captaincy, he conveyed his decision to Alec Bedser, only to discover that the selectors had already wielded the axe. Within an hour or so afterwards, Bedser contacted Brearley via a reverse charge call – he couldn't get the coins in a pub payphone – to offer him the captaincy for the remainder of the summer. He accepted for the next three Tests and immediately banged the drums of war by publicly expressing his belief that the Australians could be beaten.

Although in prime form, the decision to return to Brearley was by no means an automatic one, especially since he was no longer willing to tour. Close in particular was adamantly opposed to his return on account of his mediocre Test record and his flawed recommendation of Botham as his successor. Serious thought was given to picking Fletcher, the highly respected captain of Essex, but his cause wasn't helped by the location of the next Test, since Headingley was the ground where he'd made his ill-fated debut against Australia 13 years earlier. Chosen ahead of Yorkshire's Phil Sharpe, a specialist slip fielder, he dropped two hard chances at slip, lapses which riled the local crowd enough to heckle him throughout the rest of the match and on certain occasions thereafter.

Once Brearley had accepted the captaincy, he rang Gooch to get a feel for the prevailing mood in the England camp. Gooch said they'd fallen out of the habit of practising close catching and holding team talks, something Brearley was soon to rectify. He also rang Botham to commiserate and to assure him that he would soon be back to his best. At the selectors' meeting that Friday, the main discussion, once it had been agreed that

Woolmer would make way for Brearley, focused on Willis who'd been suffering from a chest infection. Concerned that he wasn't currently playing for Warwickshire, they provisionally agreed to omit him for Headingley, but when Bedser spoke to him the next day, Willis assured him that he would be fit. Consequently, after consulting his fellow selectors, Bedser added him to the squad provided he came through a 2nd XI match unscathed.

As Brearley journeyed to Leeds with his father, he felt a short-lived excitement at being back in the public eye interspersed with a nervousness about the critical scrutiny which accompanied it, and the reaction of the Headingley crowd, never his most avid supporters. With the nation reeling from punitive interest rates, mass unemployment and a series of urban race riots, sport was seen as one medium to help unite its people. Yet, in an age of populist nationalism when winning had become ever more paramount, the tabloid press extended little mercy to those who fell short, as Botham and his team had discovered during their unsuccessful run.

Once Brearley turned up at the ground, it seemed that he'd never been away. 'The England side was unanimous in its genuine welcome for Brearley,' Gooch wrote in his diary, 'and a feeling that, if anybody could stem the dismal slide in which we were caught up, it was Mike.'[6] Because Brearley had seen so little of the first two Tests, the pre-match discussion was fuller than normal, concentrating on what had gone wrong and how to put things right against the Australians. Their pace attack of Lillee, Geoff Lawson and Terry Alderman was formidable but their batting, without Greg Chappell, was fallible and their captain, the inexperienced Kim Hughes, lacked the support of his senior players. One anomaly that concerned England related to Lillee's habit of leaving the field to change shirts after completing a spell of bowling, a precaution against his recent bout of pneumonia.

Brearley had mentioned this to Donald Carr, the secretary of the TCCB, and Carr raised it with the Australian management, much to their indignation. They resented Brearley's failure to contact them directly and, when their hostile reaction was conveyed to him at his pre-match press conference, he raised the stakes further, only then to have second thoughts. At the England team meeting that evening, they agreed to defuse the row, knowing how controversy could rouse Lillee to greater heights.

On a slate-grey Yorkshire morning, England left out Emburey for Old and went into the match with no front-line spinner. They soon regretted their decision as Australia, having chosen to bat first, took advantage of some faulty catching to finish the day on 203/3 with opener John Dyson making a solid 102. That night Brearley slept fitfully as he contemplated his team's lacklustre showing and the omission of Emburey, but the next day he helped Botham begin his rehabilitation by encouraging him to eliminate the sidestep curb which had recently impeded his bowling. Reverting to his former run-up, his sharpness and rhythm gradually reappeared and he picked up a late haul of wickets to finish with 6-95 in Australia's total of 401/9 declared.

On the third morning, in conditions ideal for seam bowling, England wilted before Lillee, Lawson and Alderman. In front of a silent crowd, Brearley took 15 minutes to get off the mark and grafted away for an hour before Alderman had him caught behind. Had Lillee been at his best, Brearley reasoned, England would have been out for 100. Only Botham offered any resistance with a pugnacious 50. Early on he'd failed to connect with an extravagant shot and looked up at the balcony where Brearley was sitting. Brearley grinned and gestured that he should have hit it even harder, knowing that Botham performed best when attacking the bowling. All out for 174, England were forced to follow on and lost Gooch for nought before bad light brought proceedings to a premature end shortly afterwards. During a barbecue for both sides at Botham's home, it was the Australians who were naturally the more ebullient. Nothing that occurred during the first half of Monday's play disabused them of their confidence. Continuing at 6/1, Brearley was the first out, caught at slip off Lillee for 14, and after he'd seen Boycott lbw to Alderman for a stoical 46, he changed into his casuals and packed his cricket bag. By the time Dilley joined Botham, England had sunk to 135/7, still 92 adrift, and with nothing to lose both went on to the offensive, unleashing a daring array of strokes. With luck on their side and the Australian quicks beginning to tire, the score mounted rapidly and even Dilley's departure for 56 did nothing to stem the onslaught. 'When Dilley was out the lead was only 25 and then came what I thought was a brilliant piece of captaincy,' wrote Richie Benaud. 'Brearley sent in Chris Old, who was on a pair, with orders to play his own game and try to hammer the bowling … if he could! Other captains, with Botham going so magnificently, might well have told Old to play defensively and, had he done so against the pace bowling, I am convinced he would have been out very quickly. The Yorkshire all-rounder was no great shakes against the "quicks". When Dilley had joined Botham at the crease, everything had seemed lost and Dilley really had to go out there and pick up whatever runs he could. Old's departure from the dressing room was in very different circumstances and required the bravest of decisions to be made.'[7]

Old's support, and that of last man Willis, enabled Botham to finish the day 144* with England 124 to the good with one wicket left. On entering the Australian dressing room, Brearley was met with a thunderous silence, 'everyone frozen in postures of dejection', which helped convince him that victory wasn't entirely beyond England's grasp. After a fish and chips supper with Botham and several others of the team, he returned to the hotel they had booked out of that morning. Over drinks in the bar, he agreed to Willis's suggestion that the bowlers should bowl fast and straight in the second innings and he told him not to worry about bowling no-balls, a recent fault which had caused him to reduce his pace, for given the nature of the pitch he reckoned Willis possessed the pace and bounce to run through the opposition.

After England added five to their overnight total, Brearley called for more aggression and encouragement for the bowlers before they went out to field. The Australians would be the nervous ones, he stressed, and on that pitch anything could happen. Figuring that their exploits with the bat may have boosted their confidence, he opted to open with Botham and Dilley, only to quickly replace the latter with Willis at the Football Stand End. Willis, without a wicket in the first innings, struggled up the hill and into the wind and after several overs he asked Brearley whether he could switch to the Kirkstall Lane End. At first Brearley resisted but, having consulted Taylor and Botham, he then had second thoughts. (Old, who'd replaced Botham, now swapped ends.) The effect was dramatic. Willis was quickly into his stride as he charged down the hill and, in his second over, he produced a vicious lifter which accounted for Trevor Chappell. Two overs later, the last before lunch, he rocked the Australian dressing room by removing Hughes and Yallop, both without scoring, to superb catches by Botham and Gatting respectively.

With Australia lunching uneasily at 58/4, the England team spent time discussing how the remaining batsmen were likely to play. One thing was clear, Brearley stressed, they must keep running in at them and attacking the batsmen. Knowing Old's predilection for bowling at left-handers, he kept him on at the Pavilion End and shortly after the resumption, he bowled Border, Australia's best batsman, for nought; thereafter Willis disposed of Dyson for 34, Marsh for 4, helped by a fine catch at long leg by Dilley, and Lawson for 0, giving him six wickets in six overs. Australia had slumped to 75/8 but in four overs Bright and Lillee added 35, forcing Brearley back on to the defensive. Critically, he held his nerve. With a mere 21 needed, he told Willis, on advice he'd received from Gatting, to keep bowling straight at Lillee and, four balls later, Lillee chipped a straight half-volley to mid-on where Gatting took an acrobatic catch. When Willis capped a remarkable performance minutes later by uprooting Bright's middle stump, he'd bowled England to a miraculous victory by 18 runs, only the second time in Test history that the side following on had gone on to win. As the ecstatic crowd gathered in front of the pavilion, to serenade their team, Brearley went tentatively to the Australian dressing room, to shake hands and thank them for the game. 'The silence was absolute, the atmosphere heavy with the tension of dawning comprehension. It was like walking in on a major family trauma. I quietly withdrew.'[8]

Moments later, amid a cacophony of sound, he led his team on to the balcony for the post-match presentations. Grinning broadly, he waved to the crowd, greeted Fred Trueman, the man of the match adjudicator, and graciously accepted the winning cheque from the sponsors. He then retreated into the background, a beaming but self-effacing victor, to listen to Trueman award Botham the man of the match for what he called the best performance he'd ever seen in a Test match. Using up a fair slice of fortune, Botham's epic 149 had turned certain defeat into possible victory now that the team had recovered its self-belief. It needed another act of heroism by Willis to seal

England's triumph but whether he could have touched such heights without his captain's guiding hand is doubtful. 'Willis bowled fantastically,' recalled Gooch, 'but it was Brearley who instilled that will to win in us.'[9] 'Without his captaincy on that amazing last day, I doubt if we would have won, despite Bob Willis's marvellous efforts,' concurred Taylor. 'Mike was never flustered, even though he had no runs to play with.'[10]

'Brearley made the right bowling changes, field placings, squeezed the runs,' wrote Gower. 'As a captain in those circumstances you can't afford to make a wrong call. Every decision is crucial. I'd have agonized, questioned every decision ten times, but he was very decisive. He knew what he was doing. We didn't question him.'[11]

The national euphoria that greeted the victory at Headingley, and Prince Charles's wedding to Lady Diana Spencer days later, carried over to the Edgbaston Test, where the large flag-waving crowds weren't slow in expressing their support for England. Before the game began, there was one festering sore that needed healing – the deteriorating relationship between players and press now that the latter had become more critical.

Although many of Brearley's predecessors such as Jardine, Hutton and May had viewed the cricket correspondents as something of a trial, a mode of civility existed, especially on tour when players and press stayed in the same hotels and drank in the same bars. Scyld Berry recalls Brearley, during an ODI on England's tour to Pakistan in 1977/78, sauntering round to the press tent to consult him about the world's greatest 50 batsmen. By the late 1970s, however, the sheer expansion of the cricket press corps and their increasing demands for quotes made the captain's job more arduous. Confronted with all this exposure, Brearley disliked media intrusion when off duty, not least the occasion when a Brisbane radio station woke him up at

5am in his Perth hotel on the 1978/79 tour to ask him for a live interview about the Test beginning that day. He also kept the media out of the dressing room, believing that the team must have somewhere to let off steam in private. The cricket writer David Frith recalls being in the England dressing room during the Oval Test of 1981 chatting to Gower when Brearley came up to him and said, 'You're not welcome here.'

Intelligent and articulate, Brearley enjoyed press conferences, especially the opportunity to pinpoint the differences between the two sides and the defining moments in a game, which helped determine its result. Aside from his policy never to criticise the umpires, his answers tended to be thoughtful and measured, shunning triumphalism in victory and remaining philosophical in defeat. A staunch defender of his players, especially on matters which he deemed peripheral to their performance on the field, he nevertheless accepted that they weren't immune from criticism.

On a personal level he dealt patiently with the numerous comments about his own lack of form and when the BBC's Peter West used to ask him about his future place in the team, he would reply, 'That's a question you must ask the chairman of selectors.'

He also made it his business to be as honest as possible and when confronted by an embarrassing story that had become public, he wouldn't refute it as much as defuse it. On the 1978/79 tour of Australia, when allegations of a mid-pitch flare-up between Brearley and two of his bowlers in an ODI were leaked to the press, he explained that such exchanges often occurred in a match as a way of releasing tension. In Australia the following winter, a local journalist happened to catch a Boycott tirade against Brearley after Brearley had asked his opinion about the state of the Perth wicket. When the spat later became national headlines, Brearley sought to play it down while making no effort to deny it, and at Lord's in the Benson and Hedges quarter-final of 1980, he called his on-field tiff with Imran Khan 'a friendly exchange of views'.

While Brearley's demeanour towards the press was generally helpful and courteous, he could turn prickly if he thought a question facile or inappropriate. This was particularly the case with the news reporters responsible for collecting the quotes, some of whom lacked familiarity with the finer points of the game. Ian Todd of *The Sun* recalls asking controversial questions, not least after the 1978 Test at Edgbaston when he questioned England's tactics of bowling bouncers at the Pakistan tail-ender Iqbal Qasim, who was struck in the mouth, and Brearley bridled at this onslaught. 'You're being a headmaster,' he told Todd.

David Frith also felt the edge of Brearley's tongue after Botham was hit on the helmet by Australian opener Rick Darling when fielding at short leg in the fourth Test at Sydney in 1979. Having heard Brearley justify the use of helmets in light of this incident, Frith – an opponent of short legs wearing helmets, believing it gave them an unfair advantage – queried whether Botham would have been standing quite so close if bare-headed. 'Of course,' came the sharp reply. 'Fielders have been fielding there for years.'

At Headingley in 1981, Brearley took issue with the press reporting of his pre-match joust with the Australians regarding Lillee's absences from the field to change his shirt. The *Sunday Express* alleged that he'd written a letter of complaint about Lillee, when he'd merely asked for an interpretation of the laws, provoking indignation with the Australians and a major row conjured out of nothing. After the pounding Botham had taken as captain and his team-mates' grievances about the growing emphasis newspapers placed on their quotations, their simmering resentment punctured the mood of elation post-Headingley. Willis gave a tetchy interview to Peter West, and Brearley, alluding to the Lillee controversy, accused the cricket writers at his post-match press conference of concocting stories. 'If that's the way you want it, that's all right with me. I just won't talk to you in future. It's no skin off my nose. Douglas Jardine refused to talk to the press during the bodyline tour and I am quite willing to adopt the same stance. In all honesty I couldn't give a stuff about the press.'

With England threatening to break off cooperation with the press, the *Daily Mail*'s Peter Smith, on behalf of the Cricket Writers' Club, sought a meeting with Brearley to dissuade him of such a move. He stressed that writers weren't responsible for the headline attached to their copy, that requests for interviews were channelled through the appropriate authorities, and that there was something illogical about certain players complaining about the press, since they benefited financially from ghosted columns. Brearley acknowledged the force of these arguments and when the TCCB's publicity officer, Peter Lush, conveyed a similar message to him on his arrival at Edgbaston, he looked to resolve the impasse. At the pre-Test team meeting, he told his team that the rift with the press had served a useful purpose in drawing attention to the hurt inflicted on players by irresponsible reporting and comments. He would never compel anyone to talk to journalists, but recommended that they kept lines of communication open, a view that was unanimously accepted provided that the demands weren't excessive.

England omitted Dilley for Emburey and Brearley reverted to opening the innings with Boycott to enable the out-of-form Gooch to find some respite in the middle order. The two were soon batting together as Boycott and Gower went cheaply, and although Brearley was trapped on 13 for over an hour he survived to make 48, which, ironically, was to be the highest score of the match.

England batted poorly and were all out for 189 but made amends the next day by restricting Australia's lead to 69. Brearley was in his element marshalling his men and keeping his opponents on the defensive, but his day was marred by his early second-innings dismissal, lbw to Lillee for 13 with a ball that kept low.

Saturday was a day of attrition as England, 20 runs behind with nine wickets in hand at the start of play, made faltering progress against Lillee, Alderman and Bright. They were only 46 ahead when Botham was sixth out, but a belligerent 23 from Old, instructed by Brearley to attack Bright, and defiant ninth-wicket stand of 50 between Emburey and Taylor, effected a modest recovery. While the early dismissal of Wood that evening kept English hopes alive, Brearley felt less optimistic than members of the crowd as he signed autographs at close of play.

Australia began the fourth day requiring another 142 to win with nine wickets in hand before another partisan crowd. Hughes had confided to Brearley at the end of the second day that he dreaded the prospect of chasing 130 again and now his words returned to haunt him. In bright sunshine and on a dead pitch, Willis bowled magnificently to dismiss Dyson and Hughes cheaply before Border and Yallop appeared to have turned the game in Australia's favour. 'What do you think, Dickie?' Brearley asked umpire Bird as he stood next to him at square leg. 'I think you've had it, skipper,' Bird replied. 'If I were you, I'd put yourself on, bowl a few long hops and get it over with, then we can all go home.' Brearley smiled but he wasn't giving up so easily. Adjusting the field constantly and making the Australians fight for every run, he made clever use of Emburey, who bowled more than anyone else. At 87/3, Emburey had Yallop caught by

Botham at silly point and, then at 105/4, he dismissed Border, caught at short leg for 40, with a ball that turned and lifted. With the score advancing to 115/5, Brearley then played his trump card by recalling Botham, sensing that he had a psychological hold over the Australians. Brushing aside his reluctance to bowl, he told him to run in hard and, urged on by a baying crowd brandishing their Union Jacks, Botham acted entirely to script by taking the five remaining wickets for one run in 28 deliveries. While his magnetism administered the final knock-out blow, he acknowledged the great part played by Brearley. 'Mike's field placings on that last day had been magnificent. I don't recall him missing a single trick.'[12]

'It was brilliant captaincy,' concurred Benaud, 'an exhibition showing Brearley had correctly gauged the strength and weakness of the opposition, which is one of the vital things in cricket leadership. Another is to be game enough to play your hunches. I have seen a lot of captains unwilling to take with their minds the risk which they know in their hearts is worth the gamble. Brearley was never like that even in defeat and he deserves full marks for it.'[13]

Amid the celebrations, Brearley admired his opponents for the way they accepted defeat. Hughes and Lillee honoured a previous commitment to attend a dinner-dance for Willis's benefit that evening and stayed to the end, and, in conversation with Brearley, Hughes speculated on the recriminations that would now come his way back home. He later declared that had it not been for Brearley's return, Australia would have been 3-0 up in the series.

Rebutting the old adage about not changing a winning team, Brearley looked to various changes to strengthen it. Having received a favourable report from the Kent captain Asif Iqbal about the form of his team-mates Knott and Chris Tavare, he pressed for their inclusion for the fifth Test at Old

Trafford. Tavare was chosen in place of Willey, and Knott, more contentiously, was preferred to Taylor on account of his superior batting. Later, the Lancashire seamer Paul Allott replaced Old following his withdrawal because of injury.

On a slow, seaming wicket, England, batting first, once again struggled against the Australian quicks. Only Tavare stood firm with 69 until a breezy 52* by debutant Allott lifted them to a modest 231. In contrast to the previous two Tests, Australia batted with restless intensity, proving no match for Willis and Botham as they were bundled out for 130. England's lead of 101 was dissipated by their insipid second innings and when Brearley was out for 3 at 104/5 the game appeared in the balance. It needed the entry of Botham to bring the game to life and lift it to a higher level. In a flawless display of clean hitting, he pulverised the Australian attack over the course of the next two hours with shots that live in the memory, not least his three hooks for six off Lillee. His 118 off 102 balls was one of the finest innings in the history of Test cricket and after he departed to a rapturous ovation, Tavare with 78, Knott with 59 and Emburey with 57 carried on the good work. Set 505 to win, Australia, with centuries from Border and Yallop, put up a valiant fight and prolonged resistance well into the fifth day before England won by 103 runs to retain the Ashes. Both captains agreed that Botham was the difference between the two sides.

After his success, Brearley was delighted to stay on for the final Test at The Oval. He did agree, however, to a couple of changes as England replaced Gooch and Gower with debutants Wayne Larkins and Paul Parker, and Hendrick was preferred to Allott. Thinking that the pitch would be at its liveliest at the start of the match, Brearley chose to field first, only then to harbour some regrets as Australia proceeded to 120/0. With several of their bowlers less than fully fit, England did well to dismiss

Australia for 352, but with Lillee back to his very best with 7-89 it needed a century by Boycott to keep them in the game.

Australia began their second innings shakily before 84 from Border and 103 from debutant Dirk Wellham prevented a recurrence of recent collapses. As Wellham neared his century, Brearley closed the game right down, keeping him pinned down on 99 for 25 minutes, thereby depriving Hughes of a declaration that evening. Instead England had the final day to score 383 to win but they suffered the worst possible start when Lillee had Boycott lbw for 0. At 144/6 and with nearly three hours remaining they seemed destined for defeat, but Brearley, out for 0 in the first innings, now came to the rescue. In his last Test innings, he was at his most assured, making 51, adding 93 with Knott, who justified his recall with an unbeaten 70, that helped ensure an honourable draw and an unbeaten home record of 19 Tests as captain.

In addition to the absence of Gatting and Emburey, Brearley's return to Test duty was very much to Middlesex's loss, as they disappointed in the one-day competitions and could only manage fourth place in the championship. The previous year Edmonds had been made vice-captain but with Brearley in permanent residence he had few opportunities to prove himself. That all changed in 1981 when Brearley resumed the England captaincy, and although Edmonds's record as his deputy wasn't a bad one, two of the county's three championship defeats that year occurred on his watch. More important, he became engulfed in a couple of controversies, the second of which featured Selvey, his rival for the vice-captaincy. Omitted from the side against Sussex at Hove at the end of August, once Daniel had assured Edmonds he was fit, Selvey was none too chuffed, especially as Daniel lasted for only nine overs and Middlesex, fielding a depleted attack, were thrashed by ten wickets. Although it wasn't Edmonds's fault that

Daniel was incapacitated, he took the blame and this incident, coupled with his unpopularity with his team-mates, saw him replaced as vice-captain for 1982 by Gatting, another source of his resentment towards Brearley.

Outside the Test arena, Brearley remained in excellent touch. In his five remaining matches for Middlesex after his Test recall, four of which they won, he scored 58, 100, 72, 72, 21, 31, 145, putting on 338 for the third wicket with Gatting against Derbyshire, and 10, finishing the season with a county average of 51.61. For that and his Ashes triumph, Brearley was both the *Evening Standard* and the Cricket Writers' Club Player of the Year, a popular choice. He later said that the summer of 1981 was an extraordinary climax to a cricket career in which playing for England at all had been an unexpected bonus, and, needless to say, it left him with memories to last a lifetime.

Chapter 18

Festooned with Honours

BREARLEY had rarely wasted his winters and the winter of 1981-82 was no exception. Aside from his psychoanalysis training and his teaching at Westminster, he wrote much of *The Phoenix from the Ashes*, his personal account of the previous summer's events, plugged in to BBC videos, and covered two of England's Tests in India for the *Sunday Times*. The tour had nearly not taken place once the Indian government had taken exception to the inclusion of two England players, Boycott and Geoff Cook, who were both on a United Nations blacklist because they had played cricket in South Africa. It needed a clarification from the TCCB that it didn't approve of tours to South Africa and Boycott's public opposition to apartheid to resolve the impasse, only for the issue to resurface months later.

In 1971 South Africa had been subjected to an international sports boycott, a powerful weapon which helped bring home to them the extent of their isolation. In 1976 the new South African Cricket Union (SACU) was formed to administer multiracial cricket, but despite the progress made it failed to secure the readmission of South Africa to the ICC or end the boycott.

Consequently, they now instigated a number of commercially sponsored rebel tours, the first of these being an England XI, captained by Gooch, in March 1982. During the Edgbaston Test of 1981, John Edrich, an England selector recruiting for SACU, approached Brearley to ascertain whether he would lead an England XI in South Africa. Not surprisingly, he refused for, while acknowledging the efforts of SACU, he thought that the sports boycott not only demonstrated moral support for the black majority in South Africa, it also provided the most effective weapon to dent apartheid.

Once news of Gooch's tour broke, Brearley compared it to WSC, not only as a threat to Test cricket but 'also in the shabbiness and deceit of its conception and birth'.

'With predictable banality, the spokesman of the players claimed that they were in South Africa simply to play cricket. And as if to refute the idea that it was purely a business visit, i.e. cricketing visit, the South Africans, laughably, awarded Springbok caps to those picked to play against this motley crew of Englishmen assembled under the flag of the South African Breweries Company.'[1] He supported their three-year ban from Test cricket even though it included a number of good friends such as Emburey, while ensuring that it didn't become a fractious issue in the Middlesex dressing room.

In 1985, after further rebel tours to South Africa by Sri Lanka, the West Indies and Australia, he joined with John Arlott and Peter Roebuck to form the Campaign for Fair Play, which wanted no sporting contact with South Africa. Any relaxation of apartheid in sport was irrelevant until the whole system had been dismantled, a process which began in 1990 with the release of the anti-apartheid activist, Nelson Mandela, and the installation of his African National Congress as South Africa's first multiracial government in 1994.

As he began his 22nd season, Brearley announced that it would be his last. Although displaying few signs of advancing years, aside from the flecks of grey in his hair, he was about to be 40 and had lasted much longer than at one time seemed likely. (Ironically his Cambridge contemporaries were all long since retired.) With Emburey available all season because of his Test ban for touring South Africa the previous winter, and Gatting out of favour for the series against India, Middlesex's quest for honours received a major boost. They enjoyed the best of all possible starts remaining unbeaten in all competitions till the middle of June, and although they lost some momentum when chasing all four titles, they fought off a late-season challenge by Leicestershire to win the championship.

Five wins in their first six championship matches gave them an early lead and, while inclement weather consigned the next three to draws, they remained the side to beat. It was during the second of these matches at Sheffield that Brearley found himself in bad odour with the Yorkshire crowd when he took a low slip catch to dismiss Chris Old and end the innings. The ball clearly carried but some spectators thought otherwise and their jeers riled him as he walked off towards the pavilion. Flinging the ball to the ground, he ran towards the crowd and from ten yards he shouted, 'What do you think you know about it? Do you think I am a cheat – go home!' The altercation left *The Times*'s Richard Streeton unimpressed. 'It was as unnecessary for a player of Brearley's background and experience to behave as he did as it was for the spectators to query the catch.'[2]

On 9 July Leicestershire inflicted on Middlesex their first championship defeat of the season, but successive innings victories over Nottinghamshire saw them quickly return to the primrose path. In the first of these games at Trent Bridge, Brearley ended a barren patch with his second century of the summer. Opting to continue batting on the second day in the hope of forcing the follow-on, his foresight proved fully vindicated. 'Brearley, of course, has always been less prone to the stereotype than every other County captain,' wrote Streeton, 'but he gives the impression, in his last season, that he is more flexible than ever in his tactical thinking. No situation is allowed to drift for long without another experiment being tried. Watching Brearley as captain in the field is part of spectatorship and that cannot be said nowadays of too many captains.'[3] Particularly ingenious was his trap to snare Clive Rice, the Nottinghamshire captain and their leading batsman, in both innings. On a Trent Bridge wicket assisting the bowlers, Brearley noted that Rice was playing fast bowler Norman Cowans off the back foot and after he'd hit him for two off-side fours in one over, he stationed Radley, to the fielder's slight bemusement, at fly gully. Second ball, Rice hit straight to Radley 25 yards away and Radley didn't have to move. When Nottinghamshire followed on, Brearley played on Rice's tendency to clip the ball off his legs in the air by placing Radley this time at backward square leg. Immediately Rice obliged by hitting Cowans straight to him.

Bad weather continued to dog Middlesex's progress with four of their next six championship fixtures being drawn. They also lost ground in the JPL after winning their first six matches and were defeated in both one-day knockout competitions – by Lancashire in the quarter-final of the Benson and Hedges Cup and by Surrey in the semi-final of the NatWest Trophy. On the morning of 23 August, they arrived at Lord's for their championship match against Surrey only to discover that the pitch was bare and dry. By a happy coincidence Titmus, then aged 49 and working as a sub-postmaster in Hertfordshire, looked in for a chat and in no time found himself playing in borrowed kit, Brearley figuring that they could do with an additional spinner on such a wicket. Middlesex made 276 and after a rain-interrupted second day Surrey had reached 273/4 by lunch on the final day whereupon they declared. Middlesex chased quick runs before Brearley set Surrey a generous 161 in 135 minutes. He then proceeded to mark his last match at Lord's with captaincy of the highest calibre. Bowling his spinners for all but two overs, he lured his opponents to their doom by his imaginative field placings and with Titmus playing his part with 3-43, Middlesex emerged triumphant by 58 runs.

Their enterprise told against them in their encounter with Sussex at Hove after Barclay, the opposing captain, declared 53 runs behind. Brearley followed up his 58 in the first innings with an undefeated 100, one of the most spectacular of his career during which he completed 25,000 runs in first-class cricket. His declaration challenged Sussex to score 252 in three hours and after an afternoon of fluctuating fortune they won by three wickets to add to their weekend triumph of beating Middlesex in the JPL to gain the trophy. (Middlesex took second place, their highest in the league's 14th season.)

While Middlesex had led the championship all season, a late surge by Leicestershire had reduced their lead from 47 points on 17 August to two with two matches left to play. With much depending on their game against Hampshire at Uxbridge, Middlesex began inauspiciously. On a sporting wicket Brearley was out second ball, hit wicket, and they were soon 22/3, but Slack and Butcher staged something of a recovery. Their total looked all the more competitive once Edmonds and Emburey exploited the conditions to maximum effect, taking nine wickets between them in Hampshire's first innings of 178. Building on their narrow lead, half-centuries from Brearley and Gatting consolidated Middlesex's advantage only to lose their last six wickets for 19. Irked by such carelessness, Brearley gave his men a rollicking and they took his words to heart by routing Hampshire for 138. Victory by 106 runs and 22 points brought Middlesex within touching distance of the championship, since they only required four points from their final match at Worcester.

They duly secured their prize at 2.54pm the next day when Worcestershire's Alan Warner skied Emburey to Daniel at long-on. In ideal bowling conditions, Middlesex proved too formidable for Worcestershire's brittle batting, dismissing them for 168. They then batted like champions to establish a lead of 214 and, while the home team put up a better fight in the second innings, they merely delayed the inevitable. On a typical autumnal morning of mist and mellow fruitfulness, Middlesex soon disposed of their opponents, leaving them a mere 50 to win. Fortunate to survive a confident lbw appeal before he'd scored, Brearley played second fiddle to Slack before finishing proceedings with a clip past mid-on in the manner of his first scoring shot off Eric Bedser 21 year earlier. He finished with 14* to take his average for the season to 46.50. With the match all but decided, there were few people present to mark his farewell, but he was applauded off the field by the Worcestershire players. After a round of interviews, autograph signings and farewells, he packed his kit into the car. As he was about to depart, an old man stopped him and said, 'Excuse me, Mr Brearley, but what is your weight?' A surprised Brearley told him – it was 11½ stone – before he took his leave. It was only on the journey back to London that the reality of his retirement finally dawned on him. He would miss the camaraderie and the excitement of the first-class game, but, unlike many first-class cricketers, he had an alternative career mapped out and enough going on in his life to compensate.

Middlesex's fourth championship in seven years was entirely fitting in Brearley's final season, since he was the man who'd presided over their renaissance. 'In the course of his final three years,' Simon Hughes recorded, 'he had displayed the magical ability to extract the juice from the fruit and make it into a magic potion.'[4] According to Woodcock, 'Brearley was brilliantly analytical. He has worked out the modern game better than anyone else except perhaps Ray Illingworth,'[5] an assessment similar to John Arlott's. In a special appreciation in *Wisden* to mark his retirement, Arlott not only paid tribute to his exceptional intellect, but also his ability to understand and motivate players. 'There is no doubt that he was one of the best – certainly the most sustainedly successful – captain international cricket has known.' It was a legacy to be proud of and one that has stood the test of time.[6]

Chapter 19
Benign Critic

WHEN Brearley retired in 1982, he said he hoped to play some cricket of a competitive type, but family and professional commitments meant this never happened. In 1983 he'd played only four games, including captaining the Callers-Pegasus International XI in two games against a combined Northumberland/Durham XI at Jesmond, when he deputised for the injured Butcher in the Middlesex-Lancashire championship match in mid-August. His return failed to impress Simon Hughes.

> For some baffling reason, Brearley also played in the Old Trafford match. Middlesex were looking a bit short of batting experience, but this hardly justified sending out an SOS to a 41-year-old who'd retired a year earlier. But even that wasn't as incomprehensible as Brearley responding to it. With a shock of almost pure white hair emerging from beneath his floppy hat, he stood incongruously at first slip, and made a scratchy 17 going in at number five. Instead of admiring the way Brearley had gamely tried to fill the breach, I felt he'd sullied the distinguished image he had departed with. We

were reminded of most of his bad points – his stiff technique, slight irascibility and eccentric dress sense – and none of his good ones. [1]

He continued to turn out occasionally in exhibition matches, captaining the Duchess of Norfolk's XI against the Rest of the World XI in 1987, and leading various old England XIs in Australia in 1988, in Barbados in 1992, and at Trent Bridge in 1993 for Derek Randall's testimonial. That same year he enjoyed the opportunity to keep wicket to Shane Warne in a charity match in Oxfordshire, a thrill comparable to anything he'd experienced in cricket.

While generally keeping a low profile, he did participate in a revealing portrait of his good friend John Arlott, whose profound commentaries told of a most varied and eclectic career. Allies together in the anti-apartheid movement and the Cricketers' Association, of which Arlott was president, Brearley greatly appreciated the support he received from a man who'd lost his eldest son in a car accident, aged 21. He recalled:

> He was a great figure when I first knew him. I was a very ordinary county cricketer who was in his thirties and didn't look as if I'd play for England or have any expectation or much ambition of doing so. His paternal and avuncular attitude towards me was very nice, very personal and very real. I felt there was a great pride if I did well, a great pleasure and a great encouragement, and that was helpful to me. It was the generosity of a father to a loved son. [2]

Arlott was attracted to Brearley's warmth and humanity and stoutly supported him when he became captain of England, ranking him one of their very best. With poetry, politics, literature and sport in common, they flourished in each other's company, Brearley later recalling a Sunday lunch at the Arlott home where they sat down at 2pm and remained at table till 10pm.

In 1981 Arlott moved to Alderney and in 1984 Brearley was asked to go there to spend some time with him to talk about his life and interests for three Channel 4 programmes entitled *Arlott in Conversation with Mike Brearley*, subsequently turned into a book. With a bottle of Beaujolais at hand, Arlott responded to Brearley's sensitive probing with candour tinged with melancholia when recounting the premature deaths of his second wife and eldest son. It made for compelling if painful viewing.

Arlott died in 1991 and Brearley, along with Botham, another close friend, attended his funeral, and in 2014, in a tribute in *The Times* to mark the centenary of his birth, Brearley called him a great man, his words on the radio containing an eloquence and depth which others lacked.

In 1985 Brearley wrote *The Art of Captaincy*, a treatise on leadership. An occasional columnist throughout his career, he met the American-born journalist Dudley Doust for the first time during the Headingley Test of 1977 when Doust was compiling a profile of him for the *Sunday Times*. They immediately clicked and liking what he subsequently read Brearley invited Doust to co-write the book he was due to write about the Australian series. The result was *The Return of the Ashes* and, later, *The Ashes Retained*, recounting England's win in Australia in 1978/79. While Doust learned much from Brearley about cricket, his skills as a portraitist rubbed off on Brearley, who branched out on his own with *Phoenix from the Ashes*, a gripping tale about the events of 1981 told with panache. According to the sports journalist and broadcaster Mihir Bose, he brought a special dimension to cricket writing by explaining to the outside world the inside view of what happens and why.

The interest generated in that 1981 series and the requests Brearley received to talk about leadership sowed the seeds for *The Art of Captaincy*, especially since he was ploughing uncultivated land. It met with near-universal acclaim – Trevor Bailey calling it the most interesting cricket book he'd read for a long time – and over 30 years later it remains the standard text on cricket captaincy, its pages pored over by subsequent Test captains such as Michael Atherton, Nasser Hussain and Andrew Strauss. (The 14-year-old Alastair Cooke was given the book by his father but it remained on his shelf unread, although later, when captain, he appreciated Brearley's advice in person.) While Brearley offers many a fascinating insight into the tactical side of captaincy, it is his discussion on player motivation that makes the book essential reading. His ability to analyse his own leadership, warts and all, with the same clinical objectivity, only adds to its value. 'This is a modestly told book with little of the personal pronoun, which nevertheless says a lot about Brearley,' commented Swanton. 'He was an outstanding leader for the reasons that matter most. He was popular with his players, so that authority came easily and naturally.'[3]

Brearley did cause a stir by taking a swipe at two of the giants of the game: the former Kent and England captain Colin Cowdrey and the West Indian captain Clive Lloyd. The former, he contended, wasn't a good captain because he lacked decisiveness and was too concerned about how he looked, an observation which embarrassed Cowdrey when questioned about it by sports commentator Barry Davis on BBC TV's *Maestro*; the latter for allowing his side to become cynical in the exercise of power and for lacking a cricketing brain, 'as was shown by his lack of ideas when handling the ordinary Lancashire attack'.

His comments upset Lloyd who wondered why one professional would want to devalue another man's accomplishments, and Brearley, on reflection, accepted that his criticism had been hurtful. He paid tribute to the West Indian's brilliance as a cricketer and spoke of his great qualities of warmth, energy and compassion which had won him the great respect of his players.

Having written some articles for the *Sunday Times* during his playing career, it wasn't surprising that he continued to write occasionally for the paper till 1990 when he was enticed to *The Observer* by its sports editor Simon Kelner with the most generous of offers. A regular in the press box for the Saturday of home Tests, he cut a rather aloof figure, casting half an eye on the cricket and departing as soon as he filed his copy. 'For the last 15 years he has been in one of the six Test match press boxes in this country every Saturday and barely spoken a word,' noted the sports journalist Ted Corbett in 1997.[4]

Recruited for his reputation as much as for his literary gifts, Brearley felt entitled to trade on it and he could take a broad brush to his column. When lacking inspiration, he would often phone his great friend David Sylvester, the renowned art critic and cricket lover, to ask what he would like to read about the next day and he would often follow his advice.

Invariably stylish and erudite with its classical allusions and Shakespearean quotations, his writing carried weight with his readers. Among his fellow critics, John Woodcock ranks him an excellent journalist who writes very well and, to Simon Barnes, he is always interesting because he is detached, while to Mihir Bose, 'Brearley analyses and tells you something you didn't know.'[5]

Some thought that his absence from the game had rendered him less perceptive than in his pomp. Matthew Engel of *The Guardian* recalls spending a day with him at an Old Trafford Test and being surprised at how disengaged and misinformed he'd become; his colleague Mike Selvey thought he wasn't always contemporary enough, while Ian Todd felt he didn't get to the pulse of the game. Yet, according to Vic Marks, the veteran cricket correspondent of *The Observer*, when the game entered a critical phase, he would become wonderfully animated, imagining he was captaining again as he queried tactics and pondered an alternative course of action.

Rather than write about the details of a game, Brearley would present a considered overview, often focusing on a player's technique or the captain's tactics. Recalling some of his own struggles as a Test match batsman, and the hard choices facing any captain, he was generally sympathetic to his successors, so that on the rare occasions he sharpened his pen, his comments left their mark.

On one such occasion he vented his spleen on fellow columnist Christopher Martin-Jenkins, the cricket correspondent of the *Daily Telegraph*, during the Edgbaston Test of 1995. On an under-prepared wicket, England proved no match for the West Indian quicks, Curtly Ambrose, Courtney Walsh and Ian Bishop and lost by an innings in little over two days. Having dubbed the wicket a disgrace, Brearley wrote:

> Those at Edgbaston who defend such a pitch irritate me. If this is how they win championships, then roll on the deduction of points for substandard pitches. Christopher Martin-Jenkins said there was nothing wrong with the bounce of this pitch. Such a comment elicits all my atavistic professional sportsman's prejudices against the non-playing scribe; let's see him batting at No 3 against Bishop and Walsh![6]

Stung by the vehemence of Brearley's attack, Martin-Jenkins shot back the next day. Declaring that no batsman would have enjoyed facing the West Indian fast bowlers on that wicket, he continued:

> No sane cricketer would, a point which should be noted by a former England captain, Mike Brearley, who appears at matches on occasional Saturdays only, yet who, in yesterday's *Observer*, took a 'non-playing scribe' to task for an erroneous judgement as if the writer in question, who in fact has played a great deal of cricket and once defeated two Test players en route to the final of the Surrey Single Wicket Championship, had ever suggested batting was fun against very fast bowlers aiming for the body, not the stumps. [7]

Brearley also upset his former fellow opener Dennis Amiss, the chief executive of Warwickshire, with his claim that sub-standard pitches were responsible for the county's championship success the previous year and their good results so far that year. He retorted that the current wickets at Edgbaston were among the best he'd known there.

Brearley's retirement from the England captaincy in 1981 had once again left a void as captains came and went with alarming frequency throughout the decade. His immediate successor was Keith Fletcher, the much-respected captain of Essex, whom he'd marked out as a potential England captain after the under-25 tour to Pakistan in 1966/67. He took the team to India and Sri Lanka that winter but after losing to the former 1-0 in a turgid series, he was summarily dismissed by Peter May, the new chairman of selectors. His demise disappointed Brearley who declared he'd been punished unduly for a minor gesture of petulance when given out in the Bangalore Test. He considered Bob Willis, his successor, unsuitable for captaincy and when Willis gave way to David Gower in 1984, he remained open-minded about his leadership following England's 5-0 whitewash by the West Indies. A year later, after England's 3-1 win against Australia, Brearley was much more upbeat about Gower and his team's prospects in the West Indies that winter. 'So, do we have a chance in the Caribbean? I think the answer is yes, and this summer has shown us that we do. Our batting is now so powerful and confident that even the West Indies should have difficulty dismissing us twice on good pitches.'[8]

Unfortunately, it wasn't to be. On a spiteful wicket at Kingston in the first Test, England were battered into submission by the West Indian quicks and they never recovered their nerve thereafter. After another 5-0 thrashing, the selectors held Gower primarily responsible and when he lost the first Test against India at Lord's, they replaced him with Mike Gatting. That winter, Gatting won acclaim by retaining the Ashes in Australia, before losing back-to-back series against Pakistan. Unhappy with the TCCB's choice of umpires during the 1987 series in England, Pakistan proved no more accommodating when they were the hosts later that year. In the first Test at Lahore, Shakeel Khan enraged England with his officiating as they slumped to an innings defeat; then in the second Test at Faisalabad, Shakoor Rana became embroiled in an unseemly confrontation with Gatting after he'd accused him of cheating. Profanities were exchanged and with Gatting unwilling to apologise, Shakoor refused to take the field the next morning, leading to the abandonment of the day's play. While the majority of the British media backed their team's uncompromising approach, Brearley adopted a different line. He thought England had blundered by complaining publicly about the umpiring in the previous Test, and now, with a touch more sensitivity, they could have broken the impasse. 'The manager, like the captain, is in a tricky situation. Caught up in the partisan mood of the group, he feels and needs to be at one with them in their cricketing campaign, yet he, they, must keep enough distance from the group emotions to be able to offer a moderating voice.'[9]

After a winter of discontent in which England failed to win a Test in either Pakistan or New Zealand, Gatting's captaincy appeared on borrowed time, but his defenestration months later bordered on the farcical. During the first Test against the West Indies at Trent Bridge, a tabloid newspaper revealed that Gatting had invited a barmaid to his hotel room, and although the selectors accepted his assurance that no impropriety had taken place, they still dismissed him. According to Brearley, any indiscretion on Gatting's part was dwarfed by the failure of the authorities to stand up to what he perceived to be the prying nastiness of the modern media. 'For which is the greater evil: a possible sexual laxity in an England cricket captain or a sneaking, vicious, malicious and possibly libellous account in the popular press? To my mind, the TCCB has got hold of the stick at the wrong end.'[10]

After a summer in which England had four captains, any hope that the TCCB would have second thoughts about Gatting were foiled when they vetoed his reappointment for the Ashes series the following summer. The tarnished crown reverted once again to Gower, but his second coming proved ingloriously ephemeral as an inept England lost 4-0 to a resurgent Australia. 'Gower is a charming man and a charming cricketer,' Brearley concluded at the end of the summer. 'But he is not a leader.'[11] The selectors were of a similar mind and replaced him with Gooch, who over the next several years restored some pride to English cricket without ever suggesting that he was a natural leader. After Pakistan's emphatic win at The Oval in August 1992 which made them deserved winners of the series 2-1, Brearley highlighted various flaws in Gooch's captaincy. 'The fact is that

Gooch leads by example; by hard work, encouragement and by his own magnificent batting. But he still lacks the ability to respond subtly to the conditions, and his attitude to spinners borders on contempt.'[12]

There were also doubts about Gooch's regimented style of captaincy, especially the controversial exclusion of Gower from England's tour to India that winter because he was deemed too casual, especially in his approach to practice. Amid the outrage that followed his omission, Brearley offered to act as an intermediary. Gower would be expected to join in wholeheartedly in all team activities prior to the first Test, but thereafter he would be responsible for his own training programme. His offer was rejected by the cricket authorities, and England, minus Gower, were comprehensively defeated 3-0 by India.

Gooch's star continued to wane following crushing defeats to Australia at home the following summer. Reviewing England's abject performance in the fourth Test at Headingley, their third defeat in four matches, Brearley wrote that he should stand down as captain. 'A fresh mind, more open, less battered, more inspiring, is called for ... The work ethic, overstressed, can fail to value sheer flair, as most notably with Gower.'[13]

Gooch needed little persuading and he handed over to Michael Atherton, who faced calls to resign in July 1994 after becoming embroiled in a ball-tampering controversy in the Lord's Test against South Africa. It wasn't simply the fact that television cameras caught him smearing dust from his pocket on the ball, it was his misleading explanation to the match referee that rankled. While prepared to give Atherton the benefit of the doubt, Brearley castigated him for his reckless stupidity.

It seems likely, then, that Atherton was not out to alter the condition of the ball in any way that could not have been done by hands dried on a towel. And this may partly explain his openness and unguardedness. But he must have known that it lay in a grey area, and that ball-tampering is cricket's hottest issue.

No one knows what his motives were, but it could be that he experienced the idealisation that is heaped on the head of England's captain as a sort of divine shroud, a misty halo of invincibility?

Why else might he have behaved in this rather crazy way risking, if not inviting, trouble?[14]

He praised Ray Illingworth, the chairman of selectors, for his peremptory action in fining Atherton £2,000. By imposing the maximum amount, he successfully saved his captain from the strictures of the match referee. He also admired Atherton's response in the following Test at Headingley when scoring 99 in England's first innings. The innings revealed nothing about his honesty, he wrote, but a great deal about his courage and response to his critics.

Although enjoying few triumphs to savour during his 54-match stint as captain, Atherton commanded the respect of his players and there was genuine sadness when, in 1998, he voluntarily stood down. After a brief interlude with Alec Stewart, Nasser Hussain took over, against New Zealand, in July 1999, and although England lost that series 2-1 Brearley detected a ray of hope amid the gloom. 'I think there are signs that Hussain may be fostering the Chappell factor in the side ... He looks more of a captain than either Atherton or Stewart.'[15]

In company with the new coach Duncan Fletcher, Hussain quickly restored England's pride and morale, as well as getting the best out of Andrew Caddick, their temperamental fast bowler, whom Brearley had always rated. Two years later, at the end of England's tour of India, he wrote:

> Hussain was spectacularly good all series: blending, motivating, using his sense in both conventional and unconventional ways. He is afraid of neither of the orthodox nor the unorthodox.
>
> There is a tough streak in his make-up and, dare one say it, a slice of that steel most notably displayed by Douglas Jardine – also born in India. One of Hussain's chief skills was to make the best use of what each player had to offer and to arrive at a realistic appraisal of the situation.[16]

This was the pinnacle of Hussain's captaincy. Leading England in Australia the following winter, his decision to give his opponents first use of a plumb wicket in the first Test at Brisbane backfired spectacularly. Comprehensively defeated, they lost the series 4-1 and when Michael Vaughan took over the running of the England one-day team the following summer his inspirational captaincy made a great impression on everyone. Returning to lead the Test team against South Africa in the first Test at Edgbaston, Hussain found it harder to motivate his players than previously and, after getting the worst of a draw, he decided his time was up. He relinquished the captaincy with immediate effect. 'Was he brave to quit?' wrote Brearley. 'I don't think so. It would have been braver to bear with it longer, to work himself up for one last surge to see the series through.'[17]

An admirer of Hussain's successor, Vaughan, especially his willingness to embrace unorthodox field placings, Brearley hailed the 2005 series against Australia, won 2-1 by England, as the most gripping in living memory. After a 5-0 thrashing in Australia 18 months later which precipitated the resignation of coach Duncan Fletcher, he criticised the in-house appointment of his successor Peter Moores as smacking of favouritism, since he lacked the international experience.

Injury to Vaughan had forced him to miss that series but, on his return in 2007, Brearley noted that his captaincy had become too restless, especially his tendency to tinker with the field. His abrupt resignation after the third Test against South Africa in 2008 and his replacement by the abrasive Kevin Pietersen caused Brearley to question the wisdom of his appointment ahead of Middlesex's Andrew Strauss. Pietersen began well with a morale-boosting victory against South Africa at The Oval and then led England to India that November, a series blighted by the mass terrorist attack in Mumbai. On the flight from Chennai, where England had lost the first Test by six wickets, to Mohali, Brearley, covering the Tests for *The Observer*, sat next to Pietersen and found him both personable and receptive to his suggestions about field placings. England fought back to win at Mohali to draw the two-match series, a feather in Pietersen's cap, but the honeymoon wasn't to last. Weeks later he called for the removal of Moores, an act of war which led to his own dismissal as well as that of Moores's.

The captaincy now passed to Strauss who, in partnership with new coach Andy Flower, took England to the top of the Test match rankings in a little over two years. While tactical innovation wasn't his forte, Brearley approved of Strauss in every other respect, not least his feat in beating Australia home and away, and he was sorry to see him retire in 2012 after defeat at home by South Africa.

He also admired Strauss's successor, Alastair Cook, especially after engaging him in conversation in a meeting organised by the England and Wales Cricket Board (ECB) 'I found Brearley a very nice guy just trying to offer some opinions,' related Cook.

'We probably chatted for two or three hours. He didn't force anything, he never said you ought to do this or you should think that.'[18]

In 2013, disappointed never to have received a rise in remuneration at *The Observer*, Brearley moved to *The Times*, where he was welcomed with open arms, not least by their cricket correspondent, Michael Atherton. By now a more convivial figure, he established a close rapport with former team-mates working in the media. 'Part of Brearley is very gregarious,' noted Simon Barnes. 'It is always a pleasure to see him at a press box going into a huddle with Vic Marks.' Noting his own conversations with him, not least their quizzes on music and literature, Barnes says: 'Brearley enjoys good company and is good company.'[19]

Writing more frequently for *The Times* than for previous papers, he continued to give an overview of England's Tests and comment on some of the other great issues of the day. In the wake of the tragic death of the Australian batsman Phillip Hughes, he expressed relief that a freak accident hadn't led to excessive measures. 'We cannot rule out all risk in play, sport or life. Hard cases make bad law, and I am glad people are not calling for restrictions on bouncers, or other reactions of such a kind.'[20]

One matter on which Brearley shifted his position was MCC's Spirit of Cricket, introduced in 2000 as a preamble to the Laws of Cricket, traditionally their responsibility. Originally opposed to the preamble, fearing it might come across as patronising and hypocritical to parts of the developing world, he began to change tack as MCC, shorn of its former power, reinvented itself as the game's conscience. With the laws unable to provide clear-cut answers to ethical questions such as walking, dissent and sledging, he thought the preamble could help focus on values that lay beyond the laws with its call to respect the game, the umpires and the opposition.

His views were given added meaning in light of the Australian ball-tampering scandal on their tour of South Africa in March 2018, which aroused such disenchantment throughout the cricket world. While ball-tampering was nothing new and by no means the worst offence in the ICC lexicon, Australia's premeditated cheating was the culmination of its long-held contempt for the game's best traditions. Despite his scepticism that such behaviour would be eliminated, given the rivalries and aggression on parade in Test cricket, he reiterated his support for the Spirit of Cricket, an important boost for an initiative that is still feeling its way.

Chapter 20

On the Couch

DURING Brearley's final season, *The Times* journalist Ivo Tennant arranged an interview with him through the Middlesex secretary to discuss his plans for retirement. With their wires crossed, Brearley thought the interview was about Middlesex and he expressed irritation when Tennant began asking him questions about psychotherapy, nor was he best pleased when journalists quizzed him about the impending birth of his daughter, Lara. His private life was precisely that and, unlike many retiring public figures, he welcomed the retreat into anonymity, especially since it gave him time to commit to his new family after a difficult first marriage to Virginia, an English teacher at a technical school and popular with the few cricketers who knew her. After separating in 1975 she had gone back to America and, although she visited Pakistan during MCC's 1977/78 tour to rebuild bridges, things didn't work out. They were divorced in April 1980. 'I have always wanted children and it was a point of difficulty between us that Virginia did not,' Brearley told *The Sun* in July 1981. 'At the end she said she would be prepared to have children but by then it was too late.' He admitted to being difficult to live with. 'I know that during my marriage I looked for every quality in one woman. That is unfair.'[1]

After his separation from Virginia, Brearley enjoyed a brief relationship with Kari Ellefson, an attractive Norwegian, who visited him in Australia during the 1978/79 tour, but his real love lay elsewhere. On England's tour of India in 1976/77, he'd met Mana Sarabhai, a woman of beauty and charm, who hailed from Ahmedabad, the former capital of the state of Gujarat in western India and home to Mahatma Gandhi between 1918 and 1930. The Sarabhais were one of India's most affluent and illustrious families. Mana's grandfather, Ambalal Sarabhai, besides being a prominent industrialist and philanthropist, was a friend of Gandhi and a leading figure in the national independence movement. He had eight children, one of whom was Gautam Sarabhai, Mana's father, who joined Calico Mills, the family textile mill in Ahmedabad, as a director, aged 22, and another was Vikram Sarabhai, a brilliant scientist and the father of the Indian space programme. Gautam was a mathematician by training but had his interest in psychology awakened by John Wisdom at Cambridge, some 25 years before the latter achieved something similar with Brearley. He later underwent analysis with Anna Freud, the Austrian-British psychoanalyst and daughter of Sigmund Freud, and reorganised his factory floor along the lines of London's Tavistock Clinic to develop a more close-knit community ethos.

Renowned for financial and entrepreneurial acumen, Gautam succeeded his family as chairman of Calico Textiles in 1945 and by diversifying the group into chemicals, plastics and pharmaceuticals, he presided over one of the largest industrial concerns in India. A lover of culture, he also created some of Ahmedabad's finest institutions: The National Institute of Industrial Design with his sister Gina, a noted architect, and the Calico Museum, the prime textile museum in the country, managed by the Sarabhai Foundation, a non-profit organisation devoted to the promotion of art, science and literature.

His wife, Kamalini, following six years of training in child development at the British Psychoanalytical Institute and the Tavistock Clinic, became the driving force behind the foundation of the BM Institute of Mental Health in Ahmedabad, which played a pioneering role in psychological research in south-east Asia in the 1960s and 70s.

Then married to American lecturer Robert Gorchov, by whom she had a son, Mischa, Mana was at first just friends with Brearley, but things developed over the years. He went back to India on holidays, including after the tour of Australia in February 1979, she became divorced, and early in 1980 she and Mischa moved to London. It wasn't easy uprooting a boy brought up in India and used to being part of a large family, but he settled in well helped by his warm relationship with Brearley. On one occasion when Brearley went to pick him up from school and a pupil said to him, 'Look, there's your daddy,' Mischa replied, 'He's not daddy. That's Mike and he's my friend.'

After a few months Mana and Mischa moved in with Brearley, much to his delight. 'My relationship with Mana is the most important part of my life. It means much more to me than anything that can happen in cricket. I love her because she is warm and understanding. She is terrifically intelligent and has a very quick mind.'[2] When the following year she became pregnant, Brearley donned a sarong to celebrate. 'I found myself drawn to wearing the sarong that had for years lain unused in my drawer,' he told *Marriage Guidance* magazine. 'It was my way of identifying with her womanhood and also my envy of her for it.'[3]

Shortly after the birth of their daughter Lara in June 1982, they moved to 20 Provost Road, Hampstead, one of the most fashionable parts of London. 'On an avenue of cheery pastel-painted detached buildings the Brearley home is an anomaly,' reported the cricket writer Simon Lister. 'The dark bare stone has been left alone and the window sills are painted with a matt grey paint. Among its neighbours it is almost self-consciously plain.

'"Your home looks very different from the others," I say by way of an ice- breaker.

'"Yes," replies Brearley. "It does."'[4]

According to the cricket writer Rob Steen, who also interviewed Brearley at his home, the black Jaguar in the drive was the sole concession to ostentation. Inside there was an austere touch, similar to his parents' home in Brentham, the primary colours downstairs restricted mainly to paintings by the Spanish Catalan artist Joan Miro.

In 1998 he and Mana mobilised their community when Eton College lodged an application with Camden Council to demolish a historic Victorian two-storey house they owned next to the Brearleys and replace it with luxury homes. Condemning Eton for the dilapidated state of the house, Brearley publicly decried their desire to make as much money as they could from the sale with little regard for the area, while Mana wrote to the local residents, asking them to join a campaign against the plan.

In 2000 Eton sold the house to Soffair UK Properties Ltd, but their plan to build a large extension was thrown out by Camden's planning committee, much to Mana's delight since she had urged them to reject it on conservation grounds. Soon afterwards French squatters moved in and entertained the Brearleys with their displays of juggling, so much so that when the council tried to evict them, they objected, claiming that they had been very good neighbours. In time they moved on and the house was kept, with additions.

Although content to lead her own life as an architect turned silversmith, Mana shares many of Mike's cultural interests and supports his various literary endeavours. She is a consummate hostess, enjoys socialising at Lord's and is revered by the cricketing fraternity for her glamour, warmth and sense of fun, as well as for her calming influence on Mike.

Disliking the noise and bustle of London at Christmas time, the Brearleys happily decamp to Ahmedabad to the delightful family farm on the fringe of the city. Such is the Sarabhai influence there that when they have entertained England cricket teams the local factory which lets out toxic fumes is closed.

To please his father-in-law, Brearley made a valiant effort to learn Gujarati from the eminent Ahmedabad poet and activist Saroop Dhruv between 1985 and 1988, but despite buying many CDs to listen to Gujurati programmes the task ultimately proved too daunting. Yet his predilection for Indian dress, his interest in Gujarat history and love of Gujarati dishes – he is an accomplished cook of brinjal, the favourite Gujarat dish – make him, according to Mana, more Indian than English.

Aside from catching up with the family and watching the odd day's cricket, India gives Brearley time to get on with his writing, especially since 2014 when he and Mana decided to extend their winter break there to two or three months.

Since both Mike and Mana were raised in close-knit families, it was only natural that Mischa and Lara should experience a similar upbringing. Inheriting their parents' sharp intelligence, they learned the art of conversation at an early age and displayed an impressive grasp of public affairs. At first Mischa took to cricket, even adopting Mike's stance and pick-up, and was captain of Brondesbury under 11s, but this waned over time as his talents lay elsewhere. After reading Architecture at Cambridge, he has become a successful architect and has two children, Luka and Alia, by his partner Fae.

Imbued with a strong social conscience, Lara read History at Edinburgh, where she helped run a successful charity fashion show featuring the work of top designers such as Stella McCartney and an appearance on the catwalk from fellow student Pippa Middleton.

After Edinburgh and the London School of Hygiene and Tropical Medicine, she has worked overseas as a health consultant for the UN and Save the Children UK before her current job as Technical Officer at the World Health Organisation. Attached to Jaco, they have one baby daughter Maia, who, like Luka and Alia has brought much pleasure to Mike and Mana.

On a more sombre note Mike had to contend with the decline of his parents. Throughout his career his family continued to follow him closely, especially at Lord's where they were frequent spectators. One pupil recalled that if Mike went in to bat during a maths lesson, Horace would take his class to the television room. During MCC's tour to India in 1976/77, he spotted one of his class with a radio under his desk, but instead of confiscating it he merely asked the score. Retiring in 1978, Horace was able to take his wife to Australia that winter to watch Mike retain the Ashes, but, sadly, Midge was already suffering from Alzheimer's, the progressive brain disorder, which was to kill her in 1981.

Alone for the first time in 40 years, Horace kept himself occupied with his myriad of interests. Aside from his love of sport and music, he made pottery, played bridge and became an excellent cook. When he too became afflicted by Alzheimer's and was no longer able to live on his own, he moved to his daughter Jill's in Birmingham in 1995. It was soon after this that he and Mike went walking in the Black Mountains one day, a walk which took some three hours and involved a climb of 1,200 feet. They sat down for a beer afterwards and being a hot day Mike asked his father if he was tired. He thought about it, felt his legs and flexed his knees. 'I don't think so,' he said. 'Should I be?'

The last years were troubling, not least for Mike who feared that he, too, might inherit the disease. But despite the ravages, Horace kept his dignity and won affection from all those who met him for the first time. When he died at home in August 2007, aged 94, he was the oldest living Yorkshire cricketer. That October a large group of family and friends, including a number of old colleagues from CLS, gathered in Birmingham to commemorate his life. Mike gave an eloquent appreciation of a man who'd derived much pleasure from that life and who'd given back much in return.

Brearley has remained close to his sisters, both of whom have lived and continue to live full lives. The older one, Jill, was a dancer, a teacher, an Alexander Technique teacher and more recently a potter. The younger one, Margy, joined Voluntary Service Overseas and taught in Sierra Leone for two years, where she met her American husband. After taking time out to raise her four children, she worked for the Africa Centre and the BBC's Africa Service, producing programmes on a wide range of events including women's issues and an arts programme. A passionate believer in education for all children as a means of fulfilling their potential, she ran an educational improvement programme in Islington for eight years. Later she worked as an assistant to a sociologist who was researching into the best ways of improving life in estates for social housing. Her last job was for Haringey in administering a fund for projects in schools where there were a large number of deprived children.

Although Brearley was popular in the world of cricket, he was close to few of them: John Arlott, Tom Cartwright, Dudley

Doust, David Sheppard and Doug Insole were good friends, as are Clive Radley, Mike Gatting, Richard Hutton, John Stephenson, Simon Hughes and Vic Marks, but once he retired, he increasingly mixed in different circles. On the margins of a glittering world, many of his friends comprise the north London liberal intelligentsia. One of his dearest friends was the renowned art critic David Sylvester, who listed cricket among his many passions. Brearley loved him for his childlike passion and the integrity of his opinions and was devastated by his death in 2001, remarking that he'd missed no one more. During Sylvester's final weeks, he interviewed Brearley in a book published posthumously entitled *London Calling*. Asked to explain the connection between success in sport and great art, Brearley declared that they both came down to 'not turning one's face away'.

Another close friend is the social anthropologist Hugh Brody and his partner, the actress Juliet Stevenson. In 2001 he cooperated with the former to make a film on psychoanalysis and in 2008 he joined with the latter and the human rights QC, Helena Kennedy, to support a more humane detention system in this country.

One of Brearley's most avid supporters is the film director Sam Mendes, who read *The Art of Captaincy* for insights when making *American Beauty* in 1999 and dealing with his first film crew. Introduced to Brearley by Simon Hughes, Mendes became a good friend and it was through his hospitality at Lord's that Brearley met the actor Simon Russell Beale. Having heard Beale talk to the British Psychoanalytical Society on 'The Psychotherapy of Macbeth', he proposed him for the annual Ernest Jones lecture in 2009. Under his benign chairmanship, Beale, according to *The Guardian*'s theatre critic Michael Billington, gave more insights into Shakespearean characters than one could get from a heap of scholastic tracts.

It wasn't till Brearley came across John Wisdom that he had the remotest idea of psychoanalysis, a discipline established by the Austrian neurologist Sigmund Freud in the 1890s in regards to his treatment of disturbed patients. On a practical level, he joined the Samaritans at Cambridge and when speaking to people in distress, he discovered a capacity to listen and to advise. It was his first contact with such people and he harboured a desire to understand more about them and their various tribulations.

His ambition was confirmed years later in the winters of 1974/75 and 1975/76 when he worked as a nursing assistant at the Adolescent Unit of Northgate Clinic in Hendon, drawing praise from his medical chiefs for his unusual empathy and considerable vigour. Later describing it as 'one of the most exciting and interesting things I have ever done', he particularly appreciated the weekly meetings led by psychoanalyst Donald Bird, who taught them how, through self-scrutiny, they could achieve a fuller understanding of their patients. It was this experience which finally convinced him that when he retired from cricket, he would like to make a full-time career of helping people help themselves. Months later, he had a preliminary interview for training at the Institute of Psychoanalysis with Anne-Marie Sandler, a prominent analyst originally from Switzerland. He recalled:

> After the interview, she wrote, understandably, that I needed more experience with people who were in psychological trouble before making a full application. Some weeks later, I had a charming second letter from her to the effect that British members of the Admissions Committee had informed her that captaining a cricket team had more relevance to training to be a psychoanalyst than she had realised. I could proceed with my application. [5]

In September 1980 he started a full-time course in therapy at the Institute of Psychoanalysis in New Cavendish Street. It meant that when Middlesex were playing at home, he had to get up at 6am to visit his analyst. Once he fell asleep in his car. For all that, he enjoyed it, surprising himself by the range of imaginative thoughts of which he was capable, and getting to know himself much better. While qualifying as a psychoanalyst, he practised as a psychotherapist at the Camden Psychotherapy Unit, continuing there till 1987, by which time he'd established himself in private practice.

As a cricket captain, his experience handling players of different temperaments and coping with his own range of emotions proved excellent preparation for life as a psychoanalyst. Always admirably self-critical, his seven years in analysis wrestling with his own demons, aggression, envy and insecurity, helped him to understand something similar in his patients. 'We analysts have to get into a hole with our patients,' he wrote in *On Form*. 'We imaginatively have to gain a sense of their suffering, their temptations, their ways of being.'[6] Because psychoanalysis puts the emphasis on the negative feelings that the patient might express towards the therapist, it is essential that the therapist remains anonymous, which is why Brearley deliberately adopted a low profile. Simon Hughes, the cricket analyst for Channel 4, asked him to appear on the programme, but he refused because of his patients. 'For some it's difficult enough that I am even tangentially in the public eye even a little bit. The process works partly from a certain sort of anonymity; I don't talk about myself in the sessions and for the patients to be able to make use of me in whatever way they could would be much more difficult if I was to start writing about myself.'[7]

While engaged in analytical sessions, he wouldn't answer the door of his basement consultancy room or the phone, read emails or allow anyone to interrupt him. To think clearly and objectively, he would remain unobtrusive, from his understated greeting to his patients to his perfunctory farewell. As form dictated, he would sit behind them out of range to enable them to express themselves freely, rarely asking questions or directly answering theirs. His task, he explained, was not to offer sympathy, blame or advice but to help them face up to their primitive feelings.

Given the exacting nature of psychoanalysis and the tensions involved, it wasn't surprising that Brearley found the normal seven 50-minute slots per day exhausting, but never less than fulfilling. He learned the need to be sensitive enough to understand the emotional force of the anxieties and traumas that patients brought to him, and firm enough to preserve an independent outlook under that kind of pressure.

He occasionally helped cricketers who were experiencing undue stress in their game or their life, including the England slow left-arm bowler Phil Tufnell, who had three beneficial sessions with him in the mid-1990s. As he told him everything about his troubled second marriage, Brearley realised he was in a pretty fragile state and that the last thing he needed was a lecture. His approach was to let him have his say before delivering a very simple message: 'Be calm, relax and things will sort themselves out.'

An equally serious case was Brearley's former England team-mate, David Bairstow, who informed him at a cricket dinner in 1997 that he was suffering from serious depression brought on by a plethora of financial and personal problems. Brearley offered to see him privately or put him in touch with one of his professional colleagues who lived close to him in Yorkshire, but Bairstow didn't contact him again and months later he committed suicide.

That same year the ECB announced that Brearley would be available to offer confidential counselling to any England player, but three years later no one had availed themselves of the opportunity.

One person who did seek him out was the world snooker champion Ronnie O'Sullivan, a manic depressive, compounded by his enforced separation from his adored father who was serving an 18-year prison sentence for murder. At the suggestion of Clive Everton, the editor of *Snooker Scene* and television pundit, who'd suffered from clinical depression himself, he contacted Brearley in 1999. He later declared he'd been unimpressed by Brearley's suggestion that he might be struggling with his right-handed cue action because subconsciously he made a connection with the right-handed stabbing action with which his father, Ronnie Senior, killed the man in the pub brawl. 'I was a little bit sceptical about that, but for that one thing I disagreed with, Mike Brearley told me a million things that were good for me. He helped me through that stage of my life.'[8]

In 2008 Brearley, having served as chairman of its External Relations Co-Ordinating Committee, was elected president of the British Psychoanalytical Society, the umbrella body responsible for the teaching, development and practice of psychoanalysis. The honour was well merited since not only had he written a number of papers on a range of topics, he'd also been a frequent lecturer at the Institute of Psychoanalysis and helped arrange the European Psychoanalytical Film Festival.

With psychoanalysis considered expensive, elitist and unverified in its effectiveness, governments had increasingly been directing hard-pressed resources into short-term psychiatric treatments such as cognitive behavioural therapy, developed in the 1960s by the American psychiatrist Aaron T. Beck. As president, Brearley tried to win funding for psychoanalysis by explaining how much it had to offer to a world that too readily yearned for quick solutions. 'But as a source of research it's always been extremely important, in terms of understanding the mind … It's also had a great influence on group therapy, on education, in certain fringes on the arts.'[9]

At a time when society was becoming more aware of mental disorders, Brearley wasn't sure whether it was becoming more prevalent, but he did think that the cuts in intensive child psychotherapy were particularly shocking.

In 2010 the Camden Psychotherapy Unit, which had provided expert therapy at a hugely discounted rate for 40 years, was stripped of all its NHS funding as part of widespread cuts to the local council's mental health service. As a former practitioner there and one of its patrons, Brearley was well aware of the treatment it provided to those who otherwise wouldn't have the opportunity. Consequently, he helped organise a fundraising match for the unit on the nursery ground at Lord's in May 2013, captaining a team of former players against David English's Celebrity Team. Through vigorous fundraising, it has managed to keep open but with £140,000 needed each year, its future remains shrouded in uncertainty.

In addition to his work as a psychoanalyst, Brearley has permitted himself the occasional outing on the public stage, revelling in several different roles: occasional obituary writer for *The Guardian* and *The Independent*, motivational speaker on leadership and teamwork and broadcaster. In 2005 he made his radio debut with *The Complete Conductor*, talking to maestros such as Mark Elder, Harrison Birtwistle and Charles Mackerras to uncover the secrets of great conducting. His tact and sensitivity impressed as he asked the right questions and managed to get into the minds of the interviewees.

He followed this up in 2007 with *The Art of Directing*, a two-part evaluation of what makes a great director with leading figures from the theatre such as Peter Hall; then, in 2009, he introduced *The Tiger Takes Guard,* an examination of the vibrant relationship between India's emergence as an economic power and its love of cricket. That same year he delivered a talk entitled *Narcissism and Leadership* at the Free-Thinking Festival at the Sage Gateshead, later broadcast on Radio 3. The journalist and broadcaster Miranda Sawyer, anticipating some telling insights on leadership, felt deflated. 'His droning tones, his obvious points, his reasonable points, reasonably expressed, recalled a particularly sober parish priest ... Brearley seemed to be advocating a world in which everyone is modest, motivated by honesty, integrity, decency and the common good. Bye, bye Berlusconi, hello, well, Brearley. How worthy. How dull.'[10]

He has occasionally entered the political domain. Although too much of a free thinker to consider himself a typical north London *Guardian*-reading liberal, his sympathies, nevertheless, remain with the underdog. 'He is left-wing in a good and productive way,' according to John Barclay who admires his humanitarian outlook.[11] Along with several psychoanalysts, Brearley wrote to the *Independent on Sunday* in 2003 criticising the Allied invasion of Iraq, not least the manner in which it was implemented. In 2015 he signed an open letter to *The Guardian* calling on President Barack Obama to return Shaker Aamer, the last British captive at Guantanamo Bay, the American concentration camp in Cuba. He was released soon afterwards. In the 10 October 2018 edition of the *New Statesman,* he dissected the state of the Labour Party in its diary. Having accepted the basic tenets of leader Jeremy Corbyn's inner circle that they lived in an unfair society and the need to do away with zero-hours working and give workers a stake in their company he wrote:

> And yet – and yet – will the figures work out? Will the left decline into dictatorship brooking no variability? ... Should

we pull back from moves towards a more just society because we are apprehensive about the market's response to such policies?[12]

He has been a keen supporter of several charities, most notably the Schools Partnership Worldwide, an educational charity active in the developing world, and the MCC Foundation Scheme and the Lord's Taverners, both of which provide cricketing opportunities to the disadvantaged. In September 2009, in memory of the esteemed dramatist and ardent cricket lover Harold Pinter who'd died months earlier, he captained a Taverners' XI against the Gaieties, the wandering team with which Pinter was closely associated. Later that evening, when friends and colleagues gathered in the Long Room at Lord's to celebrate his life, Brearley and Gatting acted out a scene from *The Caretaker*. It was, Brearley later wrote, one of his greatest pleasures.

Chapter 21
Reform in Order to Preserve

DESPITE repeated attempts to entice Brearley back into English cricket, his work precluded him from accepting till 2006 when he joined the newly formed World Cricket Committee. (Middlesex remain rather aggrieved that, despite numerous entreaties, he has yet to serve the county in any capacity since his retirement, claiming rather bizarrely that he didn't like committees.) Once back, he enjoyed the renewed camaraderie with past and present players and the opportunity to give something back to the game he loved. In committee he didn't speak that much but when he did everyone listened, especially given his ability to offer a fresh perspective. Although not always right, his views carried weight, especially on the big issues. As chairman of the World Cricket Committee between 2011 and 2017, he sometimes opened up deliberations himself, before allowing everyone to have their say.

In 2007 he was invited by his friend Doug Insole to succeed him as president of MCC, an annual appointment with largely ceremonial responsibilities. While no admirer of MCC in his playing days, age had mellowed him, especially since the club has shed much of its fustiness to become more outward-looking, symbolised by the appointment of the Australian Keith Bradshaw as secretary and chief executive in 2006. Pleased to be asked by Insole and encouraged to accept by his wife Mana, who thought he'd enjoy it, Brearley gladly consented.

Acknowledging there were limits to what any president could achieve in one year, Brearley aimed to broaden the social composition of the crowd by reserving some cheap tickets for those on low income. With Lord's becoming ever more the preserve of the middle classes, given the exorbitant cost of tickets there, especially for Test matches, his idea merited serious consideration. Unfortunately, the practicalities of implementing it proved too taxing, although he did manage to introduce cheap seats for children of parents attending.

He also wanted to relax the dress code for MCC members in the pavilion. 'I don't like ties. I've never quite seen the point of them. I don't like something tied around my neck, so why wear one when it's hot? Especially with a jacket. I think, too, that it's socially unnecessary today, whereas perhaps 30 years ago smart dress was much more expected in certain places and certain classes of society.'[1] His sartorial tastes, slightly more conventional as the years went by, nevertheless reflected his modest, informal lifestyle. At the 2007 annual MCC dinner he was spotted waiting for a bus outside Lord's to take him home while the other top-table guests departed by limo.

Weeks into his presidency, he, along with Bradshaw, travelled to Sri Lanka to represent MCC at two of England's three Tests there and to open two recovery projects they had helped fund following the devastation wrought by the tsunami there in 2004: the MCC Centre of Excellence in Seenigama providing greater opportunities for their young people and a new cricket ground at Sri Sumangala College, a state school for some 1,600 pupils.

Brearley established a firm rapport with Bradshaw, a fellow moderniser, who later wrote: 'Mike is a very deep thinker, gentle natured, terrific to talk to about any issue. He is a psychoanalyst and there were times when I felt as if I might have been on the couch assessed but he was a fine president and an elegant speaker.' He did, however, resist Brearley's attempt to dispense with the wearing of compulsory jackets and ties in the pavilion, believing that if MCC permitted informal dress, formality would never be restored. 'Anyway, I felt this tradition was wanted and respected by members.'[2]

They also clashed over Bradshaw's co-authorship of an ECB document on a proposed nine-team city-based franchise, an English model of the Indian Premier League (IPL), leaked to the press, a plan that upset many of the smaller counties, especially those that didn't have grounds in the bigger cities. Through his column in *The Observer*, Brearley moved to distance MCC from the initiative. He defended Bradshaw's right as an independent director of the ECB to express his opinion but gently rebuked him for failing to consult his employers. 'Any proposal coming from him is liable to be seen as an MCC initiative, and, as such, to have been discussed there, so it has no backing, as things stand out, from the MCC. It might of course agree with and support the views expressed in the plan, but so far there has not been the chance either to do so or to disagree.'[3]

The plan was rejected by the ECB and the following year Bradshaw resigned from its board of directors, citing a potential conflict of interest.

Brearley wasn't against this new cricketing phenomenon. During his year as president, he acknowledged the growing appeal of Twenty20 and remarked how imperative it was that England's cricket bosses came to a mutually beneficial deal with the IPL.

At the AGM of MCC in May 2008, he nominated his former England team-mate Derek Underwood as his successor. When Underwood asked why him, he replied, 'Because I like you.' The following year Brearley was appointed one of the three club trustees, their responsibility being to guide the main committee on such matters as sale of assets, the appointment of senior staff and assessing the performance of committee chairmen. It was during his three-year stint that he became embroiled in a bitter internal dispute about the redevelopment of Lord's.

The saga began back in 1999 when Railtrack, the short-lived company which controlled Britain's railway infrastructure, decided to sell off two disused tunnels beneath Lord's at the Nursery End and invited MCC to make an offer for the main lease. The club, failing to see the commercial potential of the land and concerned about the cost, declined and the right to develop them passed to a firm of property developers, the Rifkind Levy Partnership, at auction.

On Bradshaw's initiative, MCC decided in May 2007 on a £400m overhaul of Lord's over the next decade funded by the construction of luxury flats at the Nursery End of the ground. A development sub-committee was set up under the leading planning silk Robert Griffiths comprising the former prime minister John Major, Lord Grabiner QC and Michael Atherton among its membership. They entered into a partnership with Almacantar property developers, who pledged a £100m windfall for the refurbishment of five stands in return for the lease to build luxury flats on the land. While the plan had the unanimous backing of the development sub-committee, it ran into trouble with the MCC chairman Oliver Stocken and the treasurer Justin Dowley. With recession beginning to bite after the 2008 bank crash and declining ticket sales for Test matches, they decided that the cost of expansion was too prohibitive.

Frustrated by the dragging of feet, Griffiths sent an email to Stocken in January 2011 telling him to approve the plan. Stocken, in turn, asked MCC president Christopher Martin-Jenkins to intervene, warning that unless the development sub-committee was disbanded, he and Dowley would resign. Martin-Jenkins, himself sceptical about the vision, spoke to Brearley and his fellow trustees, the award-winning lyricist Tim Rice and Anthony Wreford. They consulted widely and concluded that Stocken and Dowley should be supported. Armed with their backing, Martin-Jenkins presided over an acrimonious meeting of the full committee in mid-February, which disbanded Griffiths's sub-committee. 'Robert, I'm sorry,' Martin-Jenkins said to him afterwards, 'we couldn't afford to lose the treasurer and chairman in one go.'

'I think this is unfair,' Griffiths told Brearley. 'I think it perfectly fair,' Brearley replied.

A new working party was established under Dowley, all of whom were opposed to full redevelopment, and that November the full committee voted 18-2 to abandon the vision. Their decision prompted the resignation of Major, disillusioned at the way the club was being run.

Aggrieved by the termination of his blueprint for Lord's, in which he'd invested so much time and effort, and his ousting from the main committee, Griffiths cast a critical eye over opponents who deemed him to be too grandiose. The trustees, he thought, hadn't acted fairly and Brearley, by not engaging fully with the vision, had failed to see the practical benefits accruing to MCC, whereas Brearley for his part thought Griffiths hadn't listened to criticisms of his vision.

Brearley's pro-establishment line surprised the former editor of *Wisden*, Matthew Engel, who was strongly critical of MCC over redevelopment, when he conveyed his reservations to him.

In 2013 MCC opted for a scaled-down redevelopment plan to increase capacity by replacing five of the seven stands, to be funded out of its own resources. At the same time the appointment of Gerald Corbett, the former chairman of Railtrack, as successor to Stocken in 2015 led to a deal with the Rifkind Levy Partnership. The club agreed to consider its revised smaller-scale plan based on the construction of two luxury residential blocks at the Nursery End in return for a cash injection of over £100m.

After a lengthy consultation exercise with the membership, the committee recommended in July 2017 that it proceed with its masterplan rather than accept the offer from the Rifkind Levy Partnership.

Confronted with opposition from the likes of David Gower who thought the Rifkind Levy Partnership plan would safeguard the future of Lord's, MCC took no chances before the final decision was made at a special general meeting that September. They sent out a promotional video featuring contributions from Brearley, Gatting and the president Matthew Fleming extolling the benefits of the masterplan, a view which was overwhelmingly endorsed at the special general meeting.

The MCC World Cricket Committee was founded in 2006, on the initiative of Tony Lewis, to place Lord's at the centre of cricket thinking on the global game and to make recommendations to improve it. Although lacking any formal power, its composition of cricket luminaries such as Brearley, Gatting and Barry Richards, and, later, Rodney Marsh, Steve Waugh and Rahul Dravid, gave it a growing influence with the ICC.

The committee's first decade coincided with the startling rise of Twenty20 and the corresponding decline of Test cricket, especially in countries such as South Africa, Pakistan and the West Indies. While Brearley saw the attractions of the former, he continued to view the latter as the pinnacle of the game, and with his colleagues, made every effort to protect it. Top of their agenda was the novel concept of day-night Tests as a means of stimulating interest. MCC started experimenting with a coloured ball that would stand up to the rigours of day-night cricket and by 2011 they had done enough for the ICC to permit member nations to play day-night Tests. Despite player scepticism with the pink ball, the Australian and New Zealand boards committed themselves to a day-night Test on New Zealand's 2015/16 tour to Australia. The historic match took place at Adelaide, its novelty value attracting a crowd three times larger than normal, and Brearley was there to observe it. He thought that the pink ball had held up well, and while he appreciated that not every venue was conducive to day-night Tests he hoped that it would take off elsewhere, especially on the subcontinent.

Another proposal to boost the five-day game was a World Test Championship, to be held in England in 2013, to rival the 50-over World Cup and the World Twenty20 Championship, but this had to be shelved because of a lack of interest by sponsors and broadcasters. A further attempt to hold the tournament in England in 2017 failed again for the same reasons, leaving Brearley disappointed. Not having the World Test Championship would likely diminish Test cricket, he declared. He now looked forward to a play-off between the top-two ranked sides at the end of each four-year period, the next best option, since it would give context to Test cricket and each particular Test.

Test cricket's decline in countries such as the West Indies, Pakistan and Sri Lanka was linked to the lack of finance in these poorer parts of the world. In 2014 an ICC working party, under pressure from the powerful BCCI who thought their great commercial pull in international cricket entitled them to a greater pay-out, ceded more of their revenue to the three most powerful boards, with the BCCI receiving the lion's share.

The deal disillusioned the other boards and outraged Brearley, who wrote:

> My first reaction was shock – how could these three countries set up as a triad, to rule the world and take most of the cash. How can such a proposal represent fair play, or the spirit of cricket?[4]

He accused England and Australia of pusillanimity in not standing up to India and failing to protect the wider interests of the game. Overall earnings could well be less, he warned, if competition was diminished. It needed the election of the enlightened president of the BCCI, Shashank Manohar, as ICC chairman in 2015 to bring about change. Unhappy about the imbalance of power within the ICC and committed to a more egalitarian global structure, he instigated a review of the 2014 amendments to the ICC, and in April 2017 the BCCI was forced to accept a huge reduction in ICC revenue from $570m to $290m. Even this new arrangement still favoured the richer nations over the poorer ones and Brearley, at his last World Cricket Committee in 2017, requested a more equitable distribution. 'We are asking people to have a bit of a change of heart. We can't see how you can have long-term security for international cricket unless something along these lines happens.'

In 2013 the World Cricket Committee supported a proposal to include Twenty20 cricket at the Olympics to enhance its global appeal. The proposal was opposed by the ECB and BCCI because it would damage their broadcasting arrangements, but, in 2015, the former began to have second thoughts. When asked whether the ECB's new position would put chairman Colin Graves and chief executive Tom Harrison on a collision course with president Giles Clarke, an opponent of cricket at the Olympics, Brearley said: 'The president of the ECB is an employee of the board and has to do what he is told.' Later, in a statement issued by MCC, he sought to clarify his comments. 'I have apologised to Giles Clarke. What I should have said was that if the ECB changes its policy regarding cricket in the Olympics, then of course it would be Giles's job to present that policy to the ICC. Giles is not an employee of the ECB and I didn't intend to imply that he was.'

With the BCCI not for turning, the World Cricket Committee continued to press for a united front in applying to the host city in 2024 to include cricket.

The rise of Twenty20, for all its popularity, encouraged a burgeoning betting industry, especially on the subcontinent where huge crowds and mass television audiences generated vast amounts of revenue. Match-fixing there had brought about the ignominious downfall of South Africa's revered captain, Hansie Cronje, in 2000, and the failure of the ICC to clear out the Augean stables had left the game vulnerable to further corruption. This was particularly the case with the franchise teams in the IPL, which fell outside the jurisdiction of the ICC.

In June 2009 Brearley was part of a five-man Pakistan taskforce formed by the ICC in the wake of the terrorist attack on the Sri Lanka team bus in Lahore earlier that year. With Pakistan now deemed unsafe to host international tours – the ICC had removed it as a co-host of the 2011 World Cup – the remit of the taskforce under the chairmanship of Giles Clarke was to help bring it back into the fold.

After a constructive meeting in Dubai that December, relations began to fray the following summer when Pakistan became embroiled in a major spot-fixing scandal in the final Test against England at Lord's. Following the revelations in the *News of the World*, three of their players, the captain Salman Butt, Mohammad Asif and Mohammad Amir, were later found guilty of conspiracy to cheat and conspiracy to accept payments. They were imprisoned and were given lengthy bans by the ICC.

Unhappy with the Pakistan board's response to the crisis, the ICC taskforce broadened its remit to conduct a full-scale review of the game there. Its report, published in July 2011, called for a complete overhaul of the board's governance, in particular the power of the nation's president to appoint its chairman and members, a directive which upset them. They protested that they needed government support because of the unstable security situation there and criticised Brearley and Greg Chappell's failure to visit Pakistan in their roles as ambassadors for its cricket. Days later the board had second thoughts and indicated its intention to abide by ICC proposals to rid its cricket of political interference.

It was against this background that the World Cricket Committee asked Steve Waugh in December 2010 to lead a working party to investigate ways of removing corruption from the game. On becoming chairman in 2011, Brearley declared that corruption was the single biggest threat to cricket. He recognised that the pressure placed on players by criminal bodies and team-mates could be immense, but added that whistleblowing should become an absolute priority for everyone if corruption was to be eradicated. On his initiative, Ronnie Flanagan of the Anti-Corruption Unit (ACU) was invited to address the World Cricket Committee at Cape Town by video link the following January. He explained how corrupt gamblers and bookmakers operated, prior to the committee releasing a ten-point programme recommending undercover reporting to identify corrupt cricketers, the abolition of minimum penalties for offenders, and ACU transparency in its findings to show that its efforts to eliminate corruption were working.

The following year the committee praised the ACU for its educative and preventative work which had made inroads at international level, but warned that the problem had shifted to domestic and franchise cricket.

Following a trial the previous year, the Decision Review System (DRS), which allows batsmen and the fielding side to review contentious decisions, was introduced to Test cricket in 2009, except in games involving India because its board doubted the accuracy of the technology. At their Cape Town meeting which urged uniformity, Brearley declared that the powerful BCCI was getting away with its exemption by flexing its muscles. He accepted that DRS and its implementation weren't perfect, but it had improved both the standard of umpiring and behaviour and reduced the number of matches decided by human error.

As India continued to hold out against the flow, Brearley accused the ICC of lacking teeth. 'That the ICC allow India to veto the use of DRS in all their international matches is a symbol of what is wrong with international cricket. One country can make its own arrangements and act in the face of international opinion.'

He again berated the ICC for its submissiveness to the BCCI in his Pataudi Memorial Lecture at Calcutta in March 2016. DRS was an irresistible force despite resistance. Like Canute's waves, it couldn't be held back.

While international pressure undoubtedly helped, what ultimately shifted Indian opinion was their dissatisfaction with the umpiring in their 2014/15 series against Australia and their following one against Sri Lanka. Helped by their coach Anil Kumble's membership of the World Cricket Committee, India agreed to a trial run of DRS in their 2016/17 series against England and thereafter accepted it.

For some time MCC had been concerned that the balance between bat and ball had tilted towards the former – especially in the one-day game, given the growing number of sixes – mainly due to bat sizes getting bigger and bigger. The World

Cricket Committee was invited in 2013 to investigate bat sizes and after three years of research they agreed with the ICC that MCC should strongly consider amending the laws to restrict the width of bats to a maximum of 40mm and depth to a maximum of 67mm.

After presiding over his final committee meeting at Lord's in July 2017, Brearley once again expressed concern about the future of Test cricket. The absence of A.B. de Villiers from South Africa's Test side to play England that summer, having played in the one-day matches, spelt danger for the longer format of the game.

> The game is facing – if not a crisis – a looming potential crisis. This crisis needs to be noticed and taken seriously. For international cricket to flourish, competitive levels need to be close and teams need to be able to field their best players.
>
> The committee is worried that with the spread of privately owned Twenty20 leagues and the rapid increase in remuneration, more players from counties lacking the funds to pay them will choose these tournaments ahead of making themselves available for their countries.

It was up to the ICC to get Test cricket by the scruff of the neck and put heart and soul into promoting and marketing it, like it did with Twenty20.

In 2016, a University of Portsmouth survey of 763 umpires revealed that half of them had been subjected to verbal abuse and a minority to physical confrontation, mainly at recreational level. It made for disturbing reading. Conscious that a number of umpires were giving up because of this, Brearley said they needed to be empowered to impose on-the-spot sanctions. Weeks later the World Cricket Committee recommended that umpires be given the power to dismiss any player who threatened them or who engaged in physical assault, a recommendation MCC wrote into law – applicable from 1 October 2017.

According to John Stephenson, MCC's head of cricket, the club was rightfully proud of the World Cricket Committee under Brearley's leadership, and to his successor, Gatting, his contribution has been magnificent. While the future of Test cricket remains unclear, his committee's reforms have helped make it a better, more attractive game and one that should be fully supported at all costs.

Brearley's decision to stand for the MCC committee in 2018, warmly endorsed by the membership, signalled his continued commitment to the game. He found the England-India series that summer to be one of the most absorbing he'd watched for a long time and enjoyed the chance to meet the England captain Joe Root, to whom he was favourably disposed. As he has grown older, he has become more particular about the type of cricket he likes to watch, his ideal being close encounters featuring the top players in conditions which slightly favour the bowlers, but still derives great pleasure from learning about the game.

With his intellectual and sporting pedigree, he remains a much sought-after speaker. He gave the keynote speech at the C.L.R. James *Beyond a Boundary* 50th anniversary conference at Glasgow University in May 2013 and later that year he delivered the 11th Bradman Oration in Melbourne, while in 2016 he gave the Pataudi Lecture, set up to honour the former Indian captain, in Calcutta.

He has also stayed close to his roots. An Honorary Fellow of St John's, Cambridge, since 1998, he was president of the Johnian Society, incorporating the college alumni, in 2011, the year the college celebrated its 500th anniversary. Invited to address the final-year students, his talk was described by the Master as rather impenetrable.

In 2016 he spoke on 'Captaincy and Cricket' at CLS in aid of its bursary scheme; and in April 2018, having spoken at its centenary dinner in 2008, he returned to Brentham to open the newly refurbished pavilion.

He is also a popular fixture on the literary festival circuit, not least at Hay, close to his weekend retreat in the Usk Valley that he shares with his Cambridge friend Sir Michael Scholar. A talk he gave at the London School of Economics entitled, 'In the Zone: Spontaneity and Mental Discipline in Sport and Beyond', proved the inspiration for his book *On Form*, published by Little, Brown in 2017. In it he draws on his experiences as a philosopher, cricketer and psychoanalyst to consider the elusive nature of good form across a wide range of disciplines from drama to music and writing to tree-felling. It is an erudite book packed with literary quotes and classical allusions, and it won *The Times*, the *Daily Telegraph* and The William Hill Sports Book of the Year 2017, but its heavy academic tone made it a less rewarding read than *The Art of Captaincy*.

In 2018 he followed up with *On Cricket*, a collection of wide-ranging essays much of them taken from his previous articles and talks, some of which he has updated. With his broad historical perspective, his experiences as England captain and his general intuition, he writes with unrivalled authority about the game. 'It is Brears in mid-summer form, and makes up for the slight disappointment of *On Form* published last year,' wrote Michael Henderson in *The Cricketer*.[5] He reflects on the general influences of his youth, especially his father; he paints illuminating portraits of some of his contemporaries such as Viv Richards, Bishan Bedi, Alan Knott, Dennis Lillee and Tom Cartwright, and discusses current controversies such as match-fixing and corruption.

At the heart of the book is a lengthy evaluation on race and cricket featuring the D'Oliveira affair and the legacy of the Trinidadian writer and polemicist C.L.R. James.

In a tribute to the playwright Harold Pinter, he writes in elegiac tones when contemplating the brevity of life, in what his fellow philosopher Edward Craig calls 'Mike Brearley in a short paragraph: a willingness to stare the facts in the eye, while making your life good.'[6]

Moved by the American evangelist Billy Graham's conviction of his ultimate place in heaven when watching him on television as a 12-year-old, he felt uneasy about his father's agnosticism and he has spent his life in search of something tangible. Yet despite a detailed knowledge of the Bible and inspired by much of Christian morality, a personal faith continues to elude him. In his book *On Form*, he recounted how his grandson Luka a few years back remarked one day that he sometimes thought there was a God, sometimes not. 'I said: That's a good position, not unlike my own,'[7] a position which appears somewhat at variance with his most recent pronouncement in *On Cricket*. He wrote:

> We are confronted in life by the reality that we are specks of dust in the vast aeons of space and time; that when we die we go[I believe] into nothingness; that our importance in the long run is nil; that we live always on the brink of 'death's dateless night'. But we believe that at the same time, or in the same breadth, there are things[if one is lucky] that make life fascinating and worth living.[8]

Brearley with his many interests and accomplishments has certainly led a life that has been both fascinating and worthwhile, and in time he may even find that the future isn't quite as bleak as he now depicts it.

Mike Brearley

THE eminent historian Kenneth O. Morgan writing about Britain's greatest 20th-century peacetime prime minister Clement Attlee asserted that he was a modest man with plenty to be immodest about, and the same could be said about Mike Brearley. That he stood apart from the crowd because of his formidable intellect, multitude of interests and independent views goes without saying. No friend of the establishment, he used his probing mind to question many of the assumptions then governing cricket and come up with some fresh thinking: that sporting links with white South Africa were wrong, that county professionals should be properly rewarded and that protective helmets were a blessing not a curse. When the great schism over WSC broke out, Brearley's broad-mindedness manifested itself in his desire to compromise between the warring factions, a stance vindicated by the ultimate settlement between the cricket establishment and WSC of May 1979. Although disliked by Australian crowds the following winter when he felt compelled to oppose certain innovations imposed on his team at the eleventh hour, he has remained open to change, especially his enthusiasm for Twenty20, while continuing to defend the primacy of Test cricket.

Less obvious but no less significant was his steely personality and fierce competitiveness. In *The Art of Captaincy*, looking back over his career, he was 'surprised at how much he wanted to win', a mentality which led him to occasionally flout the game's hallowed traditions in pursuit of the numerous trophies which came his way.

Operating in an era when captains had supreme control before the introduction of team managers and coaches, Brearley, while frequently consulting his players, was indisputably in charge. A supreme tactician, he looked to shape a game by audacious declarations and imaginative bowling and fielding changes, constantly doing what the opposition least wanted him to do. Not every ploy worked, but his ability to turn defeat into victory, allied to the concern he displayed towards his players, won him their backing, even when his lack of runs made him a liability in the England line-up.

When he retired from first-class cricket in 1982, he left with his head held high and since then his reputation has continued to soar, helped by his highly acclaimed *The Art of Captaincy*, so that his leadership has remained the benchmark by which all his successors have been judged. In a recent poll of readers of *The Cricketer*, Brearley was voted England's most successful captain of all time by a landslide, with Michael Vaughan a distant second. His record of 18 wins and four defeats from his 31 Tests in charge, including three Ashes triumphs, is a highly creditable one, and his 58.06 per cent success rate is exceeded only by W. G. Grace and Douglas Jardine among England captains who captained in more than ten Tests.

Facts of course don't tell the whole story. 'The statistics suggest that he is one of the great England captains,' wrote Illingworth, 'the luckiest would be nearer the truth,' a tart observation that contained an element of truth.[1] He was certainly fortunate to play for England in the first place and he happened to be in the right place when WSC deprived Greig of the England captaincy. 'Brearley had my team,' recalled Greig. 'An Ashes-winning victory was what we were working towards and it ended up on Brearley's CV rather than mine.'[2] 'I still don't overrate him as a captain or player,' opined Lillee ... 'He marshalled the great troops he had at his disposal very well, but if you have a player like Botham in your side, you are halfway there.'[3] While Australians with their egalitarian principles have rarely subscribed to British concepts of leadership, Lillee had a point. Brearley's captaincy of England coincided with Botham's halcyon years when he was often the difference between victory and defeat.

Furthermore, Brearley never captained against the West Indies, the one side that reduced Botham to relative insignificance, and many of his 18 victories were gained against depleted sides in the Packer era. It is the opinion of Scyld Berry that had he retired after England's 3-0 drubbing by Australia in 1979/80, he would have been remembered as no more than a goodish England captain. His mythical status rests on the extraordinary events of the summer of 1981 when he returned to the front line to beat Australia 3-1. The irony is that in both the Headingley and Edgbaston Tests, before their dramatic denouements, his presence had done little to rescue England from the mire of mediocrity. At Headingley it needed an innings of outrageous brilliance and good fortune by Botham, together with some inspired fast bowling by Willis, to make history, while at Edgbaston it was Botham who once again rode to the rescue with a barnstorming spell that battered the timid Australians into submission. 'I was the luckiest man that summer,' admitted Brearley. 'If I haven't dined out on it, I've become, for better or for worse, along with Botham, Willis and others, part of the mythology. It's not easy to sort out myth from reality.'[4]

Yet, while any captain is only as good as his team, Brearley in that 1981 series played a critical part in bringing out the best in Botham and Willis, both of whom had lost their lustre over the previous year. His advice, encouragement and support allowed them to play their natural game and his composed optimism enabled the rest of the side to believe in miracles when they might otherwise have given up the ghost. From the time of his accession in 1977 he was the past master at uniting a volatile group of individuals by treating them all differently. According to Boycott, Brearley's reputation for man-management was no myth. He had no hesitation in rating him the best captain he played under. It was a view shared by the vast majority of his England team-mates. Illingworth, it is true, had his supporters, but even Edmonds, for all his disagreements with Brearley, placed his leadership on the highest of pedestals. He wrote:

> There are so many things I admire, and like, about Brears. In purely cricketing terms, he is the best captain I have ever seen. The tremendous thing was the way in which we were always trying to achieve something positive in the field when Brears was in charge. Even when the situation warranted a defensive action, it was positive defence, with a constructive aim in mind. We were not meandering about aimlessly, as has happened with some England captains. [5]

A measure of his success can be gleaned by the record of his successors throughout the rest of the 1980s. Despite having Gower, Gooch, Gatting, Botham, Lamb, Emburey, Edmonds and Dilley at the core of their side, England won a further six Test series compared to the 12 they lost and 16 victories compared to 33 defeats. Throughout the decade, they managed to win just 19.2 per cent of their games, their worst return in any decade in

Test history bar the 1940s, an era when the England team had been debilitated by the effects of the Second World War.

Brearley's impact at Middlesex was even more profound. Inheriting a weak and divided team in 1971, he gradually welded a new one of talented individuals and by playing attacking cricket they presided over a golden era. Not only did he win four championships – one of which was shared with Kent – and two Gillette Cups, he bequeathed a winning culture to his successor, Gatting, giving Middlesex another decade of dominance.

Judging by the great potential he displayed at Cambridge in the early 1960s and his consistent run-scoring for Middlesex, his failure to repeat that consistency for England ranks as the great disappointment of his career. For while an overall record of 25,000 runs and 45 centuries at an average of 37.81, in addition to 417 catches, mainly at first slip, suggests a very good county player, his Test average of 22.89 from 39 Tests speaks for itself. Although a brave and determined player, he rarely looked comfortable at the crease and failed to dominate, as indicated by his record of 29.80 runs per 100 balls. 'Looking back, it is difficult to think of one Brearley innings which stands out in the memory,' wrote Willis. 'Whenever he survived the new ball and seemed to have got set, he would just get out for no apparent reason, usually in defensive mode.'[6]

Given his late flowering as a run scorer for Middlesex, it is tempting to speculate to what extent his near-five-year absence from the first-class game between 1965 and 1971 impeded his progress. It was Brearley's contention that he would have been a better batsman, since he didn't develop a reliable technique until he was well over 30, and he may well have been right. He also attributed his modest Test record to a niggling doubt that he wasn't fit to play in such company, but this may have simply reflected Boycott's crushing assessment that he lacked Test class.

The fact that the selectors and his fellow players continued to place their faith in him when he wasn't worth his place in the side, a situation which wouldn't be tolerated nowadays, says all the more about the quality of his captaincy.

It is rare for sportsmen to prosper in an entirely new environment once their playing days are over – Imran Khan is an obvious exception – but then Brearley was no ordinary sportsman. Putting his training and practical experience to good use, he carved out a distinguished career as a psychoanalyst, rising to become president of the British Psychoanalytical Society in 2008, the year he finished as president of MCC. Now detached from battles past and the driven personality that bristled at life's imperfections, he cuts a contented figure in his role as an elder statesman feted for his Delphic utterances in print, in motivational talks and in committee. Never one to blow his own trumpet, he remains, nonetheless, the archetypal British sporting hero, who overcame setbacks to triumph, not least during those glorious summer days of 1981, when he, Botham and co. proved that dreams really can come true.

Endnotes

Introduction

1 *Wisden Cricket Monthly*,
  November 1982, p28
2 *Wisden Cricketers' Almanack* 1983, p88
3 Geoff Boycott, *The Autobiography*, p260
4 *The Sun*, 30 May 1977
5 *Daily Telegraph*, 5 December 2012
6 *Wisden* 1983, p88
7 Trevor Bailey, *The Greatest Since
  My Time*, p217
8 *The Times*, 27 September 2011
9 Rob Steen, *David Gower: A Man Out
  of Time*, p135
10 David Gower, *Heroes and
  Contemporaries*, p34
11 *The Cricket Newspaper*, 18 April 2018
12 *Sunday Telegraph*, 30 December 2001
13 *Daily Telegraph*, 29 June 2009
14 *Sunday Times*, 7 October 2009
15 Simon Wilde, *Ian Botham: The Power and
  the Glory*, p127
16 Ian Botham, *The Autobiography*, p169

Chapter 1

1 *The Gazette*, Summer 2008, p1
2 *Wisden* 1977, p102
3 Mike Brearley, *On Cricket*, p8
4 *Middlesex County Times and West
  Middlesex Gazette*, 9 July 1955
5 *Brentham CC Centenary 1908–2008*, p16
6 *Sunday Times*, 2 July 1972
7 David Bloomfield to the author,
  12 October 2018
8 Paul Fussell, *The Anti-Egotist: Kingsley
  Amis, Man of Letters*, p25,
9 Mike Brearley, *The Art of Captaincy*, p7
10 *CLS Magazine*, July 1960, p81
11 Ibid. December 1956, p151
12 *Wisden* 1958, p765
13 *CLS Magazine*, December 1960, p47

14 Mike Brearley and Dudley Doust, *The
  Return of the Ashes*, p18
15 Colin Ranger to the author, 9 July 2018
16 *CLS Magazine*, March 1960, p32
17 Ibid. July 1960, p58
18 Ibid. December 1960, p114
19 *The Times*, 6 May 1960
20 *Daily Telegraph* [India], 18 January 2019
21 *CLS Magazine*, December 1960, p131
22 *Wisden* 1961, p743
23 *The Gazette*, October 1960, p40
24 Ibid. January 1965, p137

Chapter 2

1 Kenneth Clarke, *Kind of Blue*, p32
2 Malcolm Schofield to the author,
  9 August 2018
3 *Sunday Times*, 14 August 1977
4 Ibid
5 *Daily Telegraph*, 24 June 2003
6 *The Times*, 27 March 1962
7 *Varsity*, 13 June 1964
8 *The Cricketer*, 13 May 1961, p134
9 *Daily Telegraph*, 20 May 1961
10 Richie Benaud, *On Reflection*, p38
11 Richard Jefferson to the
  author, 30 May 2018
12 *The Times*, 17 July 1961
13 Brearley, *The Art of Captaincy*, p35
14 Michael Marshall, *Gentlemen and
  Players*, p249
15 Tony Lewis, *Playing Days: An
  Autobiography*, p66
16 *Daily Telegraph*, 12 July 1962
17 John Cuthbertson to the author, 23
  September 2018
18 Alan Knott, *It's Knott Cricket*, p13
19 *Daily Telegraph*, 10 July 1964
20 *The Times*, 10 July 1964
21 *The Cricketer*, 3 July 1964, p10

22 *Daily Mail*, 22 August 1964
23 *The Cricketer*, 28 August 1964, p9
24 *The Times*, 24 August 1964
25 *The Guardian*, 24 August 1964
26 *The Cricketer,* 11 September 1964, p7

Chapter 3
1 Stephen Chalke, *Tom Cartwright: The Flame Still Burns*, p111
2 *Daily Telegraph*, 2 November 1964
3 *Daily Mail*, 4 November 1964
4 Ibid. 11 November 1964
5 Donald Carr to Billy Griffith, 12 November 1964, MCC Archives
6 *The Times*, 1 December 1964
7 Mike Brearley, *On Form*, p19
8 ibid. p21
9 *The Gazette*, January 1965, p129
10 Chalke, *Tom Cartwright*, p113
11 *The Times*, 12 February 1965
12 *Wisden* 1966, p794
13 Brian Johnston, *It's Been a Piece of Cake*, p334
14 Captain's Report of the MCC 1964–65 tour to South Africa, MCC Archives
15 Mike Smith to the author, 27 May 2018
16 Donald Carr to A. P. F. Burton, 26 February 1965, MCC Archives
17 *The Cricket Monthly* from Cricinfo, 13 January 2019
18 Colin Shindler, *Bob Barber: The Professional Amateur*, p161
19 Chalke, *Tom Cartwright*, p112
20 Ibid. p114
21 Brearley, *On Form*, p1

Chapter 4
1 *Varsity*, 30 May 1964, p15
2 *The Cricketer*, July 1964, p17
3 *The Times*, 12 July 2001
4 *Evening Standard,* 16 June 1977
5 *Daily Mail*, 21 February 1967
6 Brearley, *On Form*, p137
7 *Wisden* 1967, p705
8 Derek Wing to the author, 31 May 2018
9 *The Times*, 2 February 1967
10 *Daily Mail*, 11 February 1967
11 *The Cricketer*, April 1967, p67
12 Knott, *It's Knott Cricket*, p26
13 *Playfair Cricket Monthly*, April 1967, p8
14 Pat Pocock to the author, 1 May 2018
15 Rob Kelly, *Hobbsy: A Life in Cricket*, p86
16 Derek Underwood, *Deadly Down Under*, p102
17 Mike Brearley to the author, 23 November 2018
18 *Sunday Times*, 16 November 1969
19 Christopher Sandford, *Keeper of Style John Murray: The King of Lord's*, p160

20 John Price to the author, 30 May 2018
21 John Emburey to the author, 23 October 2018
22 David Fulton, *The Captains' Tales*, p19
23 David Lemmon, *Changing Seasons: A History of Cricket in England, 1945–96*, p282
24 *Wisden Cricketer*, February 2008, p44
25 Brearley, On Form, p137
26 Mary Midgley, *The Owl of Minerva*, p203
27 *The Courier*, 16 May 1984

Chapter 5
1 John Stern, County Dynasties, www.wisden.com
2 Fred Titmus, *My Life in Cricket*, p184
3 Brearley, *The Art of Captaincy*, p42
4 *The Times*, 24 April 1971
5 Ibid. 5 May 1971
6 Brearley, *The Art of Captaincy*, p183
7 *Wisden* 1972, p499
8 *Playfair Cricket Monthly*, January 1972, p10
9 Stephen Chalke, *Summer's Crown: The Story of Cricket's Championship*, p252
10 The Cricket Monthly, Cricinfo
11 Sportstar Magazine, 24 March 2018
12 Titmus, *My Life in Cricket*, p209
13 *The Cricket Monthly,* Cricinfo, 13 January 2019
14 *The Times*, 17 July 1973
15 Ibid. 27 August 1973
16 John Murray to the author, 13 March 2018
17 *The Cricketer*, April 1973, p37
18 Ibid.
19 *The Guardian*, 25 November 1977
20 Brearley, *On Cricket*, p248
21 Brearley, *The Art of Captaincy*, p211
22 Manager's Report of MCC tour to East Africa 1974, MCC Archives
23 *The Cricketer*, March 1974, p7
24 Brearley, *The Art of Captaincy*, p74
25 *Wisden* 1976, p492

Chapter 6
1 John Emburey, *Emburey: An Autobiography*, p131
2 Brearley, *The Art of Captaincy*, p168
3 *The Cricketer*, Winter Annual, 1976, p8
4 *The Times*, 5 July 1976
5 Titmus, *My Life in Cricket*, p206
6 Brearley, *The Art of Captaincy*, p96
7 *The Cricketer*, November 1976, p17
8 *The Times*, 3 September 1976
9 *Wisden* 1977, p104
10 Sandford, *Keeper of Style*, p183
11 *The Times*, 8 September 1976
12 *Daily Mail*, 8 September 1976

ENDNOTES

Chapter 7
1 *The Times*, 27 March 2018
2 *The Times*, 6 January 2018
3 *Daily Mail*, 17 February 1977
4 Christopher Martin-Jenkins, *MCC in India 1976–77*, p147
5 *Cricket Quarterly*, Vol 3, No 3 1977, p32
6 *The Guardian*, 19 March 1977
7 *The Observer*, 21 November 2010

Chapter 8
1 *The Times*, 14 May 1977
2 *The Sun*, 19 May 1977
3 *Sunday Times*, 29 May 1977
4 *The Times*, 22 April 1977
5 *Daily Mail*, 24 April 1977
6 *The Guardian*, 7 June 1977
7 Brearley and Doust, *The Return of the Ashes*, p15
8 *The Times*, 16 August 1977
9 Christopher Martin-Jenkins, *The Jubilee Tests*, p174
10 Knott, *It's Knott Cricket*, p99

Chapter 9
1 *The Guardian*, 25 November 1977
2 Quoted in Mark Peel, *England Expects: A Biography of Ken Barrington*, p162
3 Bob Willis, *Six of the Best*, p162
4 Stephen Chalke, *In Sunshine and Shadow: Geoff Cope and Yorkshire Cricket*, p162
5 Bob Taylor, *Standing Up, Standing Back*, p135
6 Peel, England Expects, p164
7 Scyld Berry, *Cricket The Game of Life*, p342
8 Mike Gatting, *Leading from the Front*, p64
9 Brian Rose, *Rosey: My Life in Somerset Cricket*, p62
10 Simon Barnes, *Phil Edmonds: A Singular Man*, p66
11 Peter Roebuck, *It Sort of Clicks*, p13
12 Ibid. p14
13 Ibid. p15
14 Ibid. p38

Chapter 10
1 Leo McKinstry, *Geoff Boycott: A Cricketing Hero*, p118
2 Bob Willis, *Diary of a Cricket Season*, p32
3 Taylor, *Standing Up, Standing Back*, p139
4 *The Times*, 6 June 1978
5 *Daily Telegraph*, 6 June 1978
6 *Cricket Quarterly*, Vol 4, No 3, 1978
7 Willis, *Diary of a Cricket Season*, p108
8 *The Times*, 7 August 1978
9 Brearley, *The Art of Captaincy*, p74
10 *The Times*, 16 August 1978

11 Barnes, *Phil Edmonds: A Singular Man*, p79
12 Willis, *Diary of a Cricket Season*, p126
13 Boycott, *The Autobiography*, p255
14 Ibid. p256
15 Roebuck, *It Sort of Clicks*, p129
16 *Wisden* 1979, p77
17 *The Cricketer*, October 1978, p6

Chapter 11
1 *The Cricketer*, December 2018, p100
2 Brearley, *The Art of Captaincy*, p87
3 Roebuck, *It Sort of Clicks*, p85
4 Barnes, *Phil Edmonds: A Singular Man*, p73
5 *The Guardian*, 5 January 1979
6 Brearley, *The Art of Captaincy*, p31
7 David Gower and Bob Taylor, *Anyone for Cricket?* p85
8 Ibid. p87
9 *The Guardian*, 13 January 1979
10 Brearley and Doust, *The Ashes Retained*, p74
11 David Frith, *The Ashes 1979*, p193
12 *Wisden* 1980, p937
13 Bob Willis, *The Cricket Revolution*, p26
14 Peter McFarline, *A Testing Time*, p15

Chapter 12
1 Barnes, *Phil Edmonds: A Singular Man*, p75
2 Ibid, p75

Chapter 13
1 Brearley, *The Art of Captaincy*, Introduction to the thirtieth anniversary edition, xxvii
2 Tony Lewis, *Taking Fresh Guard*, p154
3 Brearley, *The Art of Captaincy*, xxviii
4 *The Guardian*, 14 August 1979
5 Brearley, *The Art of Captaincy*, p332
6 Graham Gooch, *On Captaincy*, p3
7 John Emburey to the author, 23 September 2018
8 Brearley, *On Form*, p22
9 Boycott, *The Autobiography*, p261
10 Brearley, *The Art of Captaincy*, p309

Chapter 14
1 *Wisden Cricket Monthly*, October 1979, p27
2 *The Times*, 19 May 1984
3 Ibid. 24 May 1984
4 Geoff Boycott, *Opening Up*, p121
5 Ibid. p123
6 Ibid. p145
7 *Daily Mail*, 18 December 1979
8 Brearley, *The Art of Captaincy*, p285
9 Underwood, *Deadly Down Under*, p77
10 Boycott, *The Autobiography*, p260
11 Underwood, *Deadly Down Under*, p103

12 Brearley, *The Art of Captaincy*, p274
13 Alec Bedser, *Twin Ambitions*, p131
14 *Wisden 1981*, p924
15 Mike Brearley, *Phoenix from the Ashes*, p37

Chapter 15
1 *The Guardian*, 2 July 2011
2 Pat Murphy, *Botham: A Biography*, p59
3 *Wisden Cricketer*, July 2008, p64
4 *Sunday Telegraph*, 11 May 1980
5 Gatting, *Leading from the Front*, p98
6 *Daily Mail*, 17 June 1980
7 Brian Brain, *Another Day, Another Match*, p71
8 John Barclay, *Lost in the Long Grass*, p153
9 *Sunday Times*, 22 June 2008
10 *Wisden* 1981, p491

Chapter 16
1 Brearley, *The Art of Captaincy*, p9
2 *Daily Telegraph*, 30 June 2015
3 *Sunday Times*, 15 June 2003
4 Simon Hughes, *And God Created Cricket*, p304
5 Roland Butcher, *Rising to the Challenge*, p48
6 *The Independent*, 11 November 2006
7 Brearley and Doust, *The Return of the Ashes*, p75
8 Johnston, *It's Been a Piece of Cake*, p332
9 *The Cricketer*, November 1982, p50
10 Simon Hughes, *A Lot of Hard Yakka*, p45
11 *The Independent*, 4 July 2015
12 Hughes, *A Lot of Hard Yakka*, p93
13 Barnes, *Phil Edmonds: A Singular Man*, p38
14 Ibid.
15 Frances Edmonds, *Another Bloody Day in Paradise*, p23
16 Titmus, *My Life in Cricket*, p208
17 Taylor, *Standing Up, Standing Back*, p134
18 Hughes, *A Lot of Hard Yakka*, p22
19 Barnes, *Phil Edmonds: A Singular Man*, p58
20 Brearley, *The Art of Captaincy*, p203
21 Barnes, *Phil Edmonds: A Singular Man*, p71
22 Ibid. p69
23 Ibid. p50
24 John Emburey, *Emburey*, p133
25 Simon Barnes, *A Book of Heroes*, p123
26 Ibid. p124
27 Graham Gooch, *My Autobiography*, p70
28 Taylor, *Standing Up, Standing Back*, p135
29 Graham Dilley, *Swings and Roundabouts*, p15
30 Murphy, *Botham: A Biography*, p85
31 Pat Murphy, *Declarations*, p169
32 Robin Jackman, *Jackers: A Life in Cricket*, p144
33 David Gower, *The Autobiography*, p88

34 Taylor, *Standing Up, Standing Back*, p134
35 Brearley and Doust, *The Ashes Retained*, p48
36 Boycott, *The Autobiography*, p259
37 Brearley, *Phoenix from the Ashes*, p5
38 John Lever, *The Cricketer's Cricketer*, p66
39 Ian Botham, *The Autobiography*, p92
40 Emburey, *Emburey*, p140
41 *The Times*, 4 November 2017
42 Murphy, *Botham: A Biography*, p85
43 Wilde, *Ian Botham: The Power and the Glory*, p184
44 Brearley, *Phoenix from the Ashes*, xiii
45 Murphy, *Botham: A Biography*, p84

Chapter 17
1 Jack Simmons, *Flat Jack*, p171
2 John Rae, *The Old Boys' Network: A Headmaster's Diaries 1970–86*, p145
3 John Rae, *Delusions of Grandeur*, p83
4 *The Times*, 5 June 1981
5 Graham Gooch, *My Cricket Diary*, p113
6 Ibid. p122
7 Benaud, *On Reflection*, p41
8 Brearley, *On Form, p97*
9 Gooch, *Captaincy*, p7
10 Taylor, *Standing Up, Standing Back*, p94
11 *The Independent*, 4 July 2009
12 Ian Botham, *The Incredible Tests*, p97
13 Benaud, *On Reflection*, p42

Chapter 18
1 Brearley, *Phoenix from the Ashes*, p178
2 *The Times*, 13 May 1982
3 Ibid. 15 June 1982
4 Hughes, *A Lot of Hard Yakka*, p93
5 Ibid. 15 September 1982
6 *Wisden 1983*, p87

Chapter 19
1 Hughes, *A Lot of Hard Yakka*, p108
2 David Rayvern Allen, *Arlott: The Authorised Biography*, p314
3 *Daily Telegraph*, 7 June 1985
4 *The Scotsman*, 7 May 1997
5 Mihir Bose to the author, 24 September 2018
6 *Sunday Times*, 8 September 1985
7 *The Observer*, 9 July 1995
8 *Daily Telegraph*, 10 July 1995
9 Ibid. 13 December 1987
10 Ibid. 12 June 1988
11 Ibid. 27 August 1989
12 *The Observer*, 9 August 1992
13 Ibid. 25 July 1993
14 Ibid. 31 July 1994
15 Quoted in *Daily Mirror*, 25 January 2000
16 Ibid. 25 January 2002

ENDNOTES

17 *The Observer*, 3 August 2003
18 *The Cricketer*, October 2012, p38
19 Simon Barnes to the author, 31 May 2018
20 *The Times*, 9 December 2014

Chapter 20
1 *The Sun*, 16 July 1981
2 Ibid.
3 Ibid.
4 *Wisden Cricketer*, February 2008, p40
5 Brearley, *On Form*, p25
6 Ibid. p27
7 *Wisden Cricketer*, February 2008, p44
8 *The Independent*, 19 April 2003
9 *Prospect Magazine*, 4 July 2009
10 *The Observer*, 29 November 2009
11 John Barclay to the author, 1 June 2018
12 *New Statesman*, 10 October 2018

Chapter 21
1 Keith Bradshaw, *Memoirs*,[unpublished]
2 *Wisden Cricketer*, February 2008, p42
3 *The Observer*, 13 July 2008
4 *The Times*, 8 February 2014
5 *The Cricketer*, October 2018, p29
6 Edward Craig to the author, 9
   November 2018
7 Brearley, *On Form*, p361
8 Brearley, *On Cricket*, p294

Mike Brearley
1 Ray Illingworth, *On Captaincy*, p194
2 *The Australian,* 31 December 2012
3 Dennis Lillee, *Autobiography*, p256
4 *The Guardian*, 2 July 2011
5 Barnes, *Phil Edmonds: A Singular Man*, p79
6 Willis, *Six of the Best*, p20

Acknowledgements

This isn't an authorised biography but I'm grateful to Mike Brearley for all his help in answering a number of questions.

I'd like to thank the following who helped me with my research: John Barclay, Julian Barnes, Simon Barnes, Michael Bavidge, Scyld Berry, David Bloomfield, Mihir Bose, Professor Edward Craig, John Cuthbertson, Paul Downton, Mike Edwards, John Emburey, Matthew Engel, Barrie Fairall, Keith Fletcher, David Frith, Mike Gatting, David Gower, Mike Griffith, Robert Griffiths QC, David Hargreaves, Terry Heard, Robin Hobbs, Simon Hughes, Kevan James, Richard Jefferson, Martin Johnson, Tristran Jones-Parry, Lionel Knight, Peter Levene, Barrie Lloyd, John McGeorge, Vic Marks, John Murray, Peter Parfitt, Stuart Perrin, Judge Nigel Peters, Pat Pocock, John Price, Clive Radley, Daphne Rae, Derek Randall, Colin Ranger, Charles Robins, Anthony Rudolf, Professor Malcolm Schofield, Mike Selvey, Professor Michael Silk, Mike Smith, Richard Stokes, Ivo Tennant, Ian Todd, Dale Vargas, Brian Waters, Bob Willis, Derek Wing, John Woodcock.

I owe a special debt to the Curator of Collections at Lord's and MCC, Neil Robinson, for all his help and for permission to quote from the MCC Archives, and to the Archive and Library Manager at Lord's, Robert Curphey, for all his genial cooperation on my many visits there; also to Katherine Harrison, the chairman of the Spen Valley Historical Society, for providing me with invaluable information about the Brearleys of Yorkshire, and to Mark Saggers and Alan Henderson for enlightening me about Brentham Garden Suburb and the Brentham Club.

I'd like to express my gratitude to the following archivists and librarians for all their help: Fiona Colbert at St John's College, Cambridge, Sally Kent at Cambridge University Archives, Saven Morris at the Institute of Psychoanalysis, Ingrid Smits at Camden Local Studies and Archives Centre, Katherine Symonds at City of London School, Jeff Walden, BBC Written Archives, and Jane Whitelaw at Heckmondwike Grammar School.

I'm also indebted to the following institutions for giving me the opportunity to use material: Cambridge Central Library, Ealing Central Library, Melbourne Cricket Club Library, The National Library of Scotland, New South Wales State Library and North Tyneside Central Library.

Last but by no means least, I'd like to express my gratitude to my agent Andrew Lownie, to Andrea Dunn and Michelle Grainger for their copy edit, Ivan Butler for the proofreading, to Jane Camillin, Alex Daley and Derek Hammond at Pitch, along with Duncan Olner and Graham Hales for all their hard work on the design and typeset.

Bibliography

Allen, David Rayvern, *Arlott: The Authorised Biography* (London: Harper Collins, 1999).

Allen, David Rayvern, *Jim: The Life of E. W. Swanton* (London: Aurum, 2004).

Bailey, Trevor, *The Greatest Since My Time* (London: Hodder and Stoughton, 1989).

Barclay, John, *Lost in the Long Grass* (Bath: Fairfield Books, 2013).

Barclay, John, *The Appeal of the Championship* (Bath: Fairfield Books, 2014).

Barnes, Simon, *Phil Edmonds: A Singular Man* (London: The Kingswood Press, 1986).

Barnes, Simon, *A Book of Heroes* (London: Short Books, 2010).

Battersby, David, *In the Shadow of Packer: England's Winter Tour of Pakistan and New Zealand 1977/8* (Worthing: Pitch Publishing, 2016).

Bedser, Alec, *Twin Ambitions* (London: Stanley Paul, 1986).

Benaud, Richie, *On Reflection* (London: Collins Willow, 1984).

Berry, Scyld, *Cricket The Game of Life* (London: Hodder and Stoughton, 2015).

Blofeld, Henry, *The Packer Affair* (London: Collins, 1978).

Botham Ian, *The Incredible Tests 1981*, (London: Pelham Books, 1981).

Botham Ian, *The Autobiography* (London: Ebury Press, 2007).

Boycott, Geoffrey, *Put to the Test* (London: Arthur Barker, 1987).

Boycott, Geoffrey, *Opening Up* (London: Arthur Barker, 1980).

Boycott, Geoffrey, *The Autobiography* (London: Macmillan, 1987).

Brain, Brian, *Another Day, Another Match* (London: Allen and Unwin, 1981).

Brearley, Mike, *Arlott in Conversation with Mike Brearley* (London: Hodder and Stoughton in association with Channel 4, 1986).

Brearley, Mike, *On Cricket* (London: Constable, 2018).

Brearley, Mike, *On Form* (London: Little, Brown, 2017).

Brearley, Mike, *Phoenix from the Ashes* (London: Hodder and Stoughton, 1982).

Brearley, Mike, *The Art of Captaincy* (London: Hodder and Stoughton, 1985).

Brearley, Mike and Doust, Dudley, *The Return of the Ashes* (London: Pelham, 1978).

Brearley, Mike and Doust, Dudley, *The Ashes Retained* (London: Hodder and Stoughton, 1979).

Butcher, Roland, *Rising to the Challenge* (London: Pelham, 1989).

Chalke, Stephen, *In Sunshine and Shadow: Geoff Cope and Yorkshire Cricket* (Bath: Fairfield Books, 2017).

Chalke, Stephen, *Summer's Crown: The Story of Cricket's County Championship* (Bath: Fairfield Books, 2015).

Chalke, Stephen, *Tom Cartwright: The Flame Still Burns* (Bath: Fairfield Books, 2007).

Clarke, Kenneth, *Kind of Blue: A Political Memoir* (London: Macmillan, 2016).

Dilley, Graham, *Swings and Roundabouts* (London: Pelham, 1987).

Edmonds, Frances, *Another Bloody Tour* (London: Fontana/Collins, 1986).

Emburey, John, *Emburey: An Autobiography* (Haywards Heath: Partridge Press, 1987).

Fulton, David, *The Captains' Tales* (London: Transworld Publishers, 2011).

Fussell, Paul, *The Anti-Egotist: Kingsley Amis, Man of Letters* (New York and London: Oxford University Press, 1994).

Fay, Stephen and Kynaston, David, *Arlott, Swanton and the Soul of English Cricket* (London: Bloomsbury, 2018).

Frith, David, *The Ashes 1979* (Sydney: Angus and Robertson, 1979).

Gatting, Mike, *Leading from the Front* (London: Queen Anne Press/ Futura, 1988).

Gooch, Graham, *My Autobiography* (London: Collins Willow, 1995).

Gooch, Graham, *My Cricket Diary* (London: Stanley Paul, 1982).

Gooch, Graham, *On Captaincy* (London: Stanley Paul, 1992).

Gower, David, *The Autobiography* (London: Collins Willow, 1996).

Gower, David, *With Time to Spare* (London: Ward Lock, 1980).

Gower, David and Taylor, Bob, *Anyone for Cricket?* (London: Pelham, 1979).

Hain, Peter, *Outside In* (London: Biteback, 2012).

Hayes, Dean, *Famous Cricketers of Middlesex* (Speldhurst: Spellmount, 1992).

Hinde, Thomas, *Carpenter's Children: The Story of City of London School* (London: James and James, 1995).

Hughes, Simon, *A Lot of Hard Yakka* (London: Headline, 1998).

Hughes, Simon, *And God Created Cricket* (London: Transworld, 2009).

Illingworth, Ray, *On Captaincy* (London: Pelham, 1980).

Jackman, Robin, *Jackers: A Life in Cricket* (Durrington: Pitch Publishing, 2012).

Johnston, Brian, *It's Been a Piece of Cake* (London: Methuen, 1989).

Kelly, Rob, *Hobbsy: A Life in Cricket* (Brighton: Von Krumm Publishing, 2018).

Knott, Alan, *It's Knott Cricket* (London: Macmillan, 1985).

Knott, Alan, *Stumper's View* (London: Stanley Paul, 1972).

Lee, Alan, *A Pitch in Both Camps* (London: Stanley Paul, 1979).

Lemmon, David, *Changing Seasons: A History of Cricket in England, 1945–96* (London: Andre Deutsch, 1997).

Lemmon, David, *Cricket's Champion Counties* (Derby: Breedon, 1991).

Lemmon, David, *The History of Middlesex County Cricket Club* (London: Guild Publishing, 1988).

Lever, John, *A Cricketer's Cricketer* (London: Unwin Hyman, 1989).

Lewis, Tony, *Double Century: The Story of MCC and Cricket* (London: Hodder and Stoughton, 1987).

Lewis, Tony, *Playing Days: An Autobiography* (London: Hutchinson, 1985).

Lewis, Tony, *Taking Fresh Guard* (London: Headline, 2003).

Lillee, Dennis, *Menace: The Autobiography* (London: Headline, 2003).

McKinstry, Leo, *Geoff Boycott: A Cricketing Hero* (London: Collins Willow, 2005).

Marshall, Michael, *Gentlemen and Players* (London: Grafton Books, 1987).

Martin-Jenkins, Christopher, *A Cricketing Life* (London: Simon and Schuster, 2012).

Martin-Jenkins, Christopher, *Cricket Contest: The Post-Packer Tests* (London: Queen Anne Press, 1980).

Martin-Jenkins, Christopher, *In Defence of the Ashes* (London: Macdonald and Jane's, 1979).

Martin-Jenkins, Christopher, *MCC in India 1976–77* (London: Macdonald and Jane's, 1977).

Martin-Jenkins, Christopher, *The Jubilee Tests* (London: Macdonald and Anne's, 1977).

Martin-Jenkins, Christopher, *World Cricketers: A Biographical Dictionary* (Oxford: Oxford University Press, 1996).

McFarline, Peter, *A Testing Time* (London: Hutchinson, 1979).

Meredith, Anthony, *Summers in Winter* (London: The Kingswood Press, 1990).

Midgley, Mary, *The Owl of Minerva* (London: Routledge, 2005).

Murphy, Pat, *Botham: A Biography* (London: J. M. Dent and Sons, 1988).

Nash, Malcolm, *Not Only, But Also: My Life in Cricket* (Cardiff: St David's Press, 2018).

Oborne, Peter, *Basil D'Oliveira: Cricket and Conspiracy* (London: Time Warner Books, 2005).

Oborne, Peter, *Wounded Tiger: A History of Cricket in Pakistan* (London: Simon and Schuster, 2014).

Peel, Mark, *England Expects: A Biography of Ken Barrington* (London: The Kingswood Press, 1992).

Pocock, Pat, *Percy* (London: Clifford Frost Publications, 1987).

Rae, John, *Delusions of Grandeur: A Headmaster's Life* (London: Harper Collins, 1989).

Rae, John, *The Old Boys' Network: A Headmaster's Diaries 1970--86* (London: Short Books, 2009).

Reid, Aileen, *Brentham: A History of the Pioneer Garden Suburb* (London: Brentham Heritage Society, 2000).

Roebuck, Peter, *It Sort of Clicks* (London: Willow 1986).

Rose, Brian, *Rosey: My Life in Somerset Cricket* (Bath: Fairfield Books, 2019).

Rudolf, Anthony, *The Arithmetic of Memory* (London: Bellew Publishing Co. Ltd, 1998).

Sandford, Christopher, *Keeper of Style John Murray: The King of Lord's* (Worthing: Pitch Publishing, 2019).

Sentance, P. David, *Cricket in America 1710–2000* (Jefferson, North Carolina: McFarland and Co, 2006).

Sheppard, David, *Steps Along Hope Street: My Life in Cricket, the Church and the Inner City* (London: Hodder and Stoughton, 2002).

Shindler, Colin, *Bob Barber: The Professional Amateur* (Nantwich: Max Books, 2015).

Steen, Rob, *David Gower: A Man Out of Time* (London: Victor Gollancz, 1995).

Steen Rob, *500-1: The Miracle of Headingley '81* (London: John Wisden and Co. 2010).

Taylor, Bob, *Standing Up, Standing Back* (London: Collins, 1985).

Titmus, Fred, *My Life in Cricket* (London: Blake Publishing, 2005).

Tossell, David, *Grovel! The Story and Legacy of the Summer of 1976* (Studley: Know the Score, 2007).

Tufnell, Phil, *Phil Tufnell: What Now? The Autobiography* (London: Harper Collins, 1999).

Underwood, Derek, *Deadly Down Under* (London: A. Baxter, 1980).

van der Bijl, Vintcent, *Cricket in the Shadows* (Pietermaritzburg: Shuter and Shooter, 1985).

Vargas, Dale and Knowles, Peter, *A History of Eton Fives* (London: Quiller Press, 2012).

Wilde, Simon, *Ian Botham: The Power and the Glory* (London: Simon and Schuster, 2012).

Willis, Bob, *Diary of a Cricket Season* (London: Pelham 1979).

Willis, Bob, *Lasting the Pace* (London: Collins, 1985).

Willis, Bob, *Six of the Best* (London: Hodder and Stoughton, 1996).

Willis, Bob, *The Cricket Revolution: Test Cricket in the 1970s* (London: Sidgwick and Jackson, 1981).

Newspapers and Annuals

Age, Australian, Bognor Observer, Brentham Cricket Club Centenary History, Brentham News, Cambridge Evening News, Camden New Journal, Canberra Times, City of London School Gazette, City of London School Magazine, Courier [Newcastle University] Courier Mail [Brisbane], Cricketer, Cricket Quarterly, Cricketer Australia, Daily Express, Daily Herald, Daily Mail, Daily Mirror, Daily Telegraph, Daily Telegraph [India]Eagle, Evening Chronicle [Newcastle], Evening News, Evening News of Trinidad, Evening Standard, Guardian, Hampstead and Highgate Express, Hindustan Times, Independent, Herald Sun [Melbourne], Hindu, MCC Newsletter, Middlesex County Times and West Middlesex Gazette, Mike Brearley Benefit Brochure, Newcastle Journal, Observer, Playfair Cricket Monthly, Radio Times, Shield Weekly News, Sportstar Magazine, Sun, Sunday Telegraph, Sunday Times, Sydney Morning Herald, The Hindu, Cricket Monthly and the Cricket Newspaper, Times, Times of India, Varsity, Wisden Australia, Wisden Cricket Monthly, Wisden Cricketers' Almanack

Online Resources

BBC News Online

Cricket Archive – cricketarchive.com

ESPN crickinfo – www.espncrickinfo.com

Test Cricket Tours-test – cricket-tours.co.uk

Wikipedia – en.wikipeida.org

Also available at all good book stores

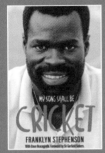

9781785315398

9781785311505

9781785314889

9781785314865

9781785314377

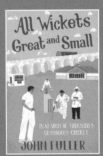

9781785311628

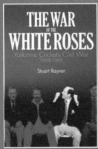

9781785314070

9781785315053

9781785311314